FILIPINO CROSSCURRENTS

Filipino Crosscurrents

OCEANOGRAPHIES OF SEAFARING, MASCULINITIES, AND GLOBALIZATION

Kale Bantigue Fajardo

University of Minnesota Press
Minneapolis
London

An earlier version of chapter 1 was published as "Of Galleons and Globalization." This journal article first appeared in *Mains'l Haul: A Journal of Pacific Maritime History,* 38(1–2) 61–65. Copyright the Maritime Museum of San Diego, 2002.

An earlier version of chapter 4 was published as "Transportation: Translating Filipino/Filipino American Tomboy Masculinities through Seafaring and Migration," from *GLQ* 14, no. 2/3, 403–24. Copyright 2008, Duke University Press. Reprinted by permission of the publisher.

All interior photographs are by Kale Bantigue Fajardo.

Published by the University of Minnesota Press
111 Third Avenue South, Suite 290
Minneapolis, MN 55401-2520
http://www.upress.umn.edu

Library of Congress Cataloging-in-Publication Data
Fajardo, Kale Bantigue.
Filipino crosscurrents : oceanographies of seafaring, masculinities, and globalization / Kale Bantigue Fajardo.
p. cm.
Includes bibliographical references and index.
ISBN 978-0-8166-6664-5 (hc : alk. paper)
ISBN 978-0-8166-6757-4
(pb : alk. paper)
1. Merchant mariners—Philippines. 2. Seafaring life—Philippines. 3. Filipinos. 4. Men—Identity. 5. Masculinity—Philippines. 6. Immigrants—Philippines. 7. Shipping—Social aspects. I. Title.
HD8039.S42P645 2011
387.509599—dc22

2010048761

Printed in the United States of America on acid-free paper

The University of Minnesota is an equal-opportunity educator and employer.

17 16 15 14 13 12 11 10 9 8 7 6 5 4 3 2 1

To my ancestors who voyaged before me and to Baía Amihan, who will learn to walk, swim, and sail soon.

CONTENTS

PREFACE

Boatmen and Boyhood

I learned early on in life that water and the sea are spaces of Filipino/a gender production (masculinities), transnational connection, and cultural translation.[1] The sea first reached out to me on the banks of the river in Atlag, Malolos, Bulakan, Philippines. Lolo[2] (Grandfather) Pete (my paternal grandfather) used to take me to Atlag as a child because that was where many of our relatives—the Fajardos—lived. The river in Atlag, simply called "ilog" (river) by locals, then and now, flows into nearby estuaries that directly connect to Manila Bay or what some fishermen call the "dagat" (the [South China] sea). The sea grabbed my attention with its airy and watery saltiness, an aroma that filled my nostrils, somehow working its way to my tongue, dancing on it, and emerging as a hint of taste. The sea's scent and flavor reminded me of eating sweet and sour sampoloc (tamarind) seeds rolled in a little salt, a popular candy in the Philippines. My mouth watered and I grew hungry.

I loved (and still love) the hums and roars of the motorized bangkas (canoes) that traveled to Atlag, transporting people to nearby villages on the river and bay. The bangkas and boatmen reminded me of tricycles[3] and "tricycle boys," adolescent boys and young men (although sometimes older men drive them too) who drive people in need of a ride to neighborhood, town, or city locations. One of Lolo Pete's siblings lived smack dab on the banks of the river and from their concrete back porch I could see the bangka drivers, men of different ages, so clearly. I admired one handsome young boatman who was brown, muscular, fit, and confident. He wore a well-proportioned straw hat, and I enjoyed watching him maneuver his bangka to slow down as he neared the docks close to the tulay (bridge) in Atlag or quicken as he sped away down the river. This boatman's way of being, that is, his masculinity, reminded me of "Edwin's," my favorite tricycle boy in Malolos. I knew Edwin's name was Edwin because his name was stitched on a leatherette sign that hung from the roof above his motorcycle. To me, Edwin was the most handsome tricycle boy, and his tricycle matched his good looks, as his Japanese motorcycle and new side car made of polished chrome glistened in the hot Bulakan sun. I always looked for Edwin near the cathedral where the tricycles zipped by the church whenever I was with my mother, "ya-ya" (nanny), or older relative waiting for a tricycle "sa bayan" (in town in Malolos.) And so in Atlag, I watched from the banks of the river, appreciating my favorite young boatman who handled his bangka with skill and style, with cool Filipino macho-ness.

After visiting with relatives, Lolo would take me to the little palengke (market) below the bridge, showing me some of the fruits of the river and bay being sold at small makeshift stands: large oysters, small blue crabs, shrimp, and fish of all kinds. My grandfather was a former fisherman when he lived in Lucena in Quezon Province (Lucena sits on Tayabas Bay in Southern Luzon), so I think he wanted me to see what the sea created and what the river baymen and fishermen caught. I was happy to see the slippery river and sea creatures with Lolo, but even happier when one day he took me on a bangka ride with my favorite boatman. In the middle section of the bangka where Lolo and I sat, we were surrounded by passengers, men, women, and children. Many of the women had pink and yellow translucent plastic bags filled with groceries, fish, and produce sitting on their laps or at their feet, as they probably went marketing in Atlag or sa bayan (in town). Our boat passed lush mangroves on the banks of the river and I watched the young boatman look calmly dead ahead, gently guiding the tiller. He always waved or moved his chin and head up (and I presume his eyebrows too [a Filipino/a bodily gesture]; I couldn't really see his face because we sat behind him), acknowledging and giving respect to the other boatmen who passed us going in the opposite direction, seemingly saying with his body language that he was part of a large circle of boatmen, fishermen, and river and baymen who proudly traveled and labored in and out of Bulakan waters.

Later on in my childhood, my family immigrated to Portland, Oregon, in the United States (in 1972–1973) as my father (a man who came from a poor family; he was the first in his family to finish a college degree at the University of the Philippines, Diliman) joined the post-1965 wave of Asian immigrants, many of them professionals, who arrived in the United States after U.S. immigration laws were liberalized due in part to President Kennedy's advocacy. In addition to professional opportunities for my father, our family also had personal connections in the United States because my parents and maternal grandmother used to host and house U.S. American Peace Corps volunteers in Malolos and many of them taught at Marcelo Del Pilar High School where my mother taught English.

One of the Peace Corps volunteers (who we called "Uncle T") provided an affidavit of support for my father when he immigrated. My mother, two sisters, and I joined my father in Portland in June 1973.

Later that summer my parents decided to take our family to the Oregon Coast for a day trip. I overheard my mother and father having a disagreement as they were getting our things together in preparation for our drive to Lincoln City, a beach town in Northern Oregon. My mother was confidently saying to my father that we (that is, their children) should pack our swimsuits, so that we could splash around in the ocean and play on the beach. My mother, having just recently arrived from Malolos, later admitted that her desire for us to have our swimsuits with us had something to do with watching U.S. American television and movies in the Philippines. Perhaps images of Elvis's *Blue Hawaii*[4] or Gidget's Southern California surfing were in her head before our drive to the coast. The Philippines in the 1970s was, of course, already saturated with U.S. American movies and television as a result of earlier U.S. colonialism and its neocolonial situation. Giving proof of this transnational media presence, my parents liked to recall that Peace Corps volunteer Uncle T enjoyed watching *Star Trek* (the original series) when it aired in the late 1960s on my parents' boxy television while he stayed at our home in Malolos.

My parents' disagreement did not seem to get fully resolved, but nevertheless we all got into my dad's Volkswagen Beetle (VW) and headed to the coast. We drove through downtown Portland and then the outskirts of the Willamette Valley. Later, we traveled on a scenic highway that crisscrossed the Oregon Coastal Mountain Range. As my father drove, I enjoyed looking at the dark forests of sitka spruce, Western red cedar, Douglas-fir, and Western hemlock, a landscape that kept me occupied until we arrived at Lincoln City.

My father stopped the car in a parking lot in front of a long brown beach full of driftwood, kite-fliers, beachcombers, and walkers. We opened the car doors and the cold Oregonian Pacific wind chilled our faces. This was shocking because in Portland the weather was warm (it was summer), but, more importantly, because we were used to the heat and humidity of the Philippines. Determined to prove her earlier point, my mother insisted that we change into our swimsuits so we could hit the beach and play in the water. Being little immigrant children from tropical islands used to playing in the hot sun and splashing around in water to cool off (e.g., on special occasions we were allowed to bath outside using a "tabo" [water dipper] and bucket near an outside faucet at my parents' house in Malolos) we quickly complied, perhaps thinking that once we had our swimsuits on we would feel better and not notice the cold Oregonian coastal air. Holding our arms and hands crossed close to our chests, we ran hoppety-hop down to the beach, trying to warm up, mimicking the tiny seabirds that jumped in and near the water's edge. Being brave, I ran closest to the water and jumped over a tiny wave, saying hello to the Pacific Ocean first. Ang lamig! (How cold!) My older sister and I (the bunso [youngest] in the family was still quite small, so she was not running around on the beach with us) did our best to perform *Blue Hawaii* on the Northern Oregon Coast for our mother, but after a while, we quickly ran back toward our parents, shivering, our teeth rattling due to the cold. "Ang lamig, ang lamig!" we declared to our parents. My parents both laughed at us and the scene. My father, being a practical man, went into the VW and pulled out extra clothes and acrylic sweaters for us. Despite my mother's earlier protests and challenges, he knew that there was a high probability that it would be cold on the Oregon coast and he wanted to be prepared. I put on a striped green and white sweater and pants and went back to say hello to the Pacific, a little wiser about Oregon's temperamental weather and a lot warmer.

I felt a strange mixture of emotions as I stood at the edge of the Pacific. Happy that our family went to the sea for the first time in Oregon, but sad as I looked out at the horizon, searching for the islands and home our family had just left. After a day of playing and exploring the beach, my mother bought some Oregon Dungeness crab at a nearby fishmonger. She was surprised to see how large they were as she was used to the small blue "alimango" (crab) in Malolos. Back at home in Portland, she cooked the crab with tomatoes and onions and served it with hot white rice, the perfect meal to end our first day at the sea on the Oregon Coast, a day I remember was full of immigrant Filipino/a cultural translations and transPacific connections and sensibilities.

My vignettes of boyhood "first seas" begin to show how oceans and seas are sites for Filipino masculinity productions and performances, labor, pleasure, mobility, cultural memory, transnational/translocal/transoceanic connection and interpretation, and processes of globalization (globalization here specifically encompasses, in part, the effects of U.S. colonialism and neocolonialism [e.g., Peace Corps] in the Philippines, my family's subsequent immigration to the United States, and United States–Philippines media exchange and cultural influence). In keeping with these broader themes, *Filipino Crosscurrents* is an interdisciplinary ethnography that addresses the cultural politics and everyday practices of masculinities, seafaring, and globalization.

The book in hand highlights the cultural meanings of the sea, ships, ports, and seamen in the context of the contemporary global shipping industry, Philippine nationalism, neoliberal economics, Filipino sea-based migration/transportation, and contemporary economic and cultural globalization. In doing so, this book reveals how these oceanic/maritime spaces, places, phenomena, and figures are important to how dominant and marginalized Filipino masculinities are produced, naturalized, and contested in the Philippines and diasporic locations.

INTRODUCTION

Filipino Crosscurrents

In 1995, scholar-artist Allan Sekula argued that the "sea has been forgotten"[1] in dominant U.S.-based scholarly debates about globalization. Here, globalization broadly refers to the flows of capital, people, goods, images, and ideologies in a capitalist world system, significantly implemented through neoliberal economics and policies.[2] By extension, Sekula is suggesting that related maritime spaces and places[3] in the global economy have also been forgotten, for example, ports, port cities, ships, shipping routes, and maritime trade and, just as importantly, the people who work, live, and move in or through these oceanic/maritime spaces, such as the Filipino seamen who work on ships that transport goods and commodities around the world and with whom I conducted components of my ethnographic fieldwork. With this forgetting of the sea and maritime space, Sekula further suggests that imaginaries of elite air travel, airports, air cargo, and digital communication networks proliferated in the early to mid-1990s, emerging as the dominant tropes, imaginaries, spaces, and industries of economic and cultural globalization.

Three years after Sekula's observations (in 1998), these kinds of air-based or digital-based imaginaries and understandings of globalization were expanded in a Southeast Asian context as the image of "capital flight" hit the front pages of newspapers, television screens, and computer monitors. This was big news in the United States and certainly in Southeast Asia where I was living in 1997 to 1998. This flight and fright of capital came about as wealthy Global North financial speculators and investors (connected to "the markets" by digital computer networks) withdrew their capital investments in large numbers as they learned of the financial troubles in Thailand, Indonesia, Malaysia, the

Philippines, and other countries. The region's economy was clearly in a capitalist crisis.[4]

As the twenty-first century opened, Sekula's once forgotten sea was quickly remembered as oceanic waters spectacularly splashed onto the pages and screens of U.S.-based media. This "hungry sea"[5] raged, drowned, and swallowed people, beaches, villages, islands, and cities through catastrophes such as the Indian Ocean tsunami, Hurricane Katrina, "perfect storms,"[6] and "inconvenient truths"[7] (i.e., accelerated global climate change). Images of flooded islands, port cities, waterfronts—Aceh, Phuket, Sri Lanka, New Orleans, and the Eastern U.S. seaboard—saturated newscasts, Hollywood blockbusters, and independent films, reminding U.S. Americans of the sea's liquid power to powerfully change local, regional, and global contexts. In 2008, as I rewrote this introduction, the sea, shipping, piracy, and globalization emerged as important news stories when Somali pirates boarded and seized ships transporting goods and commodities near and around Somalia and the Gulf of Aden, a key "choke-point" and shipping lane, demanding ransom(s) in the millions of dollars and holding seamen from around the world hostage.[8]

As oceans and seas flowed in everyday life and popular culture and as ships, shipping, and port cities became more visible and were remembered again, a lesser-known metaphorical sea, lesser known in mainstream United States, that is, but well known in the Philippines, also began grabbing headlines in the United States: the millions of hard-working global migrants (and the Filipino/a diaspora) who send oceanic-sized remittances back home to the Global South. On April 22, 2007, *The New York Times* reported on the epic proportions of global migration and the social and economic challenges migrants face. While global migrants were finally getting some mainstream media coverage in the United States, in countries such as the Philippines, migrants have been on the minds of Filipino/as (or locals) because approximately 11 million Filipino/as live and work overseas, significantly affecting the national economy and individual lives.[9] The *Times* magazine cover included a photograph of an Overseas Filipino/a Worker (OFW), a Filipina nurse, posed and photographed as abandoned, forlorn, and castaway, wearing medical scrubs, white shoes in hand, barefoot on a distant shore, aquamarine waters (the ocean) in the background, while inside the magazine a lengthy article discussed the steady flow of migrants from the Global South to North, specifically focusing on several Filipino/a migrants as miniature case studies.

So on the one hand, the sea reemerged (particularly U.S. American contexts), as an important space through which to understand "the global" (but not necessarily the global economy), and on the other hand (especially in the

United States), there was growing awareness or perhaps developing interest about the situation of Global South migrants. This interest in migration in the context of globalization is a fairly recent development in the United States. Although scholars and journalists often talk about the "flows of capital, goods, people, ideas, and ideologies," there has been a lack of sustained interest and attention on the role of migration and migrants in understanding contemporary globalization. Sociologist Saskia Sassen, for example, writes:

> The production of new forms of legality and of a new transnational legal regime privilege the reconstitution of capital as a global actor and the denationalized spaces necessary for its operation. At the same time there is a lack of new legal forms and regimes to encompass another crucial element of this transnationalization, one that some, including myself, see as the counterpart to that of capital: the transnationalization of labor.[10]

Here Sassen suggests that capital is often privileged in globalization debates, whereas poor and working-class migrants and issues of migration are underanalyzed or not seen as integral to processes of economic and cultural globalization. Because of this delinking of migration from globalization studies and the inadequate attention on global migration (identified by Sassen) and as a result of my fieldwork experiences in Manila (Philippines), Oakland (California, U.S.A.), and at sea (in the Northern Pacific), it became clear to me when I first developed this project that to understand what economic and cultural globalization means in local/regional/global contexts, I had to attend to the everyday practices of Filipino/a global migrants (especially seamen) and ideologies about them in the context of capitalism, neoliberalism, neocolonialism, and nationalism (in the aforementioned geographic scales).

Historically (i.e., precolonially, colonially, and postcolonially) in the Philippines and in the Filipino/a diaspora, the sea and related oceanic/maritime spaces and phenomena have been important cultural, economic, and environmental sites. The Philippines is an archipelago of more than 7,000 islands, and many Filipino/as historically relied on or continue to rely on the sea for travel, commerce, and economic livelihoods. If you have ever spent time in the Philippines, you know that the sea or water is a part of everyday life for thousands, indeed millions, of people. It is not uncommon to see fisherfolk working in all kinds of waters—"sa laut o sa ilog" (at sea or in the river) or to travel by *bangka* (canoe) or ferries to visit relatives and friends on another part of one's island or perhaps to a different island altogether.

In the early part of the twentieth century, many Filipinos migrated or immigrated to the United States not by plane, but by steamship. If you consider water more broadly, thousands of Filipino male migrants worked in water-related industries, such as fish canneries and irrigated agriculture.[11] Since the 1970s, however, the sea has become important in the Philippines and the Filipino/a diaspora because of the hundreds of thousands of Filipino seamen (also called seafarers, OFWs, "marineros," or sea-based migrants) who live and work on board industrial cargo or container ships transporting goods and commodities that comprise a significant part of global trade.

The Philippines is currently the top supplier of shipping labor. Filipino seamen comprise about 20 percent (one-fifth) of the 1.2 million international ship workers. In 2007, 266,553 Filipino seamen worked on thousands of international container and passenger ships for nine to twelve months (the usual length of their contracts).[12] Another important statistic is that 90 percent of the world's goods and commodities are transported by ship. This percentage speaks to the crucial role Filipino seamen play in worldwide maritime trade. According to the Trade Union Congress of the Philippines secretary-general Ernesto Herrera, citing records from the Bangko Sentral ng Pilipinas (BSP/Philippine Central Bank), in the first nine months of 2008, Filipino seamen sent $2.393 billion back home to the Philippines. This amount reflects an increase of 43.35 percent compared with the $1.669 billion they remitted over the same time frame in 2007. These figures suggest that the demand for Filipino seamen's labor has increased.[13] Herrera estimates that "each Filipino sailor now sends home an average of $760 monthly." In October 2008, the BSP reported that remittances contributed by overseas Filipinos (land- and sea-based) increased by 15.5 percent to $13.707 billion from January to October of 2008 compared with $11.866 billion in 2007, suggesting further that the demand for global Filipino migrant labor has increased (not just for seamen).[14] The increase in Filipino labor in the shipping industry since the 1980s and their top-dollar remittances informs the now well-known cliché that overseas Filipino/as "keep the Philippine economy afloat." The previously outlined statistics and economic and social trends reveal that Filipino seamen are key laborers in contemporary economic and cultural globalization as they literally work to transport the world's goods, while also contributing millions of dollars to the Philippine economy.

Keeping these late twentieth century and early twenty-first century developments in mind, in conducting researching for and writing *Filipino Crosscurrents,* the following questions guided me: What would it mean to remember and rethink the sea, shipping, seafaring, and sea-based migration in the context of economic and cultural globalization in the Philippines, Southeast Asia, the Pacific, and the Filipino/a diaspora?

(Diaspora here includes both land and sea sites.) How an oceanic or maritime-based cultural politics and political important in the Philippines, the United States, Southeast Asia, the Pac and the Filipino/a diaspora? What are the cultural politics of Filipino maritime/migrant masculinities vis-à-vis other masculinities, and how do Filipino men or masculine subjects negotiate and understand these cultural politics? How do Filipino seamen working in the global shipping industry understand, embody, and create their masculinities through their work and everyday practices on ships, in ports, and at sea? And why are the cultural politics of Filipino masculinities significant in the context of economic and cultural globalization, capitalism, and global Filipino/a migration?

Based on fieldwork in the Philippines (mostly in Manila, but in some provinces too), in the United States (primarily in Oakland, California, and the San Francisco Bay Area), and at sea (on board an industrial container ship that sailed from Oakland to Hong Kong [China]) through cultural studies–inflected ethnographic research, over the last twelve years I have been exploring the cultural politics of oceanic/maritime space (i.e., port cities, ports, seas, and ships), Filipino masculinities, and globalization(s). In this ethnography, I culturally interpret and illustrate how differently situated Filipinos—Philippine state and governmental officials, corporate executives, seafarers' advocates, working-class seamen, and even ethnographers—engage seafaring, shipping, and maritime trade to imagine and produce heterogeneous Filipino masculinities and alternative trajectories and epistemologies of globalization. Based on my research, I argue that as an outcome of the advancement of neoliberal economics, capitalist globalization, and Filipino/a overseas migration as long-term development plan in the Philippines, as well as the feminization of Filipino/a global labor and the feminization of the Philippine nation-state, Filipino seafaring and seamen emerged as *key masculine cultural and economic spaces and figures* for the Philippine state at the end of the twentieth and beginning of the twenty-first century. It is precisely through seafaring and the figure of the seaman that the Philippine state seeks to discursively perform, reiterate, enact, and consolidate Filipino masculinities at this particular historical, cultural, and political juncture.[15] However, rather than absolutely conforming to Philippine state–sanctioned seafaring or maritime masculinities, some Filipino seamen have been able to find alternative spaces and nonconventional or nonnormative ways to create, embody, and imagine other kinds of Filipino masculinities.

Taking a step back for a moment, what do Filipino masculinities mean in the context of this book? Although established masculinity scholars such as Jack Halberstam have acknowledged that masculinity is difficult to define[16] (and I agree with him especially in cross-cultural local/global contexts), in *Filipino Crosscurrents,* I use the terms masculinity and masculinities in an inclusive and, more importantly, queer manner. Masculinities, for me, refer to a heterogeneous spectrum of differently situated masculine racialized, classed, and geographically, historically, culturally, economically located and situated sex/gender formations and performances, largely in Philippine and diasporic contexts, which were important sites in my study, but also in other overlapping Asian, Indigenous/Pacific, African American, and European/white contexts, which were also relevant to my fieldwork but not central to the project.[17] While masculinities have historically been connected with dominant, heterosexual, elite manhoods, maleness, and/or patriarchies, my understanding of masculinities is more wide-ranging and definitely queer. That is, I am interested in these kinds of Filipino male masculinities (dominant, heterosexual, elite, connected to manhood, maleness, and patriarchies), and I address specific aspects of them in all chapters of this book, but at the same time, my broader ethnographic analysis of masculinities and how I approached fieldwork has been informed by queer studies, a field that has critiqued these kinds of dominant/normative understandings and formations of gender and, in doing so, has opened up other possibilities.

Consider, for example, the scholarship of Judith Butler and Jack Halberstam. Both theorized, developed, and made popular (in academic as well as in nonacademic/community spaces) the notion that gender (i.e., notions, constructions, and embodiments of femininities and masculinities) are socially, historically, and culturally created, performed, repeated, reinforced, and policed through discourse, institutions, and material practices such as clothing, fashion, or "drag." Moreover, and quite significantly, both suggest that masculinities (or femininities), that is, "gender," need not be forever or essentially linked to biology or anatomical "sex." Indeed, Halberstam argues in *Female Masculinity* that "masculinity must not and cannot and should not reduce down to the male body and its effects."[18] While I agree with Halberstam that female masculinity can be a "masculinity without men" (a central premise of his book), in chapter 4, I engage and analyze Filipino examples in which (Filipino) tomboy masculinities and manhoods (which I argue can be interpreted as an indigenous/Filipino formation of fe/male masculinity and manhood) are created precisely through proximities and social intimacies with Filipino males/men, specifically alongside working-class Filipino seamen. While Butler and Halberstam do the important work of theorizing gender in a broader and more queer sense, both primarily address white or European gender and sexuality formations (queer or transgender, a significant contribution of their scholarship). Although their critical theories inform my research questions and the way I approached fieldwork and fieldwork questions, it is highly important to consider how masculinity, race, class, culture, sexuality, citizenship, and space/place intersect and coconstitute each other through what women of color feminist scholars and writers theorize as an "intersectional" approach or framework where we cannot see gender in isolation from these other axes of difference, nor is it simply an "additive" process.[19] Rather, these axes of difference interact, intersect, and cocreate each other in complex ways.

To begin doing this, we must think about how sex/gender are conceptualized in Filipino and diasporic contexts and how sex/gender have been theorized in Southeast Asian contexts. While I agree with the broad strokes of Butler and Halberstam's theorization of gender, in the Filipino language (and thus in multiple Filipino/a contexts), sex/gender are not separated in the same manner as in European, white, feminist, gay, and/or lesbian formulations or contexts.[20] The Filipino language is gender-inclusive or gender-neutral; that is, there is fluidity, flow, and nonduality among notions, performances, and embodiments of sex/gender.[21] Indicating this fluidity and nonduality, the Filipino language does not have gendered pronouns (e.g., "he" or "she" in English). Social and interpersonal contexts are more important than anatomical understandings or biological readings of "the body," revealing how notions of personhood are generally more dynamic and definitely less dualistic compared with dominant European notions of sex and gender as definitely distinct. To give a brief example, the word "lalaki" means both "male" *and* "man." This somewhat paradoxical formulation (particularly if you are used to separating sex/gender) reveals how sex/gender are connected, interdependent, or collapsed within each other, not in a dualism. Moreover, the more holistic gender inclusiveness and gender neutrality of Filipino and the way in which the language emphasizes fluidity, flow, nonduality, and context in understanding sex/gender suggests further (and this may be obvious by now, but I want to make sure it is clear) that there need not be a fixed correlation between "maleness" and "manhood" or "femaleness" and "womanhood." In chapter 4, I elaborate on these points and I discuss specific examples of "noncorrelations" and analyze their significance in the context of Filipino global migration and seafaring.

In taking an intersectional approach, it is clear that working-class, maritime, and/or migrant Filipino masculinities cannot be understood without thinking about the effects of colonialism—in the case of the Philippines: Spanish, U.S. American, and Japanese colonialisms. While it is not in the scope of this book or introduction to fully address these larger local/global histories and processes, I will discuss an important text in Philippine Studies, which significantly informs the ethnographic analysis of Filipino masculinities developed in *Filipino Crosscurrents,* José Rizal's

Noli Me Tangere. Although perhaps an unconventional or queer choice in my discussion of masculinities and masculinity studies, based on my reading of *The Noli* (as Rizal's famous novel is commonly called in the Philippines) and my understanding of the novel as an example of what black feminist literary scholar Barbara Christian called "narrative theorizing,"[22] I suggest that in *The Noli* Rizal critically and imaginatively suggests how to read Filipino masculinities and maritime space. In doing so, he offers creative and productive ways to understand and approach Filipino migrant and maritime masculinities situated in the twentieth and twenty-first centuries, central thematics of this book.

Published in 1897, Rizal's *Noli Me Tangere* radically ignited and helped to propel the indigenous Philippine revolution against colonial Spain in the late nineteenth century. The story takes place in the nineteenth century and revolves around Juan Crisóstomo Ibarra y Magsalin, a mestizo who has just returned to the Philippines after seven years of living in Europe. Ibarra (as he is called in the book) seeks to participate in political and social reforms in the Philippines. The novel provocatively questions how to accomplish this (e.g., political reforms? native education? armed struggle?). Romance is also a key trope in *The Noli*. Ibarra loves the beautiful Maria Clara (a mestiza), the biological daughter of Father Damaso, a Franciscan Spanish friar, and a native woman. Father Salví, another friar, also lusts after Maria Clara. (Damaso's fatherhood and Salví's lasciviousness reveal the Spanish clergies' sexual exploits and relationships with native women of the Philippines, one of the reasons *The Noli* was banned and Rizal was persecuted). Through melodramatic and satirical twists and turns of intrigue, dialogue, and everyday life, the narrative successfully exposes the multiple social, political, racial, gender, and class inequalities among and between the lively cast of characters in the town of San Diego during the twilight of Spanish colonialism. Owing to space limitations, I am unable to fully elaborate on this riveting story[23] (and its sequel *El Filibusterismo*), but what is critical to the discussion here is that in several scenes of the novel, boats, water, and masculinities are key tropes that reveal Rizal's narrative theorization of Filipino masculinities and maritime space.

In chapter 23, "A Fishing Expedition," Ibarra and Maria Clara, along with several of her female cousins, their sweethearts, friends, and chaperones, go boating and fishing at a lake in preparation for a large outdoor feast in the woods. It is on a boat *(bangka)* that Ibarra first encounters Elías, a mysterious and capable native boatman. Rizal describes Elías:

> Their boatman, was silent, remaining apart from all this merriment. He was young, with an athlete's body and quite interesting features, large,

> sad eyes, and a severe cast to his mouth. Long, black, unkempt hair fell around a muscular neck. Through the folds of a shirt fashioned from dark tacking one could make out powerful muscles on his strong naked arms, which helped him manipulate, like a feather, the oar that served as the tiller to guide the boat.[24]

Here, Rizal beautifully, and I would add homoerotically, encapsulates the significance of boats and maritime space in the creation and embodiment of Filipino masculinities. Rizal as male/man writer imagines, visualizes, and acknowledges the boatman's powerful masculinity and manhood, produced and enabled precisely through Elías's dynamic relationship to his boat, oar, and, ultimately, the water.

As a self-identified queer, transgender, and tomboy (Filipino American immigrant) ethnographer, like Rizal, my narrative analysis and theorizing also include homoerotic moments and sensibilities (homoerotic in the broadest and most inclusive sense of the term that black lesbian feminist scholar, Audre Lorde, proposed).[25] And again, like Rizal, I make similar discursive and analytical moves, revealing the cultural significance—or centrality—of diverse Filipino maritime and migrant masculinities in ports, port cities, ships, and seas in contemporary contexts. In particular and informed by Rizal, I develop and engage a postcolonial and decolonized ethnographic optic that seeks to represent the beauty and complexities, as well as the cultural and political problems, related to specific kinds of Filipino maritime and migrant masculinities (e.g., state or corporate sanctioned). (I will elaborate on this point shortly.)

In addition, in chapter 45, "The Persecuted," Rizal writes about the dialogue between Ibarra and Elías (who we subsequently learn is an Indio [native] "outlaw" who fights for the common tao [people]). The two men ride and talk in Elías's bangka before sundown into dusk on the lake where "there are no witnesses," to exchange their social and economic viewpoints, as two differently situated Filipino men, and their differing strategies for social change in the Philippines. In sum, Ibarra represents the masculinity and manhood of landed mestizo elites (the less corrupt kind?), while Elías represents Indio masculinity and manhood (although because of his specific life history, Elías is an educated Indio, unlike most natives of his time). Ibarra primarily believes in expanding education for natives and gradual political reforms, whereas Elías believes in a more urgent and far-reaching agenda, including "radical reforms in the armed forces, in the clergy, in the administration of justice . . . respect for human dignity, more security for the individual, less force on the part of the armed forces, fewer privileges for the body of people who abuse [the common people] with impunity."[26]

In this important maritime and lacustrine scene of *The Noli,* Rizal again highlights the centrality of maritime spaces (boat, lake) and activities (paddling) in the production of Filipino masculinities and manhoods. Indeed, Rizal precisely spotlights these spaces and everyday practices. Quite importantly, he also engages with the Filipino notion that native/Philippine society can be understood or imagined as a boat. The Filipino word for society or community is "barangay," a term derived from "balanghai" (large outrigger canoe or boat with or without sails). Filipino writer-artist Nick Joaquin suggests that natives/ancestors migrated to the archipelago, sailing/paddling with their kin and clans. As a result of this precolonial maritime history, maritime notions and sensibilities are central to understanding community and identity in particular/specific Philippine contexts.[27] (This is not a universal origin or arrival story; it cannot and should not be applied to all heterogeneous Filipino/a communities based in the archipelago and diaspora.) While Filipinas were also in the boat (in "The Fishing Expedition"), in this chapter, Rizal showcases two specific kinds of Filipino masculinities and manhoods, suggesting Rizal's more masculinist rather than proto-feminist imaginative or political orientations.[28]

In short, Rizal narratively theorizes that Filipino masculinities and manhoods are heterogeneous, not homogeneous, and he powerfully imagines them as differently situated and in tension as a result of race, class, political beliefs, and relationships to place/location (i.e., Ibarra has recently returned to the archipelago after living abroad, and Elías is a native and a seasoned local). Although Rizal does not fully address sexual difference as an important axis of difference in this boat scene, what is important, especially in terms of understanding what Filipino masculinities in this ethnography mean, is that Rizal understood and theorized sex/gender, that is, masculinities/manhoods, as intersectional, heterogeneous, and differently situated (due to race, class, politics, and relationship to place). Without a doubt, he also shows the effects of colonialism on various masculinity formations. Taking great inspiration from Rizal's thinking and narrative theory of Filipino masculinities and maritime space, in this ethnography, I tried to approach and write about Filipino masculinities with a Rizalian sensibility and optic by analyzing the beauty, complexities, contradictions, and political differences among and between particular kinds of maritime and migrant masculinities and manhoods (articulated through discourse or embodied/created through everyday practices) in postcolonial, neocolonial, neoliberal/globalization contexts in the Philippines and diaspora.

To understand Filipino masculinities in these twentieth and twenty-first century contexts, we must consider the significance of the (racialized and classed) feminization of Filipino/a (migrant) labor (in its own right, but also in relation to Filipino masculinities). As Philippine Studies and feminist scholar Neferti X. Tadiar[29] compellingly argues, the racialized, classed, gendered, and sexualized disempowerment of the Philippines, manifested through political and economic emasculation or feminization, historically developed in the nineteenth and twentieth centuries as a result of colonial and postcolonial structural inequalities and "fantasy-productions," which intensified and worsened as a result of the unequal and triangular international political and economic dynamics between the United States, Japan, and the Philippines.[30] Structural inequalities, for example, include the Philippines's massive financial debt to U.S.-backed institutions such as the International Monetary Fund (IMF) and World Bank, as well as connected structural adjustment and deregulation of industries through neoliberal "free trade" economics, which expanded in the 1970s and 1980s and which consolidated in the 1990s. According to a special report written by the nongovernmental organization (NGO) Freedom from Debt and published in *The Manila Times,* as of August 2007 the Philippines's debt to the IMF–World Bank was P3.871 trillion (equivalent to US$81.91 billion).[31] This means that, as of mid-2007, every Filipino owes P43,649, with each individual having to pay P7,012.12 annually just to service the debt. Freedom from Debt also notes that Philippine president Gloria Macapagal Arroyo (president at the time I wrote this introduction) has been particularly notorious for her "addiction" to this unsustainable and exploitative debt scenario. The NGO also writes that "from 2001 to 2006, Mrs. Arroyo borrowed a total of P2.83 trillion shaming the total P1.51 trillion combined borrowings of the Aquino, Ramos and Estrada administrations spanning 14 years."[32] The remittances that Filipino seamen and other OFWs contribute generate the foreign revenue needed to finance these massive international debts.

Tadiar's notion of fantasy-productions, however, elaborates and expands upon analyses of structural inequalities as primarily economic. As I understand Tadiar's concept, the term refers to the interconnected processes of neoliberal capitalist development and heteropatriarchal state and corporate desires and erotics, which work to construct or disempower the Philippines and Filipino/a subjects and labor through racialized, classed, and sexualized (supposedly) subordinate femininities, for example, through United States and Japanese state and corporate discourses and tropes of the Philippines or "the Filipino/a" as "mistress," "hooker," or "DH" (domestic helper).[33] This imagery is buttressed and maintained by orientalist and neocolonial discourses that construct the United States as the ultimate heterosexual heroic man (who is married to Japan [respectable femininity] but keeps the Philippines as his mistress [unrespectable/supposedly marginal femininity]). Keeping Tadiar's theoretical interventions in mind, through colonial, capitalist, racist, misogynistic heteropatriarchal and heteronormative cultural and political logics and discourse (which Tadiar and other feminist and postcolonial scholars such as Cynthia Enloe, Jacqui Alexander, and Gayatri Gopinath have argued are central to international politics and relations [building on Edward Said's earlier critique in *Orientalism*]), one way of reading the abandoned, forlorn, and castaway Filipina nurse depicted on *The New York Times* Sunday magazine cover discussed earlier is that she represents a genealogy of unrespectable and supposedly victimized Filipina femininity (i.e., the nurse is historically linked to the mistress, hooker, and DH). Moreover, the Filipina female migrant worker signifies the Philippines's similarly unrespectable and supposedly marginal femininity in international politics. That is, through repetitive orientalist, misogynistic, and racist discourse (coming out of the "West"), the Philippines as an "imagined community"[34] is (again) depicted as hyperfeminine, supposedly weak, marginal, and without agency.

Processes of racialized and classed feminization also affect contemporary Filipino seamen in the global shipping industry. As such, it is important to remember that feminization not only affects "women" or "females" but can also affect "men," "males," or "tomboys" (as well as other possible gender expressions and presentations). While some Filipino migrant men were historically seen as hypermasculine or threatening, especially to white labor, white men, and/or white women, other Filipino migrant men were constructed as "feminine."[35] For example, historian Linda España-Maram documents how whites socially constructed Filipinos (in the mid-twentieth century) who were employed in domestic industry positions as "house boys" and gardeners as feminine "Orientals."[36]

Filipino men who worked in the U.S. Navy also experienced this kind of racialized and classed feminization. Sociologist Yen Le Espiritu documents that from 1898 to 1992 the U.S. Navy actively recruited Filipino men to work in "feminized" ratings; that is, as stewards and mess boys who were often seen and understood as doing "women's work" (especially by white Navy sailors). Espiritu writes,

> Barred from admission to other ratings, Filipinos enlistees performed the work of domestics, preparing and serving the officers' meals and caring for the officers' galley, wardroom, and living spaces. When they were ashore, their duties ranged from ordinary housework to food services at the U.S. Naval Academy mess hall. Unofficially, Filipino stewards also

have been ordered to perform menial chores such as walking the officers' dog and acting as personal servants for the officers' wives.[37]

Working in this U.S. naval "brown-skinned servant force," Filipino Navymen in Espiritu's study reported frustration, resentment, and anger at the U.S. Navy's racialized, gendered, and classed exclusions and everyday practices. To survive the racialized, classed, and gendered oppression they experienced, Espiritu documents that one strategy Filipino Navymen relied on was to "reclaim masculinity instead of fighting patriarchal oppression." This reclamation often occurred in the Philippines upon their return home where Filipino Navymen became economically and socially upwardly mobile.

More recently in the context of contemporary global shipping, sociologist Steven C. McKay documents and analyzes similar yet different dynamics on multiracial, multinational cargo ships. McKay writes that contemporary Filipino seamen also experience racialized and classed feminization. McKay cites a study in which Norwegians who worked with Filipinos on board an industrial container ship described their Filipino shipmates as "physically weak, feminine, negligent, and irresponsible. . . . Filipinos [we]re regarded as feminine and quite often labeled as homosexual [by Norwegian shipmates]."[38] This narrative reveals orientalist logics whereby Asian subjects (in this case, Filipino) are feminized precisely because of race (and class). Like their historic counterparts in the U.S. Navy, contemporary Filipino seamen also experience racialized emasculation and feminization through their close working relationships with (racist) European or European American sailors. It important to keep in mind, however, that context matters. When in the Philippines, seamen's masculinities are often seen as exemplary, not secondary or marginal, especially by the (Philippine) state and other institutions. (I elaborate on this in other chapters of the book.)

Given the regional and global economic and cultural feminization of the Philippines and migrant, one goal of this ethnography is to document and analyze how and why seafaring, shipping, and seamen emerged as important masculine economic, political, and cultural spaces and figures at the end of the twentieth and beginning of the twenty-first century. I argue further that because processes of economic and cultural feminization have intensified in the last several decades, differently situated Filipinos engage maritime industries, narratives, and masculinities in what appear to be attempts to counter neocolonial and orientalist[39] international relationships and political economies that seek to materially and discursively disempower or subordinate the Philippines and Filipino/a subjects and labor. More often than not, however, these counternarratives are usually an attempt by the Philippine state, multinational corporations, and private manning agencies (employment agencies) to control or manage Filipino maritime labor (seamen). As a result of on-going Philippine/Filipino/a feminization (attempted, imagined, and/or actualized), it might appear politically and culturally strategic to simply replace feminized Philippine/Filipino/a subjects and imaginaries with masculine ones. Although this is a predictable masculinist and nationalist move, this is not the most strategic or productive tack to take.

Instead of uncritically reinforcing or attempting to naturalize Filipino sea-based masculinities in the context of regional/global feminization, I engage a critical ethnographic and decolonized optic to analyze dominant discourse, imaginaries, and everyday practices of sea-based masculinities and political economies. While I certainly appreciate and admire many aspects of Filipino maritime masculinities (as I discuss, I am influenced by Rizal) and can understand some of the impulses to celebrate Filipino maritime or seamen's masculinities (especially because Filipino seamen have significantly contributed to the Philippines and diaspora socially, economically, and historically), in *Filipino Crosscurrents,* my goal is to stress the complexities, fluidities, and contradictions of racialized and classed Filipino masculinities by acknowledging and critically reading cultural, economic, and political differences and power, that is, the role of race, class, gender, sexuality, nationality, immigration status, and location, in local/national, regional, and global contexts and in processes of economic and cultural globalization.

In doing so, I reveal how dominant constructions of Filipino maritime masculinities are socially constructed and reiterated (in the Butlerian sense discussed earlier) for particular conservative/neoliberal/neocolonial socioeconomic agendas. To do this, I ethnographically analyze how Filipino maritime and migrant masculinities (produced through discourse, imaginaries, and everyday cultural practices) are implicated and deployed in the context of specific national, regional, and global politics. In doing so, I show that although dominant maritime Filipino masculinities are naturalized, they are in fact culturally, politically, and economically created, contested, and/or in tension (with other masculinities) on shores and ships, in ports, and at sea.[40] At the same time, when appropriate (and through a postcolonial and decolonized ethnographic optic) I emphasize and stress the beauty and pleasures of Filipino maritime or seamen's masculinities, rather than pathologizing them, which sometimes occurs in colonial discourse or feminist analysis. In taking this critical approach to Filipino seafaring, masculinities, and globalization, I hope the analysis presented here contributes to scholarly dialogue about heterogeneous racialized and classed genders and sexualities and to local, regional, and global social justice efforts that seek to confront exploitative and unjust masculinist power, including Philippine and U.S. state, multinational corporate, IMF–World Bank, and global capitalist formations.

In addressing the cultural politics and political economies of the sea, sea-based migration (seafaring), and shipping, I foreground how the Philippines and its sea-based diaspora (e.g., seamen[41]) actively participate in the production of past and present global economies and interconnections through maritime trade and shipping, rather than telling an ethnographic story about contemporary economic and cultural globalization through the more dominant discourse and imaginaries of air travel and digital communications or finance discussed earlier.

Although Sekula innovatively documents and theorizes multiple maritime spaces, places, and workers in his impressive book *Fish Story* (e.g., he analyzes and photographs ports in Los Angeles [U.S.A.], Hong Kong [China], Gdansk [Poland], and Ulsan [Korea], as well as container ships in the open sea), Philippine-based maritime locations and Filipino sea-based diasporic spaces and subjects (e.g., Filipino seamen in ports and on ships) are absent or rendered illegible in Sekula's photographic and written text. Sekula writes,

> Things are more confused now. A scratchy recording of the Norwegian national anthem blares out from a loudspeaker at the Sailor's Home on the bluff above the channel. The container ship being greeted flies a Bahamian flag of convenience. It was built by Koreans working long hours in the giant shipyards of Ulsan. *The underpaid and the understaffed crew could be Honduran or Filipino.* Only the Captain hears a familiar melody.[42] [emphasis added]

Sekula's port and ship scene describes a late twentieth century port affected by a deregulated shipping industry, manned by many men of color from the Global South.

Shipping was one of the first industries to become "globalized." In the 1940s the "flag of convenience" ship registry system was established, resulting in an industry "less hindered by territorial and jurisdictional barriers."[43] The open ship registry or flag of convenience system works in this way: 40 percent of ships carrying goods between two nations must be registered in either the importing or exporting country (totaling 80 percent). Similarly, the labor on board these ships must also be from either the importing or exporting country. The remaining 20 percent of ships transporting goods may be registered in a different country, that is, a country that is not one of the importing/exporting countries. Through the flag of convenience system, shipping companies are allowed to register ships in countries with minimal regulations, labor standards, and corporate taxes. In this context, the crews of ships registered through flags of convenience often comprise nationals from different or multiple nations, with laborers from the Global South working in large numbers or, to borrow Sekula's phrase, the seamen are often from "old and new third worlds . . . Philippines, Indonesia, India, China, Honduras and Poland, with Asians in the majority."[44] In the open ship registry system, seafarers, like land-based factory workers, are economically and socially vulnerable. For example, their wages are often quite low (especially those of lower rank working on ships registered through flags of convenience), the shipping companies may threaten labor by suggesting they will hire in a different country if labor agitates or organizes, their salaries may be withheld, they may be abandoned in port(s), their working conditions are often unsafe, their hours are long, their food is insufficient, their drinking water is unsafe, they may receive poor or no health care, and they have little recourse if labor violations occur.[45]

As a result of the flexibility of the shipping industry, Sekula concludes, "things are more confused now." The ship he describes moving into the channel was manufactured in Ulsan, Korea and registered in the Bahamas, the captain is Norwegian, and the "underpaid and understaffed crew" are Honduran or Filipino. One reading of Sekula's latter comment (about the interchangeability of brown Honduran and Filipino seamen) is that it seems to mark a lack of research or photographic intimacy/proximity with these two specific national maritime labor groups, but it also suggests how lower paid and usually lower ranked seamen of color from the Global South are seen as ubiquitous, and, therefore, exchangeable as labor in the cultural and economic logics of the global shipping industry.

Paul Chapman's *Trouble on Board: The Plight of International Seafarers*[46] also addresses many of the labor problems associated with flexibility of the flag of convenience system. Like Sekula, Chapman's writing broadly covers the situation of working-class seamen from the Third World. While Chapman's book makes important critical contributions to maritime studies; that is, he documents the contributions and challenges of Filipino and other Global South seamen in the context of the open ship registry system, describing in detail some of the problems they face (discussed previously), established scholars of global shipping and seafaring such as Sekula and Chapman inadequately address the cultural politics and political economies of Filipino seafaring and masculinities in the context of globalizations. This is a noticeable gap in the literature, especially because Filipinos have a long history in precolonial, colonial, and postcolonial maritime trade and since the 1970s and 1980s Filipinos have been working in high numbers in the contemporary global shipping industry.[47]

My research and sociologist Steven C. McKay's research begin to address some of the gaps in available maritime studies scholarship. In his essay, "Men at Sea: Migration and the Performance of Masculinity," McKay documents and analyzes "the intimate link between patterns of global labor market segmentation/incorporation and workplace hierarchies [and] the making of multiple masculinities, and shifting processes and prestige of labor migration." McKay also addresses the "role of the Philippine state in promoting and regulating the labor market niche and crafting narratives of heroism and masculinity to reinforce it," and the role of the "Filipino seafarers themselves" and their "exemplary styles of masculinity." McKay's sociological analysis is important because he documents and addresses how shipping is segmented by race and gender and he reveals how "Filipino seamen endure the harshness of workplace conditions." While our research has similarities, for example, we both address Filipino seamen's masculinities and the political economy of global shipping and thus our work can be seen as complementary, our scholarship differs in that instead of focusing on "exemplary styles of masculinity," which can also be understood as more *gender-normative* performances, embodiments, or expressions, my ethnographic or analytical foci have turned more toward the gaps, fissures, tensions, and contradictions of Filipino maritime masculinities. So like McKay, I also focus on state- and corporate-generated narratives of seafaring, shipping, and Filipino masculinities, but instead of stressing exemplary masculinities, I read against the grain of dominant narratives, performances, and everyday practices of Filipino seafaring, masculinities, and globalization, and I focus more on cultural politics and political economies that are regularly sidelined, unrecognized, and/or abandoned by narratives and everyday practices of normativities. In doing so, my approach to Filipino seafaring, masculinities, and globalization engages a more Filipino queer and postcolonial or decolonized ethnographic analysis. In other words, I am invested in addressing non-normative cultural phenomena and figures through intersectional Filipino/a American Studies, Asian American Studies, feminist studies, and queer studies approaches.

Ocean/Diaspora Studies

Although oceanic amnesia took hold in some U.S.-based academic circles in the 1990s, some scholars working in critical race theory, Native Pacific Cultural Studies, cultural anthropology, Indian Ocean Studies, Caribbean

Studies, and Asian American Studies began retheorizing culture, race, diaspora, and identity/subject formation by engaging oceans, seas, seafaring, and port cities. Influential texts published during this period include Paul Gilroy's *The Black Atlantic: Modernity and Double Consciousness,*[48] Epeli Hau'ofa's "Our Sea of Islands" and "The Ocean in Us,"[49] Amitav Ghosh's *In an Antique Land: History Disguised as Travel,*[50] Edouard Glissant's *Caribbean Discourse*[51]*;* and Antonio Benitez-Rojo's *The Repeating Island: The Caribbean and the Postmodern Perspective.*[52] Although not necessarily seen as central to mainstream economic and cultural globalization debates at the end of the twentieth century, these texts provide important postcolonial oceanic/maritime interventions in diaspora studies, regional studies, and global studies. In doing so, these postcolonial/anticolonial and/or diasporic scholars collectively demonstrate *how oceans connect*—waterways, islands, continents, ports, and diasporic networks—facilitating translocal, transnational, regional, and global identities, cultural practices, and political economies.

To elaborate on how these kinds of scholars have influenced my thinking and approach in writing *Filipino Crosscurrents,* I address three specific works here: Gilroy's *The Black Atlantic* and Hau'ofa's "Our Sea of Islands" and "The Ocean Is in Us." Gilroy argues in *The Black Atlantic* that the "Black Atlantic," the space between Africa, the Americas, the Caribbean, and Europe, is a black African diasporic space, a "web" or "network" that historically produced culturally heterogeneous and hybrid African diasporic cultures, and he uses the image of the ship as his "central organizing *symbol*" [emphasis added]. Gilroy writes,

> The image of the ship—a living, micro-cultural, micro-political system in motion—is especially important for historical and theoretical reasons. . . . Ships immediately focus attention of the middle passage, on the various projects for redemptive return to an African homeland, on the circulation of ideas and activists as well as the movement of key cultural and political artifacts: tracts, books, gramophone records and choirs.[53]

In this passage, Gilroy underscores the importance of ships in creating African diasporic communities that traverse the vast expanse of the Atlantic Ocean and Atlantic Rim.

In particular, he emphasizes how ships were a key technology used by Europeans to transport African peoples across the Middle Passage (the Atlantic Ocean) to Caribbean islands and the Americas, uprooted and transplanted through chattel slavery. At the same time, Gilroy reminds us that ships were also the technology or vessel for resistance, redemption, and cultural exchange across the Black Atlantic. *Filipino Crosscurrents* takes inspiration from Gilroy's theory that oceans or oceanographies are diasporic spaces. And like Gilroy (and Michel Foucault), who read ships as "heterotopias,"[54] I see oceans—and ships—as complex time-spaces that can hold and transport oppression and resistance, multiple subjectivities, and racialized and classed gender realities. Gilroy argues that it is the *image* of the ship, the ship as a *symbol,* that is critical to his theory of the Black Atlantic. Beyond brief mentions of ships and a handful of black or African American mariners, most of Gilroy's text does not actually address the sea or ships as a material space.[55] Rather, seas and ships remain primarily in the realm of the metaphorical, as Gilroy focuses more on African diasporic cultural productions such as music, literature, and Pan-African political organizing. *Filipino Crosscurrents* builds on Gilroy's idea of oceans and ships as diasporic spaces, but engages the sea and ships and maritime routes and maritime trade as material sites *and* as effective metaphors of masculinities and globalizations.

Further, in a Pacific Ocean(ic) context, Hau'ofa[56] in "Our Sea of Islands" argues that the oceanic space of the Pacific *connects* Pacific Island nations and peoples, rather than dividing, isolating, and making Pacific Islands and Pacific Islanders appear small and insignificant on an international political world-stage (central imaginaries in European colonial epistemologies). I quote Hau'ofa's highly influential essay at length:

> Do people in most of Oceania live in tiny confined spaces? The answer is yes if one believes what certain social scientists are saying. But the idea of smallness is relative; it depends on what is included and excluded in any calculation of size. When those who hail from continents or from islands adjacent to continents—and the vast majority of human beings live in these regions—when they see a Polynesian or Micronesian island they naturally pronounce it small or tiny. Their calculation is based entirely on the extent of the land surfaces they see.
>
> But if we look at the myths, legends, and oral traditions, indeed the cosmologies of the peoples of Oceania, it becomes evident that they did not conceive of their world in such microscopic proportions. Their universe comprised not only land surfaces but the surrounding ocean as far as they could traverse and exploit it, the underworld with its fire-controlling and earth-shaking denizens, and the heavens above with their hierarchies of powerful gods and named stars and constellations that people could count on to guide their ways across the seas. Their world was anything but tiny. They thought big and recounted their deeds in epic proportions.[57]

In Hau'ofa's theorization of the Pacific and Pacific Islander identities, we see how his shift toward the sea expands and extends Pacific Island geographies, moving from small islands to oceanic/vast waters, that is, the larger Pacific, which ultimately emphasizes great and impressive oceanographies of Pacific Islanders or Oceanians. (Oceanians is the term Hau'ofa uses for Polynesians, Micronesians, and residents of the Pacific/Oceania in his follow-up essay, "The Ocean Is in Us.") Hau'ofa writes further:

> There is a world of difference between viewing the Pacific as "islands in a far sea" and as "a sea of islands." The first emphasizes dry surfaces in a vast ocean far from the centres of power. Focusing in this way stresses the smallness and remoteness of the islands. The second is a more holistic perspective in which things are seen in the totality of their relationships.[58]

In other words, Hau'ofa argues that the Pacific Ocean is a more suitable space through which Pacific Islanders/Oceanians can imagine and build transpacific identities, communities, and social/artistic movements. And like Gilroy, Hau'ofa sees the diasporic possibilities and connections around the Pacific. Hau'ofa observes, "The world of Oceania may no longer include the heavens and the underworld, but certainly encompasses the great cities of Australia, New Zealand, the United States, and Canada."[59] Here Hau'ofa refers to the transnational, transoceanic migrations of Pacific Islanders/Oceanians that have created diasporic communities across the Pacific, both in the basin and on the rim.

Filipino Crosscurrents is informed by Hau'ofa's cultural theories and poetics of the Pacific and Oceania. Hau'ofa dazzlingly demonstrates that island peoples cannot or should not remain island-locked or landlocked, materially, culturally, politically, or epistemologically. Hau'ofa's writing inspires us to think oceanically, to reflect on how oceans are temporalized and spatialized and I would add racialized, classed, gendered, sexualized, and nationalized, as well as the importance of remaining mindful of the historical and contemporary power inequalities and dynamics involved in temporal/spatial practices. Hau'ofa, for example, critiques European mapmaking, which resulted in small island geographies and mentalities, as well as U.S. American, Australian, and Japanese "modernization" policies that favored rich Pacific Rim nations while making Pacific Island nations poorer and more dependent.[60]

In Hau'ofa's follow-up essay, "The Ocean Is in Us," he makes the following observation:

> Pacific Ocean islands from Japan, through the Philippines and Indonesia, which are adjacent to the Asian mainland, do *not* have

> oceanic cultures, and are therefore not part of Oceania. This definition of our region delineates us clearly from Asia and the pre-Columbian Americas and is based on our own historical developments, rather than on other people's perceptions of us."[61] [emphasis added]

Through these comments Hau'ofa attempts to articulate what makes Oceania and Oceanians different from other cultural/racial formations, namely those associated with or more connected to (mainland) Asia and the Americas. While Hau'ofa's desire for Oceanian specificity is clearly important and we are in agreement that the Philippines, Indonesia, and Japan are not geographically or culturally part of Polynesia or Oceania, especially in terms of how Polynesia and Oceania have been historically defined (most importantly by contemporary indigenous peoples, but also by national or colonial governments), from my perspective, Hau'ofa relies a little too much on closed systems of European-created categories and colonial technologies that historically categorized "unknown" or "undiscovered" geographies and peoples, rather than allowing for a sense of fluidity in understanding what might constitute oceanic (small "o," not Oceanian) cultures.

Charles De Brosses, a French magistrate and scholar who published *Histoire Des Navigations Aux Terres* in 1756, was the first to "la[y] down the geographical divisions of Australia and Polynesia . . . which were afterwards adopted by. . . succeeding geographers."[62] This reveals the role of colonial geography in imagining and socially constructing "Polynesia," which also significantly informs Hau'ofa's understanding of "Oceania" and hence, his categorization of the Philippines, Indonesia, and Japan as non-oceanic. In marking Oceanian culture as oceanic and as something entirely different from cultures found in the Philippines, Indonesia, and Japan,[63] Hau'ofa unequivocally argues that Philippine, Indonesian, and Japanese archipelagic formations "do *not* have oceanic cultures" [emphasis added]. In making these distinctions between Oceania, island Southeast Asia, and Japan, Hau'ofa incorrectly identifies the Philippines as *not* having oceanic cultures. The Philippines and the Filipino/a diaspora both have long histories with the sea and seafaring. As I will show in *Filipino Crosscurrents,* there are significant components of Philippine and diasporic cultural formations that are undeniably and unforgettably oceanic.

More recent twenty-first century scholarship on oceanic/maritime space, seafaring, and transoceanic mobilities includes: Pacific Studies scholar Teresia Teiawa's doctoral dissertation "Militarism, Tourism, and the Native: Articulations in Oceania" and article "Native Thoughts: A Pacific Studies Take on Cultural Studies and Diaspora," historians

Peter Linebaugh and Marcus Rediker's *The Many Headed Hydra: The Hidden History of the Revolutionary Atlantic* (2000), historian John Kuo Wei Tchen's *New York Before Chinatown: Orientalism and the Shaping of American Culture, 1776–1882,* ethnographer Jacqueline Brown's *Dropping Anchor, Setting Sail: Geographies of Race in Black Liverpool,* historian Dorothy Fujita-Rony's *American Workers, Colonial Power: Philippine Seattle and the Transpacific West, 1919–1941,* poet/scholar Dionne Brand's *A Map to the Door to No Return,* and Caribbeanist Omise'eke Natasha Tinsley's "Black Atlantic, Queer Atlantic: Queer Imaginings of the Middle Passage," among others.[64]

In sum, Teaiwa theorizes a Native (Oceanian) feminist and anticolonial cultural critique to interrogate European and U.S. American mili-tourism and colonialism in Oceania. Linebaugh and Rediker historically document and interpret race, ethnicity, and class in the seventeenth century maritime Atlantic world. Tchen historically documents and interprets patrician, commercial, and political orientalisms in the United States (in the eighteenth and nineteenth centuries) and New York's role as a key port city in these processes. Brown ethnographically analyzes how black communities in the port city of Liverpool draw on complex histories of African seafaring to forge local identities and politics. Fujita-Rony historically documents and interprets how transpacific trade and militarism encouraged Filipino migration to Seattle in the 1920s and 1930s, subsequently contributing to Seattle's development as a major port city on the U.S. west coast. Brand poetically imagines the contemporary relevance of the sea, the Middle Passage, and slavery to black Caribbean and African diasporic identities (especially in Trinidad and Canada). And Tinsley theorizes a queer Black Atlantic by analyzing Caribbean/Caribbean diaspora literature and ethnography that imagine shipboard Middle Passage same-sex eroticism and lifelong friendships between African women who were enslaved.

Like these texts, *Filipino Crosscurrents* engages diverse histories and critically reads the cultural politics of maritime discourse, the sea, port cities, and seafaring, but rather than the geographies and oceanographies previously noted, this ethnography is largely rooted and routed through the port cities of Manila and Oakland and the Pacific region. This recent scholarship published in ocean-based/diaspora studies and/or Pacific/Atlantic/Indian Ocean World Studies reminds us that it is important to think historically and intersectionally as we document, interpret, and critique sea-based diasporas, cultural politics, and political economies. At the same time, this compelling body of literature also begs the question and response: Where are Filipino/as and Filipino/a stories of the sea? (Fujita-Rony's book is clearly an exception; her book focuses on Filipinos who contributed to transpacific migration and Seattle's development as a port city.)

The marginalization of Filipino/as in studies of oceans or seas reveals serious gaps in maritime/ocean-based scholarship. Although, in my opinion, significantly underaddressed in ocean-based/maritime studies, Filipino/as (and Malay, Indio, and/or Native predecessors or ancestors) have centuries-old traditions of seafaring and maritime trade, which are clearly oceanic and continue today. For example, Malay/Indio/Native sailors with knowledge of monsoon winds helped to connect Africa, Europe, Central/East/Southeast Asia in the thirteenth century,[65] and in the Spanish colonial period, "Indio" sailors from the Philippines sailed the galleons that traversed the Pacific and connected Manila and Acapulco. Many of these seafarers, also known as "Manila men," jumped ship and resettled in present-day Mexico and the United States (e.g., California and Louisiana) in the seventeenth and eighteenth Centuries.[66] Even prior to the galleons era, there was a Malay/Indio/Native seafarer named Enrique de Malacca who is claimed by present-day Philippines, Indonesia, and Malaysia.[67] De Malacca played an important role as a language interpreter during Ferdinand Magellan's attempted circumnavigation during 1519–1521. Moreover, the Philippine archipelago has one of the most biologically diverse seascapes on the planet,[68] has several important maritime ports, and currently leads the world in supplying global shipping labor. This historical sketch shows that although underanalyzed in Atlantic/Pacific/Indian Ocean World Studies, the Philippines and its sea-based diaspora are important in maritime realms and oceanic worlds.

An important feature of some of the texts previously introduced (e.g., Teaiwa, Brown, Fujita-Rony, Brand, and Tinsley) is that they also address racialized and classed gender and sexuality in intersectional ways. *Filipino Crosscurrents* seeks to participate in this critical and scholarly debate in ocean-based/diaspora studies by engaging feminist, postcolonial/decolonized, transnational, diasporic, and queer intersectional aproaches to develop an ethnographic cultural critique that aims to denaturalize and culturally interpret Filipino masculinities in the context of seafaring, sea-based migration, and global shipping, rather than leaving masculinities unremarked upon or naturalized.[69]

Crosscurrents Framework

Four elements comprise the crosscurrents framework I develop and use in this book: (1) crosscurrents as oceanic or maritime border zones; (2) crosscurrents as oceanic trajectories of seafaring, sea-based migration, maritime trade, and global shipping; (3) crosscurrents as alternative temporalities and spatializations of globalization; and (4) crosscurrents as heterogeneous masculinities.

First, rather than privileging a more land-based or geographic cultural framework, I develop and use a water-informed and inspired *oceanographies of culture* approach that highlights *crosscurrents as oceanic or maritime border zones,* for example, oceans, seas, port cities, ports, ships, bays, rivers, currents, maritime routes, shipping lanes, choke-points, and monsoon winds. Differently situated people (differently situated because of race, class, gender, sexuality, citizenship, and differences in immigration status) move in or through these kinds of crosscurrent sites through travel, seafaring, shipping, and other migrant and immigrant practices. For example, in the context of my fieldwork, I observed Philippine and U.S. state officials, port developers, yachtsmen, working-class dockers of various racial formations and nationalities, working-class seamen from the Global South and North, sex workers, local vendors, seafarers' union members, faith-based seafarers' advocates, manning agency representatives, local residents, journalists, and ethnographers moving in and out of port spaces, ships, and seas, resulting in different paradigms, practices, and narratives of race, class, gender, sexuality, citizenship, and location coming together. As a result of these social encounters, discursive and epistemological interactions and everyday practices of power that can occur in crosscurrents or maritime border zones, race, class, gender, and sexuality are potentially/regularly reconfigured or retranslated. As such, it is critical to attend to the complex, hybrid, and often contradictory dynamics and outcomes of cultural practices and intersecting narratives in crosscurrents border zones.

This kind of ethnographic focus is useful because of the different and overlapping histories, narratives, and practices of power and identity that operate in and help to constitute the crosscurrents. For example, in the Philippines and the diaspora, indigenous/native/precolonial histories, narratives, and practices of seafaring, masculinities, and globalization overlap, flow into, and counter other histories, narratives, and practices of seafaring, masculinities, and globalization, including U.S. American, Spanish, Japanese, and Singaporean, among others. Crosscurrents border zones are, therefore, critical locations to ethnographically analyze because oceans, seas, ports cities, ports, ships, bays, rivers, currents, maritime routes, shipping lanes, monsoon winds, and choke-points are the oceanic or maritime border zones that can powerfully illustrate and reveal the relationships, dynamics, and tensions between different social actors, knowledge and power,[70] ideologies, and political economies in an archipelago nation like the Philippines, one with a sea-based diaspora working in global shipping and the global economy. While this book does not address all the examples of crosscurrents border zones listed previously, I suggest these examples here to indicate possible future research directions and locales.

The crosscurrents framework developed in this book dialogues with and is partially informed by Chicano/a/Latino/a Studies and South Asian Studies borderlands cultural theory as developed by writers and scholars such as Gloria Anzaldúa,[71] Renato Rosaldo,[72] Mary Louise Pratt,[73] and Amitav Ghosh. Focusing largely on terrestrial border, "contact zones,"[74] or "shadow lines," these writers theorize the *geographies* of hybrid[75] Chicano/a, Latin American, and South Asian cultures and identities through a border*lands* or terrestrial "contact zone" approach, and they examined land-based borders or contact zones to illustrate the cultural maneuvers, dynamics, and outcomes of peoples, cultures, and politics meeting, clashing, dominating and resisting. In the process, they also developed situated and antiessentialist historical analyses of the cultural politics and everyday realities of crossing borders or, just as importantly, borders crossing people, communities, and terrain.

Facets of how I conceptualize Filipino crosscurrents as oceanic/maritime border zones also dialogue with recent Asian American Studies, for example, historian Dorothy Fujita-Rony's ideas about the necessity to address both "water and land" in U.S. American and Asian American histories and historian Gary Okihiro's suggestion that scholars of U.S. American history move beyond the agrarian-maritime binary. Fujita-Rony observes,

> The most familiar way we understand the role of water and land in relation to Asian Americans is in considering people's ocean passage to the United States, especially in the era prior to regular air travel. Doing so directs our attention to the major significance of trans-Pacific shipping companies like the Empress Lines and President Lines that crossed between Asia and North America. Militarism, colonialism, and capitalism bound together sites across the Pacific and created ocean highways, leading Indians to travel to Vancouver, Chinese to go to San Francisco, and Filipina/os to migrate to Seattle.[76]

By taking into account water and the sea, Fujita-Rony reminds us that the Pacific in particular was an important "transit space"; in other words, a fluid meeting place for mobile subjects—Asian migrants, immigrants, and what she calls "water workers" (e.g., Asians working in the U.S. merchant marines or Filipinos working in the U.S. navy) gathered and encountered each other as they voyaged by boat or ship.

Taking a broader view, Okihiro comments,

> The Asian American subject pushed to the foreground of history helps us to rethink both the agrarian and maritime traditions. It reminds us that the United States and the Americas are surely elements of the Atlantic world. . . but also are parts of a Pacific world. . . . In that sense, the United States is an island surrounded by lands north and south, but also oceans east and west. And as an island, in contrast to the imagined insularity of the agrarian tradition, the United States must be viewed not only as a center with its own integrity but also as a periphery and fluid space of movements and engagements that resist closure and inevitable outcomes.[77]

Okihiro here imagines the United States as an island connected to other geographies and oceanographies, an island that is not closed or bound, but more open and fluid, part of a "center" and also a "periphery," recalling Hau'ofa's poetic theorizations.

Fujita-Rony and Okihiro's scholarship on the importance of disrupting cultural and epistemological binaries, their more fluid account of historical events in the United States and Asian America, and their emphasis on oceans and ships as critical sites of encounter resonates with my own understanding of crosscurrents as maritime border zones.

Finally, it is also useful to recall anthropologist and Pacific Studies scholar Greg Dening and his theory and cultural history of "islands and beaches." Dening wrote,[78]

> "Islands and beaches" is a metaphor for the different ways in which human beings construct their worlds and for the boundaries that they construct between them. It is a natural metaphor for the oceanic world of the Pacific where islands are everywhere and beaches must be crossed to enter them or leave them, to make them or change them. But the islands and beaches I speak of are less physical than cultural. They are the islands men and women make by the reality they attribute to their categories, their roles, their institutions, and the beaches they put around them with their definitions of "we" and "they." As we shall see, the remaking of those sorts of island and the crossing of those sort of beaches can be cruelly painful.[79]

Dening emphasized islands and beaches as cultural spaces ("less physical" or geographical), which enable(d) Europeans and Marquesan Islanders to define the contours and borders of appropriate cultural categories, roles, and institutions. He also evoked how islands and beaches are land-based (or geographic), but he reminded us they are also water-based, that is, "oceanic" (or oceanographic). In other words, islands and beaches function as *hybrid* geographic and oceanic border zones.

By uprooting and extending Dening's island and beaches metaphor and theory and conceptualizing Filipino crosscurrents as something that is extendable outside of the land and water (national) territorial borders of the Philippines and the United States, I build on his cultural and historical theory by modifying it in Philippine and Filipino/a American transnational/diasporic contexts. That is, I ethnographically address different crosscurrents border zones inside and outside the archipelago. As such, the crosscurrents framework I develop is not nation- or island- or beach- or archipelago- or continent-bound, but aspires to more fluidity in its transoceanic and transnational cultural interpretations. In addition, like Dening, I work to similarly to expose the cultural disruptions, social and economic inequalities, and epistemological violence that develop and emerge as diverse subjects move in or through crosscurrents border zones, revealing the cultural politics and oceanic or maritime political economies that inform sea-based discourse, masculinities, global shipping, and the global economy.

In this ethnography a key crosscurrents border zone that I researched to understand Filipino seafaring, masculinities, and globalization is the city of Manila, a major port in Southeast Asia. Other crosscurrents border zones that are critical to this book include Manila–Acapulco galleon trade routes and histories and the Manila Harbour Centre (chapter 1), "Rosca" (a pseudonym for a town in the Western Visayas) and the San Francisco Bay Area (chapter 2), as well as ships docked in Oakland and Manila and the *Penang Prince,* an industrial container ship that voyaged from the Port of Oakland to the Port of Hong Kong via the Northern Pacific Ocean (chapters 3 and 4).

Second, since mobilities are central to crosscurrents border zones, that is, ships and boats dock in port, but then they depart and sail to other oceanic or maritime border zones, crosscurrents also refers to *oceanic or maritime trajectories of seafaring, sea-based migration, maritime trade, and global shipping*. Geographer Doreen Massey stresses this insight when she writes, "a town or city (a place). . . consists of a bundle of trajectories"[emphasis added].[80] Massey uses a train ride in her book, *for space,* instead of a transpacific industrial container ship to explain this idea. She writes,

> You are, on [a] train, travelling not across space-as-surface (this would be the landscape—and anyway what to humans may be a surface is not so to the rain and may not be so either to a million micro-bugs which weave their way through it—this "surface" is a *specific relational*

> *product* [emphasis added] you are travelling *across trajectories* [emphasis Massey's].[81]

Massey reminds us that space or place is not natural, not an already preexisting transparent location, but rather, space is created through social and political relationships, materiality, power, and flows of people and ideas in and through space. Another way of thinking about this is that geographic/oceanographic space *and* mobility/movement are coconstitutive; that is, they work in tandem, coproducing each respective cultural phenomenon.

Because I am attentive to mobilities created through seafaring, sea-based migration/travel, maritime trade, and global shipping, as mentioned previously, I address multiple locations instead of analyzing a single ethnographic site—historically conceptualized as "the village or island" in colonial or foundational anthropology. I also stress how sea-based movement, travel, and transportation (seafaring/shipping) are constitutive of Philippine and Filipino/a diasporic cultures by ethnographically addressing how differently situated Filipinos reinforce, navigate, and/or contest cultural formations and ideologies in different geographies and oceanographies. In addition, I show how race, class, gender, sexuality, nationality, and immigration status are potentially reconfigured as a direct result of movement or mobility; that is, through seafaring, shipping, and migration. In doing so, this book dialogues with the Aihwa Ong's *Flexible Citizenship: The Cultural Logics of Transnationality,* Martin F. Manalansan IV's *Global Divas: Filipino Gay Men in the Diaspora,* and Robert R. Alvarez's *Mangos, Chiles, and Truckers: The Business of Transnationalism,* among others.[82]

While many scholars address cultural processes when migrants or immigrants arrive in the "host country," in *Filipino Crosscurrents,* I address what some may imagine as "in between" traveling/migrating/seafaring spaces—oceans, seas, ports, ships, shipping lanes, and maritime routes. Indeed, as James Clifford reminds us, "travel is constitutive of culture."[83] In other words, from a seafaring or oceanographic perspective, these sites or trajectories are not simply in between spaces or inconsequential routes; rather, they are central to and help constitute Filipino seamen's everyday lives and cultural practices. As a result, in this book I illustrate how cultural phenomena in and through these oceanic or maritime border zones and mobilities, the crosscurrents of seafaring, shipping, travel, and transportation, are constitutive of heterogeneous Filipino masculinities and alternative trajectories and epistemologies of globalizations. This book resonates with Alvarez's ethnography in that he too addresses the specificities of transportation (in his case, trucking). However, while Alvarez is interested in the transportation of commodities (mangos and chiles) and supply chains, I am more interested in the spaces/places/trajectories of transportation (seafaring/shipping) and the dynamics of oceanic or maritime border zones and mobilities and how they inform, produce, and/or challenge cultural politics and political economies related to racialized and class Filipino masculinities and globalization(s).

Third, as a result of focusing on oceanic or maritime border zones and sea-based mobilities and trajectories, crosscurrents also refers to *alternative temporalities and spatializations of globalization.* So, instead of imagining globalization through crisscrossing jet streams of air travel or interconnected networks of digital communications and finance that hinge on "global cities,"[84] the dominant tropes and spaces of globalization at the end of the twentieth century/beginning of the twenty-first century, I chart alternative lesser-known (working-class and migrant Filipino) geographies and oceanographies of globalization, which are produced precisely through alternative oceanic or maritime border zones and working-class migrant mobilities. Moreover, whereas dominant time-space models and discourses of globalization often center the United States or other "core"[85] geographies through "time-space compression" (through notions of speed, instantaneous contact, and the "annihilation of space through time" in established or well-known global cities such as New York, London, and Tokyo, *Filipino Crosscurrents* seeks to explain globalization through supposedly "peripheral" or "marginal" spaces and trajectories—Manila, the Philippines, the Filipino/a diaspora, and Filipino seafaring.[86] This engagement with how time-space works in the shipping industry, especially among working-class Filipino sea-based migrants, dialogues with Saskia Sassen's notion that "feminine circuits of survival" (e.g., domestic work, trafficked women, and low-wage manufacturing), in tandem with elite forms of labor, monies, and goods, are central to globalization.[87] My research reveals masculine, working-class, and Filipino migrant time-spaces and circuits of globalization, the crosscurrents of survival and maritime work in the global economy created precisely through seafaring and shipping.

In contrast to dominant notions of time-space compression and global interconnection through global cities, I show how globalization can also be temporally, spatially, and epistemologically understood through different routes and circuits (of seafaring, migration, shipping, and cultural politics) that flow in and out of the Philippines and the Filipino/a diaspora, two sites that were once considered "backwater" sites or subjects in the academy. To show how Filipino seafaring and sea-based migration contribute to and create alternative spatializations and interconnections in globalization and to illustrate that the Philippines and the Filipino/a diaspora have actually been quite active and central to past and present globalizations, I engage the historical and contemporary links between Manila and Acapulco (Mexico), two former Spanish colonial port cities that were integral to the Spanish colonial empire (chapter 1), the contemporary economic and political competition between Manila and Singapore (also in chapter 1), the various seafaring routes of Filipino seamen, past and present, who have jumped ship in ports outside of the Philippines (chapter 2), the transport and transnational links between Manila/Philippines and Oakland/U.S.A. (chapters 3 and 4), and the time-space dimensions of a Northern Pacific voyage of a container ship that transported goods and commodities from the Port of Oakland to the Port of Hong Kong via the Ports of Tokyo, Japan; Osaka, Japan; and Kiaoshung, Taiwan (chapter 4).

Finally, crosscurrents also refers to how differently situated Filipinos (e.g., seamen, state and corporate officials, seafarer advocates, and ethnographers) imagine, narrativize, and/or experience heterogeneous sea-based Filipino masculinities through everyday cultural practice and discourse. Responding to the feminization of Filipino/a global migration (which I discussed earlier in this introduction), in the last several years, U.S.-based scholars began publishing works that focus on Filipina migrants and their everyday lives and practices. Scholarly texts with this emphasis include Rhacel Salazar Parreñas's *Servants of Globalization: Women, Migration, and Domestic Work,* Nicole Constable's *Maid in Hong Kong: An Ethnography of Filipina Workers* and *Romance on a Global Stage: Pen Pals, Virtual Ethnography and "Mail Order Marriages,"* and Catherine Ceniza Choy's *Empire of Care: Nursing and Migration in Filipino American History.*[88] My research dialogues with the work of these scholars, as well as scholars such as Espiritu, España-Maram, and McKay (discussed earlier) who address the feminization of Filipino male or men's labor. Indeed, it is precisely because of the feminization of Filipino/a global migration that we need to continue interrogating Filipino/Asian masculinities. In this ethnography, I engage with the feminization of Filipino/a global migration and labor as important historical, political, and cultural turns, but I give focused attention to issues of masculinity and Filipino male and/or masculine identified migrants. Because processes of feminization affect multiple genders and as a result of the on-going circulation of feminizing narratives, it important to analyze the cultural politics of Filipino masculinities to see how masculinities are shifting, consolidating, and/or becoming naturalized in the context of neoliberal capitalism, neocolonialism, and Philippine nationalism.

When the fields of Filipino/a American Studies and Asian American Studies first developed in the United States in the 1960s and 1970s, Filipino male migrants were central research subjects in these new fields because Filipino migrant/immigrant communities were overwhelmingly composed of Filipino "men" or "males" and many of the earlier scholars were men who perhaps subjectively chose to focus on "men's histories" instead of "women's histories."[89] In this wave of foundational scholarship on Asian/ Filipino male migrants who migrated to the United States in the first half of the twentieth century, texts overall tended to emphasize race, class, nationality, and heterosexuality, as these axes of difference intersect with social phenomena such as labor niche, racism, and community formation. While this early scholarship on Filipino men's immigrant and work experiences in the United States contributed significantly to our understanding of broader Filipino/a American and Asian American histories and cultural formations, much of the foundational scholarship naturalizes (conventional) Filipino masculinities, manhood, and heterosexuality.[90] That is, in this earlier scholarship, scholars essentialized maleness/manhood/ heterosexuality precisely by stressing "male anatomy," rather than opening up these categories for analytical interrogation or questioning how racialized, classed, and sexualized genders are culturally constructed, naturalized, and/or policed through repetitive and socially sanctioned discourse, ideologies, performance,[91] and everyday practice.

My ethnography seeks to intervene into this body of ethnic nationalist and unmarked masculinist Filipino American Studies and Asian American Studies scholarship by showing or exposing how racialized, classed, and sexualized Filipino masculinities are culturally constructed, heterogeneous, and contingent, rather than "natural," "essential," and/ or "transparent." This book, is therefore, allied with recently published works such as Linda España Maram's *Creating Filipino Masculinity in Los Angeles's Little Manila*, Martin Manalansan's *Global Divas: Filipino Gay Men in the Diaspora*, and Allan Punzalan Isaac's *American Tropics: Articulating Filipino America*, which respectively address the complexities and social constructions of Filipino masculinities in the context of racism, white supremacy, U.S. colonialism, anti-Asian immigration policies, and labor exploitation in the United States (in the case of España-Maram), in the context of dominant and/or racist white gay cultural practices in New York or in the context of a globalized gay discourse (in the case of Manalansan), and in the context of U.S. imperial desires, projects, and tropes in the Philippines and continental United States (in the case of Isaac).

To illustrate Filipino crosscurrents as heterogeneous masculinities, in chapter 1, I analyze and critique how Philippine state officials and corporate leaders engaged Manila–Acapulco galleon maritime histories at a new port development/free trade zone in Manila through a "commemorative regatta" that sought to imagine and celebrate a masculine, maritime-based, national identity in the context of neoliberal economics and the Asian Financial Crisis. In chapter 2, I show the cultural politics of Philippine state–sanctioned and promoted narratives and imaginaries of Filipino seamen (and other OFWs) as "bagong bayani" (new heroes and heroines), as well as the cultural politics of more marginalized masculinities, such as those of Filipino seamen who have jumped ship or "deserted." In chapter 3, I address Filipino seamen's labor and lives at sea and in port(s), paying particular attention to temporal and spatial notions in the context of contemporary globalization and how shipboard life and nautical time contribute to alternative time-space realities, affects (e.g., loneliness and alienation), and working-class migrant and maritime masculinities. And last, in chapter 4, I analyze the overlapping social spaces among and between working-class Filipino seamen and Filipino tomboys. Tomboy here refers to an indigenous/Filipino practice of fe/male manhood.[92] This ethnographic analysis developed in part because Filipino seamen began sharing stories about tomboys in their past and present lives with me (I elaborate on our encounters in this chapter). As in the preface of this book, chapter 4 also includes an autoethnographic discussion of my own masculinity as a self-identified queer, transgender, tomboy, and immigrant Filipino/American ethnographer doing fieldwork in Filipino crosscurrents.

Ethnography on the Move

To develop this ethnography I engaged a research methodology that is perhaps best described as *situated traveling fieldwork*. Rather than conducting a long-term "village study" that focuses on or seeks to find ahistorical cultural continuities or notions of closed and fixed "culture(s),"[93] situated traveling fieldwork maximizes short-term ethnographic encounters in transnational/translocal/transpacific crosscurrents border zones and trajectories to reveal and emphasize cultural contact and exchange, contradictions, tensions, and solidarities. As described previously, oceans and seas (and other crosscurrents border zones and trajectories) are critical sites for a variety of people. Given these dynamic social geographies or oceanographies and because identities and understandings of culture are forged through coconstitutive axes of race, class, gender, sexuality, nationality, and/or immigration status, attending to the contradictory or affirming dynamics of encounters and cultural contact in crosscurrents border zones and trajectories is methodologically critical.

This mobile and situated approach to ethnographic fieldwork also reflects the changes in the field of cultural anthropology as outcomes of feminist, postcolonial, and/or anticolonial challenges in "post–civil rights"[94] and/or postcolonial contexts. Ethnographer Kirin Narayan, for example, argues that it is important to attend to shifting identifications amid a field of interpenetrating communities of power relations while conducting ethnographic fieldwork and in the process of writing. Narayan writes,

> The loci along which we are aligned with or set apart from those whom we study are multiple and in flux. Factors such as education, gender, sexual orientation, class, race, or sheer duration of contacts may at different times outweigh the cultural identity we associate with insider or outsider status.[95]

In other words, because categories and everyday practices of identity and belonging are unstable and because fieldwork occurs through a spectrum of "duration[s] of contacts" where boundaries between "(cultural) insiders and outsiders" are often blurred, it is analytically productive to be aware of all sorts of differences (or at least strive towards heightened awareness) when conducting ethnographic fieldwork and to situate ethnographic knowledge when we write.[96]

Because differently situated people move in or through crosscurrents border zones through traveling, seafaring, shipping, and/or migratory practices and because the crosscurrents are constituted by overlapping and/or shifting local, national, regional, and global contexts, during fieldwork in the Philippines and United States and in writing this book, I aimed to be mindful of particular and specific—*yet shifting*—political, historical, and economic contexts and how these interrelated contexts affected ethnographic moments and my own ethnographic accounts. Moreover, when deemed appropriate and hopefully useful, I ethnographically analyzed and wrote in reflexive ways to better explain the complexities of translocal, transnational, and/or transpacific cultural logics; the coconstitutive axes of race, class, gender, sexuality, immigration status, geographies, and mobilities; the dynamic positionalities of my research subjects or research participants; and my own shifting positionalities "in the field." Moreover, the writing approaches I deploy also try to address specific yet overlapping interdisciplinary translocal/transnational readerships in the United States, Philippines, and larger diaspora.

Use of a situated traveling fieldwork approach was well suited for the kind of fieldwork I was able to conduct in the Ports of Manila and Oakland and in broader port cityscapes (1997–2002) where conversations and encounters of shorter duration were common. Conducting research

Port of Manila, 1998.

Port of Manila, 1998. Container ship and indigenous bangka (canoe) docked in port.

on board a ship (one that was sailing in the open sea) as a graduate student-ethnographer was initially difficult to arrange and cost-prohibitive as my dissertation funding was for fieldwork *in* the Philippines. To take advantage of research opportunities in Manila (and later in Oakland), I decided the best way to conduct ethnographic fieldwork in a port city was to go to the port to talk to seamen whose ships were docked and to spend time in neighborhoods where seamen congregated.

In Oakland, the latter strategy was more difficult to implement because Filipino seamen do not get substantial shore leaves and there is less of a portside seamen's culture or community because of economic, historical, and political shifts in the larger shipping industry (e.g., containerization and mechanization in the 1970s and post–September 11, 2001, anti-immigrant policies, to mention a few of the changes). When I conducted research on board ships docked in port (in Manila and Oakland), I gained access to Filipino seamen by accompanying seafarer advocates who were visiting ships largely for religious or advocacy reasons, for example, to conduct different kinds of religious outreach and/or to provide counseling and other social services. I also boarded ships independently.

My conversations with seamen in port(s) generally lasted for a few minutes up to one hour. The relatively brief duration of conversations is partially due to the fact that while ships are docked in port, seamen are

Port of Oakland, 2006. City of Oakland in the background.

Cargo containers at the Port of Oakland, 2006.

quite busy attending to their respective duties, and as a result of mechanization and increased time and profit pressures, working in port can be more stressful and fast-paced than when working at sea, although this depends on the seaman's position and whether or not he has time off. As a result of these shipboard/portside realities, while conducting research on ships docked in port(s), I met and spoke with Filipino seamen who were eating meals in mess halls or galleys, hanging out on deck during work breaks (often smoking cigarettes), and, in some cases when time permitted and it was safe, I spoke with them while they were working or attending to their duties.

In Manila, I also spoke with many Filipino seamen in Malate and Ermita, neighborhoods where many manning agencies (employment agencies) are located and where Filipino seamen's labor unions also have offices. Because of these geographic particularities, on any given day hundreds of Filipino seamen are in this area of Manila. In and around Malate and Ermita, I regularly met Filipino seamen who were back from sea and/or looking for work and those who had professional business in the neighborhood. I also met and spoke with Filipino seamen who were traveling through this part of Manila on buses and jeepneys, as well as those who were hanging out in restaurants and bars, on the streets, and in parks. In contrast to conversations on board docked ships, in Manila (and in some cases, in the provinces), I had longer conversations with seamen who were back from sea, those who were looking to begin or renew contracts with shipping companies, those still attending maritime schools or academies, and seamen retired from the profession.

To expand my understanding of the cultural politics of Filipino seafaring and global migration and to better comprehend the contemporary and historical maritime and global migration landscape of Manila, I attended maritime/shipping industry events and I also spoke with Philippine state officials, corporate leaders, and seafarer and migrant rights advocates. To strengthen my historical understanding of Filipino seafaring, I conducted library-based research in Manila, as well as archival research at one of the seafarers' union's offices (which had old union newspapers and other written materials). In the San Francisco Bay Area, in addition to fieldwork at the Port of Oakland, I interviewed several San Francisco Bay Area–based faith-based seafarers' advocates and trade union representatives and conducted library/archival research at the Oakland Public Library (downtown branch). A key piece of my Oakland-based research also involved spending time with and interviewing a key research participant, a Filipino seaman who jumped ship and resettled in California.

Later, as a member of the faculty at the University of Minnesota, Twin Cities (with additional research funding), I was able to conduct research on board a ship that was sailing in the open sea. In the summer of 2006, as a passenger-ethnographer, I conducted follow-up fieldwork and traveled by industrial container ship from the Port of Oakland to the Port of Hong Kong, China, via the Northern Pacific Ocean with stops at the Ports of Tokyo; Osaka, Japan; and Kiaoshung, Taiwan. The photographs that are included in some of the chapters were taken during fieldwork in Manila and Oakland (1997–2002) and during more recent research trips (2006–2009). Last but not least, it is important to note that in addition to the ethnographic knowledge gained through fieldwork, several points of analysis developed in this book emerged as a result of on-going life experiences and travel in the Philippines (1968–present).

The writing approach I take in *Filipino Crosscurrents* is informed in part by James Clifford's idea of narrative "collage," Anna L. Tsing's use of a "portfolio of [writing] methods," and Mary Louise Pratt's call for new tropes in ethnographic writing and cultural anthropology. In *Routes: Travel and Translation in the Twentieth Century,* Clifford states that he experimented with "travel writing and poetic collage along with formal essays" to "evoke the multiple and uneven practices of research. . . and [the] borders of academic work."[97] In other words, Clifford suggests that no single writing style can handle every type of research situation or academic inquiry and so he argues that a combination or collage of writing styles is often necessary and appropriate. Similarly, Tsing in *Friction: An*

Ethnography of Global Connection states that she engaged a "portfolio of methods" to develop her ethnography of global connection, resulting in knowledge that is "variously ethnographic, journalistic, and archival."[98] Like Clifford, she makes a strong case for engaging a variety of methods to respond to different kinds of fieldwork situations and ethnographic inquiries, which in turn helps to produce different kinds of knowledge.

In "Fieldwork in Common Places,"[99] Pratt also contributes to the scholarly dialogue about ethnographic method and writing. She writes,

> Anthropologists stand to gain from looking at themselves as writing inside as well as outside the discursive traditions that precede them; inside as well as outside the histories of contact on which they follow. Such a perspective is particularly valuable for people who would like to change or enrich the discursive repertoire of ethnographic writing. . . . A first step toward such change is to recognize that one's tropes are neither natural nor in many cases, native to the discipline. Then it becomes possible, if one wishes, to liberate oneself from them, not by doing away with tropes (which is not possible) but by appropriating and inventing new ones (which is).[100]

In this passage Pratt suggests that ethnographers or anthropologists are always implicated in "(ethnographic) discursive traditions" and "(anthropological/colonial) histories of contact." Thus, to displace colonial or neocolonial narratives, having an awareness of the cultural politics of this body of knowledge (ethnography/anthropology) is a good beginning. To move beyond this initial start, she also suggests that experimenting with or "inventing" new tropes in ethnographic writing is needed to create effective discursive interventions for, indeed, as Pratt makes clear, tropes always exist and cannot be fully eliminated, but new ones can be developed and engaged.

Echoing Clifford, Tsing, and Pratt's postmodern "writing culture" sensibilities, to make sense of the Filipino crosscurrents of seafaring, masculinities, and globalizations, the array of methods I use includes situated traveling ethnography, discourse analysis, travel reportage, and personal reflection, while the knowledge I present in this book is a combination of ethnography and autoethnography, cultural criticism, travelogue, and documentary photography. In addition, I engage and develop an alternative trope and analysis that I hope will be useful to multiple interdisciplinary fields including Philippine Studies, Filipino/a American Studies, Asian American Studies, American Studies, Gender Studies, Queer Studies, and postcolonial studies—namely, the trope and theoretical framework of Filipino crosscurrents. In culturally interpreting the complex nexus of Filipino seafaring, masculinities, and globalization and by engaging the different theoretical, ethnographic, and writing approaches discussed in this introduction, *Filipino Crosscurrents* ultimately shows that the Philippines, its citizens, and those in the diaspora cannot be reduced to neocolonial tropes, imaginaries, and figures such as the supposedly disempowered DH, the marginalized navy steward, or the forlorn and castaway nurse. However, neither can or should the Philippines, its citizens, or Filipino/as in the diaspora be reduced to the figure of the heroic sailor or macho seaman. Instead, I urge readers to reflect on the Philippines and the diaspora, especially the sea-based diaspora, as crosscurrents where differently situated subjects (people), discourse, imaginaries, and ideologies come together on shores, ships, and at sea, through difference, in dissent and solidarity, revealing exploitation and alienation, sometimes resistance and pleasure, but always the complexities of Filipino seafaring and masculinities in the context of economic and cultural globalization.

CHAPTER ONE

The Race of the Century

Galleons and Global City Desires in Manila

It was on the Manila Galleon that we began to become the Philippines.

NICK JOAQUIN, *Manila, My Manila*

You have to ride the boat. You can't miss the boat. There's only one boat.

J. M. LAMORENA (representative of [former] President Joseph Estrada's administration), personal communication.

Manila Bay, Tondo, Metro Manila, Philippines, 1998

Dockside. A band in red uniforms plays traditional fanfare music. A small crowd waits eagerly for boats to arrive. A television helicopter flies overhead, apparently broadcasting live. Everyone is excited, full of anticipation, but no boats arrive. Tired of the waiting and playing during false alarms, the band eventually sits down along a ledge to rest. I sit close to the band members and listen to their conversation.[1] "Maybe they've hit an iceberg," a trombone player jokes, speculating on why the boat has been delayed. We laugh at his ironic imagery. We are in tropical latitudes, after all, thousands of miles away from the nearest iceberg. It is the year of the megahit film *Titanic,* starring Leonardo DiCaprio and Kate Winslet, but we are not in the Northern Atlantic. We are standing at the edge of Manila Bay in Tondo in Manila. The event we are attending is advertised as the Race of the Century. In other promotional materials it is called the Manila–Acapulco Commemorative Regatta.

In trying to ethnographically interpret the maritime land- and seascapes of Manila, I read newspapers daily, learning about shipping and seafaring matters. One morning, I notice an advertisement for the Race of the Century in *The Inquirer*, a leading newspaper in Manila. The event appears to bring together many different things that I love and am interested in: Philippine maritime history, seafaring, sailing, and Manila Bay. On the day of the closing events for the commemorative regatta, I wake up early in Quezon City and take two jeepneys (a form of local transportation) and a taxi, eventually making my way to Tondo where the *Karakoa-MHC* (Manila Harbour Centre), a yacht, is supposed to arrive.

The *Karakoa-MHC* is named after "karakoas," the ancient indigenous boats that once sailed the seas of Mindanao and the Moluccas in the sixteenth century; the Manila Harbour Centre is the yacht's corporate sponsor. The *Karakoa-MHC* has just sailed across the Pacific from Acapulco, Mexico, and according to race organizers, it is the first officially sanctioned boat in centuries to retrace the old Manila–Acapulco galleon trade route, a maritime circuit of trade between two of Spain's former colonies (Las Filipinas [present-day Philippines] and New España [present-day Mexico]), which was active for 250 years (1565–1815).

When I started ethnographic fieldwork in Manila, I observed a strong interest, appreciation, and nostalgia for Manila–Acapulco galleon trade histories. Upon return to the San Francisco Bay Area, I noticed similar sentiments. The Race of the Century was, therefore, not the only time in Manila that Manila–Acapulco galleon trade histories were evoked by locals. For example, when I spoke to Filipino seamen on docked ships in the port or where they congregated in Ermita, many discussed the Manila–Acapulco galleon trade, the Indio/Native sailors who sailed the galleons back and forth across the Pacific, and some of the challenges seamen (past and present) face(d).

"Rudy,"[2] a young seaman from San Carlos, Negros Oriental, when asked why he thought Filipinos were considered "number one" in the global shipping industry, replied, "We're a seafaring people. We've been sailing and working on the seas even before the Spaniards arrived, but during the galleon times, *that* is when we proved ourselves as seamen."

Another young seaman, "Romeo" (from Zamboanga City), commented, "The history of Filipino seafaring is long. Native seamen worked on ships for centuries and now we are just carrying on that tradition." Seaman "Victor" (from Mandaue, Cebu) observed, "Just imagine, the Native sailor didn't have modern instruments during the galleon times like we have now. The Native sailor was a real sailor. Their life was hard. Our life is hard too, but their life was harder." As a final example, seaman "Totoy" (from San Fernando, La Union), a chief cook, commented:

> Sometimes the galleons and the Native seamen come to mind when I'm at sea. Our ships are so much larger than what they sailed and their voyages took longer. They really had guts. But it's like we're the same. Filipino seamen still have to have guts today. Our lives are still hard.

Manila–Acapulco galleon histories for Rudy, Romeo, Victor, and Totoy, as well as for many other seamen whom I do not cite here, were a source of pride for Filipino seamen. This pride, as I understood it, was not necessarily one filled with bravado but rather, imbued with humility because these men had experienced the pleasures and pains of the sea, the ocean's solitude, beauty, and dangers, and the simultaneous feelings of loneliness, displacement, and connection that the sea can potentially bring. In recalling the galleons and Native sailors, they shared an elegant pride that was filled with respect—for themselves as seamen and for their historical counterparts. Their narratives speak to how many of the Filipino seamen I spoke with understood contemporary Filipino seafaring labor and seamen's masculinities through a historical horizon that emphasizes the bygone Manila–Acapulco galleon era and the courageous masculinities of the Indio or Native seamen who traveled the vast expanse of the Pacific during the Spanish colonial period. And so, for a specific group of people—Filipino seamen I met during fieldwork—Manila–Acapulco galleon trade histories were important historical and cultural spaces through which they were able to link their current occupations, shipboard realities, and notions of (working-class Filipino) manhood with the Indio or Native sailors who they considered to be important "Filipino" maritime ancestors or models.[3]

Yet, it was not only Filipino seamen who talked to me about Manila–Acapulco galleon trade histories. Others involved in different aspects of the shipping industry also evoked the galleons and Native sailors during interviews. For instance, Nelson Ramirez (president of United Filipino Seafarers [UFS]), Father Savino Bernardi (priest and advocate at Apostleship of the Sea, an Episcopalian faith-based nongovernmental organization that serves sea-based migrants), and Isabelo A. Samonte (representative of the International Labor Organization) all discussed the importance of Manila–Acapulco galleon trade histories to contemporary Filipino seafaring.

Ramirez, a dapper and charismatic leader of UFS who was formerly a seaman before taking up labor union advocacy, commented,

> Filipino seamen are highly skilled; they're responsible and they're brave. Our history is long and goes back to the Manila–Acapulco galleons

> and beyond. The Indio sailors were mistreated by the Spaniards and similarly, Filipino seamen sailing on ships flying "flags of convenience" are also mistreated.[4]

Bernardi shared these thoughts:

> There is a high demand for Filipino seamen because they are good sailors; they speak English; they are responsible; and they cost less than seafarers from developed countries. Filipinos have an impressive maritime history. They were especially important during the Manila–Acapulco galleon trade. In the present day, we have to remember that Filipino seamen are also migrants. We have to be aware that they also experience problems that are similar to what land-based migrants experience; for example, depression, isolation, loneliness, and abandonment (in port).

And last, Samonte observed,

> We have a seamen's culture here in the Philippines. It is a unique culture because many Filipinos live by the sea. People are impressed with how Filipinos work at sea. Filipinos have an excellent reputation for their seamanship, a reputation that goes back to the galleons. The galleon period is a very important period for Filipino seafaring and for the Philippines.[5]

Like the Filipino seamen previously discussed, seamen's advocates such as Ramirez, Bernardi, and Samonte make similar historical and cultural connections between Manila–Acapulco galleon trade histories and contemporary Filipino seafaring. That is, they link the courageous masculinities of present-day Filipino seamen and past Indio/Native sailors, they highlight the parallels between the high-quality Filipino seamanship found in the present and what they believe existed in the past, and they recall that like past maritime ancestors, contemporary Filipino seamen face hardships in ongoing transpacific and more global maritime trade. In doing so, these seamen's advocates highlight the contributions of Filipino seamen as workers and migrants, as well as the difficult working and social conditions they must face in a globalized shipping industry.

And still, there were others situated outside the shipping industry who also evoked and engaged Manila–Acapulco galleon histories. For example, the U.S. Ambassador to the Philippines at the time, Thomas C. Hubbard, in collaboration with the Ayala Museum in Makati City, helped to develop and distribute a CD-ROM titled, *Castles of the Sea*.[6] The CD-ROM documents the Manila–Acapulco galleon trade with the goal of educating users about the transpacific trade route and Manila's role in sustaining the trade. I met Ambassador Hubbard at a U.S. Embassy event in Manila to which Fulbright scholars were invited. There, I asked him why he got involved with the project and how he became interested in the galleon trade. Ambassador Hubbard replied,

> It's a very important period in Philippine history. The trade was extremely important to the Spanish and I think Filipinos also contributed a great deal to its overall success. It's a history that all Filipinos should be proud of and that's why I wanted to take part in creating this CD-ROM.[7]

As a part of their historical and cultural work, the Ambassador and the Ayala Museum, digitized Manila–Acapulco galleon trade histories, an act of remembering meant to educate people about the transpacific trade, creating media for "all Filipinos" to enjoy.

Manila-based filmmaker and Philippine cinema studies scholar Nick Deocampo, organizer of a centennial film festival (which I attended during fieldwork), also engaged Manila–Acapulco galleon trade histories, most notably *Memories of Old Manila*, a film that poetically explores the legacies of Spanish colonialism and the Manila–Acapulco galleon trade in Manila, as well as themes of memory, contemporary urban poverty, decay, and resistance. While conducting library research in Intramuros (an area that I frequented because of its close proximity to the Port of Manila), I found a copy of Deocampo's provocative film. The narrator in *Memories. . .* , an elderly Filipino man, bears witness to the comings and goings of Manila, currents that brought people and things from all corners of the world.

> This is Intramuros, the walled city, the old Manila. What memories these walls keep after all these centuries? Past its moats walked emissaries from God and princely characters, pagan, sorcerers and Christian martyrs, sacred women and whores. On these streets walked commerce and religion, the pomp and pageantry of our glorious past. This ancient city was Babylon in its commerce and a Jerusalem in its faith. These walls lay witness to the march of History. . . . Here the West first met the East. Here two cultures danced in a maddening encounter between thought and desire, strength and courage. But only one had to win.[8]

Here, Deocampo poetically and cinematically looks to Intramuros, the geographic heart of Manila during the Spanish colonial period, and its haunted postcolonial landscape and architecture, which hold memories from Manila's illustrious and violent port city past. Manila and Intramuros were/are crosscurrents spaces where commerce flourished/flourishes and where "two cultures danced in a maddening encounter." Although not directly articulated by the film's narrator, in the broader context of Deocampo's film, the narrator's comments allude to the Manila–Acapulco galleons, which were the mode of transportation for "emissaries from God and princely characters" and which facilitated Spain's global imperial conquest and commerce, contributing to Manila's "Babylon"-ish and "Jerusalem"-like atmosphere.

As these ethnographic examples suggest, many Manila-based men, from Filipino seamen to seamen's advocates to cultural workers, regularly evoked Manila–Acapulco galleon trade narratives during my fieldwork in Manila. Thus, when I learned that the Race of the Century/ Manila–Acapulco Commemorative Regatta was being celebrated at the Manila Harbour Centre, my ethnographic curiosity was running high. I was motivated to explore why the commemorative regatta was being held and to what political, cultural, and economic end(s). Indeed, histories in and of themselves are not necessarily "positive" or "negative," but rather what is more crucial is understanding and unpacking the ideologies and resulting everyday practices that are often entangled with particular histories and discourse.

In short, at the Race of the Century/Manila–Acapulco Commemorative Regatta, Philippine state and corporate leaders were evoking the galleon trade and Filipino seafaring in more troubling, ideologically conservative ways. In the remainder of the chapter, using the Race of the Century as an ethnographic departure point and crosscurrents portal, I culturally critique the problematic ways that state and corporate officials evoked Manila–Acapulco galleons. I also address the gendered cultural logics and political economies that helped constitute (late 1990s) state and corporate Manila–Acapulco galleon discourse, how these narratives were/are connected to "global city" and "manning capital of the (shipping) world" discourses and desires, and why these gendered cultural logics and political economies were significant in Manila at the end of the twentieth century, but also in the broader geopolitical contexts of the Philippines, Southeast Asia, and Asia and the Pacific. In taking these ethnographic turns, this chapter outlines a more macroeconomic and macrocultural interpretation of the cultural politics and political economies of Filipino seafaring, masculinities, and globalization. In the next chapter, I tack away from the macrolevel and address the cultural politics and political economies of more micro or interpersonal dynamics of seafaring, masculinities, and globalization.

Manila–Acapulco Galleon Trade Histories

Although I often observed different Filipino/as in Metro Manila and the San Francisco Bay Area evoking Manila–Acapulco galleon trade histories, quite often discussions were not historically deep or specific enough. It is a history many Filipinos are aware of, but often our historical understanding is generic or superficial. Especially in the United States, it is a history that is completely marginalized in the history books used in elementary, high school, or university curricula, precisely because the history precedes the "birth" of the United States as a nation-state, the trade route primarily took place outside of the contemporary borders of the United States, and institutionalized U.S. American histories tend to be nationalistic and historically/geographically narrow or limited. Yet, Manila–Acapulco galleon trade histories are important histories to know because the transpacific trade influenced and had an impact on a number of geographies and oceanographies important to Philippine Studies, Filipino/a American Studies, Asian American Studies, and American Studies. In the spirit of providing readers with some historical and cultural context to understand the significance of Manila–Acapulco galleons in a contemporary context, the following paragraphs outline key aspects of the trade.

According to historian William L. Schurz, the Manila–Acapulco galleon trade route is considered the "longest continuous navigation in the world" and also one of the most "treacherous."[9] The 250-year-old trade route (1565–1815) connected Spain's colonies in the Americas (i.e., New Spain/Mexico), the Pacific Basin (Guam and Marianas), and Southeast Asia (Philippines), but the central ports of contact were between Manila and Acapulco. According to statesman and historian Robert A. Underwood, the galleons sailed and stopped in Guam, but there was no official station there for many decades. Subsequently, galleon travel to Guam in the early phase of the trade was irregular.[10] In 1668, by royal order, galleon captains and their crews were officially directed to establish a port of call in Guam. This practice, however, did not regularly occur until the Spaniards established a Jesuit mission in Guam during the same year. Because of the length of time for communication to reach Spain's far-reaching colonies, royal decrees were often ignored or unimplemented. In other instances, Spaniards living in far-away colonies or those sailing the galleons simply did not agree with decrees and regulations, which literally originated from the other side of the planet. As a result, new rules or policies were seen as out of touch or irrelevant. Thus, there was no efficient or effective way for Spanish authorities and regimes to ensure that

Spaniards living in the colonies or sailing the galleons, "their" colonial subjects, actually obeyed royal decrees.

Putting the Manila–Acapulco galleon trade route in a more global perspective, from Acapulco, Mexico, Asian goods and commodities were transported overland by mules, carts, and men to the Port of Vera Cruz. The Asian goods and commodities were stored in warehouses, and eventually, other Spanish galleons and armadas, which had sailed from Spain, would transport the Asian goods and commodities to Spain's primary port in the Caribbean, Havana, Cuba. From Havana, the Spanish galleons sailed to the Canary Islands (another Spanish colony) and then continued to the Port of Cadiz in Spain. In the context of Spain's global empire, the Manila–Acapulco galleon trade route represents an important trajectory within Spain's circulatory system of global imperial maritime trade. That is, the galleon trade between the Philippines and Mexico greatly facilitated a *transpacific* maritime exchange and flow of goods, commodities, people, wealth, and culture, but it was also *transatlantic*. In other words (colonial Spanish) Pacific worlds and Atlantic worlds came together through the galleons, connecting Spanish colonies in Southeast and East Asia, the Pacific Islands, the Americas, the Caribbean archipelago, and Spain itself.

According to historian John Kuo Wei Tchen and documentary filmmaker Loni Ding, a significant aspect of the Manila–Acapulco galleon trade was that it facilitated commerce of Chinese commodities and spices from Southeast Asia that were in high demand in the Americas and Europe.[11] Indeed, as Tchen and Ding's research shows, "the West" had been looking to "the East" for centuries. Chinese silks were the primary goods transported to Acapulco, but other commodities such as mangoes, local textiles and wares from Mindanao and pearls from Sulu were also transported to the Americas. In return, merchants in Manila were compensated with silver from Mexico and Peru. Manila merchants also imported goods such as corn, pineapples, arrowroot, peanuts, lima beans, chocolate, and cassava.

The maritime trade between Manila and Acapulco facilitated important economic and cultural exchange, and it also facilitated political relationships between the Philippines and Mexico. The ties between the two Spanish colonies were so significant and substantial that historian Carlos Quirino suggests that in many ways the Philippines was a like a colony of Mexico.[12] As mentioned previously, during the Manila–Acapulco galleon trade era communication and travel between Spain and its colonial outposts were slow. Mexico was closer to the Philippines (compared with Spain, especially prior to the Suez Canal opening), so much of Spain's political, cultural, and economic influences were "filtered" through

Mexico. As an outcome of this dynamic, Quirino suggests that Mexico's colonial influence on the Philippines was stronger than Spain's.

Political relationships were forged but cultural exchange also flourished. Quirino suggests further that some of the Aztecs who crewed the galleons traveling to Manila brought with them their language, which locals and Natives in the archipelago eventually borrowed. For example, some Tagalog words that have Nahuatl origins are *balsa* (a light wood), *calabaza* (a kind of squash), *chocolate*, *nana(y)* (mother), and *tata(y)* (father). However, as anthropologist Olga Nájera-Ramírez points out (in a personal communication), Quirino's cultural explanation may not be completely accurate because many indigenous/Nahuatl words were incorporated into Spanish. Although linguistic exchange/linguistic colonialism occurred in Mexico, one cannot assume that Spaniards or Indios in Manila learned of Nahuatl words directly from indigenous sailors from Mexico (although it may be possible that they did). Quirino's specific point about indigenous sailors from Mexico being present in Manila is, therefore, debatable, but Quirino's broader point that there was significant cultural and political exchange between the Philippines and Mexico during the galleon trade era is well founded. Through the Manila–Acapulco galleon trade, in addition to trading goods and commodities, the Philippines and Mexico also exchanged popular culture such as fashion and music. For example, the barong tagalog (the native dress of Filipino lowland Christian men; Filipino Muslim men and indigenous men often have different styles of "traditional clothing") is said to have originated in Mexico, and musical compositions such as "La Paloma" and "Sanduanga Mia" are said to have been first heard in Mexico, before becoming popular in the Philippines.

Because of the influx of goods and commodities and cultural and political influences in the Philippines that the galleons facilitated, the Manila–Acapulco galleon trade was extremely important to the city of Manila. Spaniards in Manila (or "Filipinos" as they were often called in contrast to Spaniards from Spain who were called "Peninsulares") greatly focused on the galleon trade to the detriment of other forms of economic livelihood such as agriculture. Quirino suggests that agricultural activities were inadequately developed in the archipelago during the height of the galleon trade. Life in Intramuros, the "walled city," the racially segregated Spanish section of Manila, revolved around the galleon trade and schedule. Although it often took five to seven months for a galleon to reach Acapulco, the return voyage to Manila was usually faster (by one or two months) because of the more favorable winds and currents, which flowed in the direction toward Asia. Inhabitants of Manila anxiously awaited the departures and arrivals of the galleons because significant wealth and cultural exchange were at stake. As such, life in Manila economically and socially revolved around the Manila–Acapulco galleon trade during the 250-year life span of the maritime trade.

Although it is commonly believed that during the Manila–Acapulco galleon trade, Manila was an ultra-wealthy city, historians such as Schurz point out that the city's economy was actually more tenuous or irregular. That is, the success or failure of Manila–Acapulco galleon ventures significantly affected Manila's economic situation. Storms, shipwrecks, and piracy were some of the most common dangers that ultimately affected Manila's economy, as goods were either lost at sea, stolen, or destroyed, never arriving at designated ports of call.

Despite the numerous dangers that could prevent the galleons from reaching Acapulco or Manila, the galleon trade continued throughout the years. Eventually, specific Spanish individuals or their families, for example, Antonio Pacheco and Francisco David, controlled significant parts of the transpacific trade. Year after year Pacheco's and David's names appeared regularly on manifest lists, suggesting that they were prominent merchants involved in the Manila–Acapulco galleon trade.[13] Less prominent merchants or other local people also participated in the trade. Although not necessarily of extreme wealth, they could buy space from larger merchants (e.g., Pacheco and David) or from sailors (e.g., Spanish, Indio, or Chinese) who often sold their allotment of (one) trunk space to Manileños who needed to transport goods to Mexico, other parts of the Americas, the Caribbean, or Europe.

Spanish merchants and traders became prominent in Manila, but Chinese merchants, traders, and elites were a key force to be reckoned with in Manila (and surrounding areas) as well because they significantly influenced the economic success or failure of the Manila–Acapulco galleon trade and the economic and social climate of Manila. Chinese merchants and settlers had been in the Philippines for centuries, but like the mid-to-late 1800s gold rush in California, the transpacific galleon trade drew more Chinese people, mostly men, who eventually intermarried with Native women and participated in maritime and land-based trade. As a result of intermarriage and long-time residency in Manila and other nearby towns, Chinese or Chinese mestiza (women) merchants and traders were also successful traders in Manila and in other locales. One such Chinese mestiza businesswoman was Tecla Chichioco, a successful trader whose parents also had businesses ventures in different "palengkes" (markets) in Malolos and other parts of Bulacan (province), as well as in other provinces in Central Luzon. According to scholar

Nicanor Tiongson, Chichioco established a trading business in Malolos rather than Manila because Manila was already saturated with Chinese- or Chinese mestizo-run operations.[14] This suggests that Chinese and Chinese mestizos were well established in Manila, a key port city of the Manila–Acapulco galleon trade.

Chinese traders and merchants operated on small-scale levels, but many also had vast wealth and were thus part of an elite social and economic class.[15] Although already established in Manila (and other parts of the archipelago) prior to the Spanish invasion, Chinese merchants and traders served as the dominant suppliers of cargo to residents of Mexico and the broader Spanish empire, so the galleons were also called the "Nao de China" (ships from China). Chinese communities were segregated in Manila, geographically limited to an area called the Parian. Tiongson suggests, however, that over time the Chinese intermarried and eventually became part of local Filipino culture and communities (especially in and near Manila).[16] And although politically and socially subordinate to the Spanish who maintained colonial rule (indeed, the Chinese were often the victims of anti-Chinese violence and injustice) Chinese merchants and traders supplied the significantly large volume of China-based goods and commodities and their presence greatly affected the rhythms and ultimately the economic successes or failures of the trade. For example, during times of heightened Chinese–Spanish conflict, the galleon trade either declined or temporarily ceased.

Spanish, Chinese, and mestizo/as were not the only ones who contributed to the Manila–Acapulco galleon trade. Natives (Indios) also participated, sometimes by force, and other times more freely. Sociologist and historian Rolando G. Talampas,[17] for example, writes about the brutal contributions and extreme sacrifices of Natives in shipbuilding and crewing the ships that sailed back and forth between Manila and Acapulco. In both of these areas Talampas suggests that Natives were subjected to harsh treatment, economic exploitation, death, and partial or full enslavement. Native men carried out the difficult and dangerous work of cutting down and dragging the lumber to the shipyards, which were, for example, located, in Cavite (south of Manila). A significant number of Native men also labored in the crews that transited the Pacific. As already discussed, the transpacific voyage held many dangers. It is fair to speculate, then, that many of those who died at sea were Native/Indio sailors. Moreover, as the galleons were constructed in larger sizes, they transported more cargo and passengers and the number of crew members increased from approximately 60 to 150. In this transpacific maritime trade, Native sailors or seamen primarily occupied the position of "common seamen" (what would be called ordinary seaman today). Social hierarchies and economic and social inequalities between Spaniards and Natives were common on board the galleons; for example, compared with their Spanish counterparts who received 100 pesos for their labor, Natives received 48 to 60 pesos.[18]

The voyage from Manila to Acapulco was long and arduous, averaging five to seven months depending on the weather, winds, currents, danger from pirates, and health of the crew. In hindsight, some may wonder why the Spaniards never stumbled into Hawai'i, as this would have made the voyage significantly easier because galleon crews would have had the opportunity to replenish supplies and water as well as give sick passengers or crew members a place to recuperate. Historian Carla Phillips suggests that the primary reason Spaniards never (officially) sailed to Hawai'i is that the galleons generally sailed conservatively because of the commercial interests that were central to the trade. Commanders of galleon vessels tried not to disrupt established patterns of navigation because they were fearful of sailing into trouble by voyaging into unknown and perhaps dangerous waters. Phillips suggests further that commanders were under strict orders "not to explore," as colonial administrators and royal officials did not believe this was the galleon's primary role. In conclusion, Phillips argues that there is significant material and oral (traditions) evidence to support the idea that there was indeed contact between Spanish mariners and Native Hawaiians during the two and a half centuries between Magellan and Cook.[19]

Not only long, the voyage across the Pacific was also uncomfortable. Passengers who paid the 2,000 to 4,000 pesos for safe passage across the Pacific, as well as the seamen who crewed the ships, had to endure harsh conditions: bad food, illness, overcrowding, cramped quarters, boredom, and bad weather. Although significant amounts of food were carried on board for the transpacific voyage (one manifest from 1590 listed 40,000 pounds of biscuits; 2,388 pounds of salted meat, garbanzos, and beans; 50 bacons; 900 cheeses; large quantities of oil and vinegar; and 405 pounds of onions and garlic), according to Schurz, it was not unusual for galleons to run out of food or for crews and passengers to find themselves with low supplies. When the food started to run out, some could rely on the chocolate or sweetmeats they brought on board for the long voyage, but, generally, it was the poorer passengers and ordinary seamen who received the least rations during shipboard food shortages. Passengers and seamen also did not have sufficient space to move on board the ships because all the decks and the spaces below in the hold were usually filled to capacity with cargo. Shippers and merchants filled the galleons to such extreme capacities that they sometimes had to pull excess cargo on raft-like platforms behind the ships. At other times, galleon crews threw cargo overboard if their ship was not sailing efficiently or was under attack or in danger from a storm.

Despite the difficult voyage, passengers and seamen coped with many of the difficulties on board, and there were clearly moments of pleasure and recreation. For example, passengers and seamen gambled to pass the time (although by royal decree, gambling was supposedly illegal), or they danced when weather and space permitted. Sometimes women who worked in prostitution accompanied wealthier Spanish men, thereby providing sexual labor and companionship. Passengers and seamen also organized fiestas at first sight of land. In these ways, during the many months it took to sail across the Pacific, passengers and seamen creatively sought out activities that made their journeys a little more pleasant or pleasurable.

The Manila–Acapulco galleon trade had a significant impact on the economic, social, and cultural life of Manila. Linking the former Spanish colonies of Mexico and the Philippines, the transpacific maritime trade linked Asia, sometimes the Pacific Islands, and the Americas, attracting more Chinese settlers, merchants, and traders to the Philippine archipelago and in the process facilitating economic, political, and cultural exchange. The maritime trade's success ebbed and flowed but not without human costs. Although many Spanish and Chinese shippers and merchants profited from the transpacific trade, in the context of Spanish colonialism, Natives were exploited and many lost their lives as they labored to build ships and sail the Pacific. A significant outcome of the Manila–Acapulco galleon trade was that Manila's strategic location as a Spanish colonial entrepôt between the "East and the West" was established. Subsequent colonial powers in the Asia and the Pacific region (e.g., British, U.S. American, and Japanese) looked to the archipelago for its strategic geographic position in Southeast Asia. After operating for 250 years, the Manila–Acapulco galleon trade ended as a result of the Suez Canal opening, which provided an alternative and more efficient route to Europe. In 1810, Mexico declared independence from Spain, which severed or lessened political and economic ties between the Philippines and Mexico because at the time of Mexico's declaration, the Philippines remained a colony of Spain (the Philippines did not declare independence until 1896).

Neoliberal Economics and Corporate Globalization in the Philippines

When I saw the newspaper advertisement for the Race of the Century (Manila–Acapulco Commemorative Regatta) and when I later decided to attend the event, I was not aware that the race and postrace celebration were part of a plan to promote Philippine President Fidel V. Ramos's neoliberal economic plan Philippines 2000. I assumed that the regatta was part of Philippine Centennial celebrations since there were many government-sponsored centennial events planned that year. I was partially correct. The regatta was part of state-sponsored efforts to celebrate the nation, but it was also intended to celebrate the state's love of neoliberal economics, as manifested through Ramos's Philippines 2000, a development scheme created through the economic and cultural logics of neoliberal "free trade."[20] The plan's ultimate objective was for the Philippines to achieve Nic-hood (Newly Industrialized Country) status by the year 2000. While Nic-hood appears to be a "neutral" or reasonable economic goal, Philippines 2000 actually emphasized the following ideologies and approaches: free trade and the opening up of markets to international/global competition; expanding deregulation and the privatization of industries; decreasing governmental regulation of price controls on basic commodities and services; cutting public expenditures for social services such as education and healthcare (also known as "structural adjustment"); and stressing and prioritizing "individual responsibility" and eliminating or minimizing the concept of the "public good" or "community." As Chicana feminist activist Elizabeth "Betita" Martinez and immigrant rights and social justice activist Arnoldo Garcia argue, the economic philosophy of neoliberalism seeks to further pressure the poor, the working poor, and the working classes to individually find solutions to larger social problems such as lack of health care, education, or poverty.[21]

In the case of the Philippines, the Ramos administration deregulated a number of sectors, including telecommunications, banking, and insurance, which resulted in the opening up of local Philippine markets. This in turn allowed and enabled more multinational corporations to enter, compete, and/or take over local companies in the aforementioned sectors. In addition to deregulation, creating "regional growth centers" was another objective of Philippines 2000. Under Ramos's plan, for example, more than 118,000 hectares of irrigated land were designated for conversion into "industrial corridor(s)." According to (Maoist) radical social and economic justice advocates, this plan would have displaced 130,000 families in the Philippines.[22]

Two key pieces of legislation undergird Philippines 2000, namely, the Special Economic Zone Act and the amended Build-Operate-and-Transfer law. The Special Economic Zone Act governs the creation and administration of Export Processing Zones and Free Trade Zones, whereas the Build-Operate-and-Transfer law allows wholly owned foreign firms to participate in these programs.[23] Incentives for multinational corporations in "special economic zones" include tax- and duty-free importation of inputs, corporate welfare or income tax holidays, and a 5 percent gross income tax in lieu of regular taxes and exemption from many other fees.

Philippines 2000 (what many in the Philippines believed was simply a new name for an old agenda of elite and multinational corporate control of the Philippines) received intense criticism from the political left and progressive or radical communities and organizations in the Philippines, including the National Democratic Front, indigenous peoples, feminist and women's organizations such as GABRIELA, environmentalists, trade unionists, and migrant rights advocates. Diverse participants in these social justice/nationalist movements argued that economic elites and foreign multinationals were touting Philippines 2000 or corporate globalization solutions to improve economic and social conditions in the Philippines. Progressive and radical social, economic, and environmental justice advocates pointed out, however, that the opposite was true. According to different constituents of the previously mentioned progressive social movements, Philippines 2000 and other corporate globalization schemes of neoliberal free trade actually make the Philippines and its residents more vulnerable to multinational corporate expansion, multinational corporate exploitation, environmental destruction, and widespread poverty. Moreover, they argue that neoliberal economic schemes continue the Philippines's long-time dependence on foreign capital, investments, trade, technologies, and ideologies.

The Philippine state, in promoting Philippines 2000 and its agenda of neoliberalism and special economic zones, during the last several decades of the twentieth century, closely collaborated with global financial institutions such as the International Monetary Fund (IMF), World Bank, the World Trade Organization, and multinational corporations to expand neoliberal economic schemes. In many cases the collaboration was unequal, with the IMF and World Bank *forcing* different national governments, particularly those of the Global South, to implement and institutionalize free trade, structural adjustment, and other corporate globalization policies.[24]

Political scientist Alison Brysk has argued, however, that globalization, that is, not the excessively corporate kind, has produced some positive social effects and benefits.[25] Brysk discusses how globalization has improved telecommunications; created a freer flow of information; provided more opportunities for improved global awareness of social, economic, racial, and environmental justice; and facilitated more effective transnational grassroots activism and resistance, to outline a few more positive political and cultural impacts. Despite these advances in telecommunications and cross-border or transnational social justice organizing, it is important to remain aware of how neoliberalism and *corporate* globalization have created or continue to create more exclusion, poverty, and human rights abuses, especially for people in the Global South, including the Philippines.

As a result of neoliberalism and corporate globalization in the last several decades, multinational corporations have increased profits and political power and are now more than ever in the advantaged position to dictate the terms of production and trade. Multinational corporations (including shipping companies) can now move production (or sea-based transportation) to any country they choose (via open ship registry), usually one with minimal or nonexistent labor and environmental protections, monitoring, and scrutiny. In sum, multinational corporations have increased mobility and flexibility—opening and closing manufacturing plants, registering ships in different countries, or hiring seamen of other nations, at will, if local challenges emerge. Challenges may include, for example, union organizing, demands for higher wages, higher corporate taxes, or expanded regulation of industries. The same mobility and flexibility also apply to foreign investments or capital. At the end of the twentieth century and in the early years of the twenty-first century, capital has moved much more freely and quickly around the globe than in other historical periods. This was the case during the Asian Financial Crisis of 1997–98 when investors quickly withdrew capital from local (Southeast and East Asian) economies, and this was the case in 2008 when the United States–led global financial crisis emerged. Both crises of capitalism created intense local and regional economic and social disruptions.

In this more globalized context, national governments have become largely unable or unwilling to regulate multinational corporations to protect their citizens, workers, communities, and environments; this includes, in particular, the Philippine government.[26] Those who are vulnerable in this far-reaching economic system include those who come from historically marginalized communities around the world: poor people, the working class, the working poor, people of color, indigenous peoples, women, children, and sexual minorities. According to sociologist and activist Walden Bello, the Executive Director of the Bangkok-based nongovernmental organization Focus on the Global South, inequality and poverty around the world dramatically increased as neoliberal economic policies were implemented in many regions of the world. I quote Bello's sobering assessment at length:

> Structural adjustment and related free-market policies that were imposed beginning in the early 1980s were the central factor that

> triggered a sharp rise in inequality globally, with one authoritative UN study covering 124 countries showing that the income share of the richest 20 percent of the world's population rose from 69 to 83% between 1965 and 1990. Secondly, adjustment policies were a central factor behind the rapid concentration of global income in recent years—a process which in 1998, saw Bill Gates, with a net worth of $90 billion, Warren Buffet, with $36 billion and Microsoft cofounder Paul Allen, with $30 billion, achieve a combined income that was greater than the total combined income of the 600 million that live in the world's 48 developed countries, a great number of which had been subjected to adjustment programs.[27]

Bello clearly shows that the effects of neoliberalism, free trade, and structural adjustment have been catastrophic for the poorer countries of the world, whereas wealthier nations and individuals have clearly benefited from neoliberalism and corporate globalization.

How were the IMF and World Bank allowed to negatively influence the Philippine economy and social conditions in the archipelago? In 1972, when Philippine President-cum-Dictator Ferdinand Marcos declared martial law in the Philippines (creating a police state to impose "stability"; that is, the dictatorial regime used military/police force to combat oppositional social movements such as Maoist-based communism, women's movements, indigenous peoples' movements, and radical student organizing), IMF and World Bank loans, multinational corporations, and foreign investors quickly entered the archipelago, facilitating the deepening of social and economic inequalities. The Philippines's cycle of debt and dependency worsened in the 1980s with structural adjustment programs that decreased government investments in education and health, deregulated previously nationalized industries, and forced massive debt repayments.

In the 1990s with the (Fidel V.) Ramos administration in power, the Philippines experienced its second wave of neoliberal economics. Bello writes,

> During the Ramos period, we had a second wave of trade liberalization . . . imposed by doctrinal technocrats who were in command at that point, like Ciel Habito. They aimed to bring down, across the board, all tariffs between 1 to 4%. Their model in this exercise was the Pinochet government in Chile, because at that time in Chile they brought down, across the board, the average tariff to 11%. Their thinking was that if the Chileans can withstand tariffs being brought down to 11%, then of course we Pinoys can bring down our

> tariffs to 1–4% and we will survive. What that accomplished was to accelerate the crisis of our industries during the Ramos period. More and more firms fell into bankruptcy; the investment atmosphere was so bad that the local industry refused to invest significantly. So basically, this process tied into the process of globalization that really became the official ideology and the official push in the Philippines in the 1990s.[28]

Along with this opening up of the markets, implemented in part through what Bello notes are practically nonexistent tariffs, in the 1990s, the United States and its allied institutions the IMF, World Bank, and Asian Development Bank distributed $557 million worth of loans and grants to the Philippines. In 1998 the Philippines had a foreign debt burden of $46.4 billion, and the annual debt service amounted to $4.4 billion or 8.8 percent of the Philippines $52.6 billion GDP.[29] Using a 1997 estimate, 32 percent of the population lived below the poverty line and the unemployment rate was 9.6 percent. (This rate would be considerably higher if the 7 million Filipino/as who are forced to leave the Philippines to work in more than 180 countries worldwide are taken into account; 7 million is a 2000 statistic.[30]) As noted in the Introduction (as I write in 2009), there are now approximately 11 million Filipino/as working outside the Philippines.

A decade later in 2008, the People Against Illegitimate Debt (PAID!) movement in the Philippines, a partner of the Freedom From Debt Coalition, a nonprofit organization that organizes for social justice and debt relief reported the following debt statistics:

> To date, the National Government has a debt of P3.78 trillion or $81.6 billion. Our total consolidated public sector debt as [a] percentage [of] our Gross Domestic Product (GDP) is 81.9 percent. Each Filipino soul from the newly born baby to a dying septuagenarian is indebted by as much as P43,487, paying P7,012 annually to service the debt.[31]

Doris Dumlao, a journalist writing for the *Philippine Daily Inquirer*, writes, "The new poverty line for Asia-Pacific is $1.35 a day and about 23 million Filipinos, or 27 percent of the Philippine population, are living below it."[32] Moreover, reflecting on Philippines 2000, Lyn Resurreccion, the Nation and Science editor for *Philippines Today*, writes, ". . . NIC-hood in 2000 never materialized. It showed that the country needed some catching up to do with its more technologically dynamic neighbors."[33] In light of the ongoing poverty and increasing debt burdens of the Philippines, this suggests the debt and dependency cycle for the Philippines has continued to deepen in the last twelve years since I began fieldwork, poverty for millions of Filipino/as persists, and the Philippines did not reach Nic-hood by 2000, nor did the Philippines catch up with its more prosperous industrialized neighbors.

The Philippines's dire economic situation and social realities speak to the critical need for ethnographers and other cultural analysts and cultural workers to document, expose, and culturally critique how governments and multinational corporate leaders use particular narratives and ideologies in their attempts to legitimize, naturalize, and/or ultimately institutionalize neoliberal free trade corporate globalization agendas. This ethnographic focus on "the top" or on elites is important because the state and capital working together have significant material and ideological power. In the remaining sections of this chapter, I disentangle the interconnections between the Race of the Century (Manila–Acapulco Commemorative Regatta), Philippine state/corporate "global city" desires, the Asian Financial Crisis of 1997–98, Philippine state/corporate hopes that Manila maintains its position as the manning capital of the (shipping) world, and intersectional discourses that seek to disempower and feminize the Philippines, Philippine citizens, and Filipino/a overseas/diaspora populations through gendered heteropatriarchal and neocolonial cultural logics.

Race of the Century (Manila–Acapulco Commemorative Regatta)

The band and I continue to wait for the yachts that have just finished sailing the Race of the Century. This race began in Acapulco Bay (Mexico) in January 1998 and ended in Mactan (Philippines) in mid-March 1998 and was composed of three separate races: race 1 from Acapulco Bay (Mexico) to Waikiki Beach (Hawai'i, U.S.A.); race 2 from Waikiki Beach to Guam (U.S.A.); and race 3 from Guam to Mactan (Visayas, Philippines). Having won the earlier races, the *Karakoa-MHC* yacht was declared the overall winner of the regatta. To celebrate the race and to commemorate Manila–Acapulco galleon trade histories in Manila (i.e., not in Mactan) and to help launch the Manila Harbour Centre, the *Karakoa-MHC* is scheduled to arrive soon at the docks, where a small crowd lingers and waits. In the crowd, there appear to be many upper-class Filipino families who either arrived by chauffeur or in self-driven luxury cars or SUVs, dressed in Sunday-best-meets-cruise-wear fashion: lots of leather Sperry topsiders, white cropped capri pants, and preppy navy blazers. Other participants include the Mexican ambassador to the Philippines, Enrique Michel, his diplomatic colleagues, local journalists covering the regatta, and onlookers from nearby barrios in Tondo where the Manila Harbour Centre is located.

After waiting for a few hours, the band and the crowd are rewarded for their patience. The *Karakoa-MHC* approaches the dock, cruising

Marching band playing (and waiting) at Race of the Century at Manila Harbour Centre, 1998.

comfortably by motor, a Philippine flag on board waving in the wind. Several yachts from the Manila Yacht Club join the *Karakoa-MHC* sailing into the vicinity. Sailing enthusiasts on shore enjoy the views of sailboats skimming across a medium denim-blue Manila Bay. The skies are clear, and there is plenty of sunshine. The marching band greets the yachts and sailors, competently performing several entertaining numbers. Tuba sounds and drumbeats hang in the salt air.

Finally, the *Karakoa-MHC* is at the dock. A number of *Karakoa-MHC* sailors dismount to secure the boat by tying lines to the dock cleats. Curiously, most of the crew (there are eight of them) are white and appear to be in the forty to sixty age range. I find out later that most of the crew are from the United States. The sailors look sunburned, sea salted, and joyful. They dress in Land's End or Nautica type clothing, Teva sandals adorn their feet, and baseball caps protect heads and faces. In fine spirits, the sailors assemble themselves on deck, and Filipino photojournalists line up to take photos of the *Karakoa-MHC* and the sailors who have sailed from North America.

After all the boats have docked, there is more fanfare and photo ops, cocktails and light food are served, and a postregatta ceremony is scheduled. During the reception, I learn from a Filipino journalist that there

"The Race of the Century is on. . . ." Advertisement for Commemorative Regatta, Manila Harbour Centre, 1998.

was one Mexican man and one Filipino on board sailing with the white U.S. Americans. One middle-aged heterosexual couple with whom I spoke identified themselves as sailing enthusiasts from San Francisco, California. "Barbara" looks at me with surprise when I approach and ask her a few questions; she was perhaps not expecting to meet a Filipino American graduate student–ethnographer from University of California, Santa Cruz, at the arrival point of her transpacific voyage. Barbara tells me that when they were sailing across the Pacific, the crew did indeed think of the Manila–Acapulco galleon trade and the galleon sailors. "It was extremely rough," she commented. "We tried to imagine them sailing on ships which were not equipped with modern technology. We were in awe and developed tremendous respect for what they had accomplished." Her sea-based observations and reflections echo those of Filipino seamen I spoke with at the Port of Manila and in Ermita and Malate in the weeks and months prior to the arrival of the *Karakoa-MHC.*

Next, the event sponsors and honored guests address the small crowd. Mexico's Ambassador Michel reflects on the momentous occasion and the cultural connections between Mexico and the Philippines. The Ambassador evokes several points raised by historian Carlos Quirino in his classic essay, "The Mexican Connection; the Cultural Cargo of the

Regatta scene at Manila Harbour Centre, 1998.

Karakoa-MHC crew at Manila Harbour Centre, 1998.

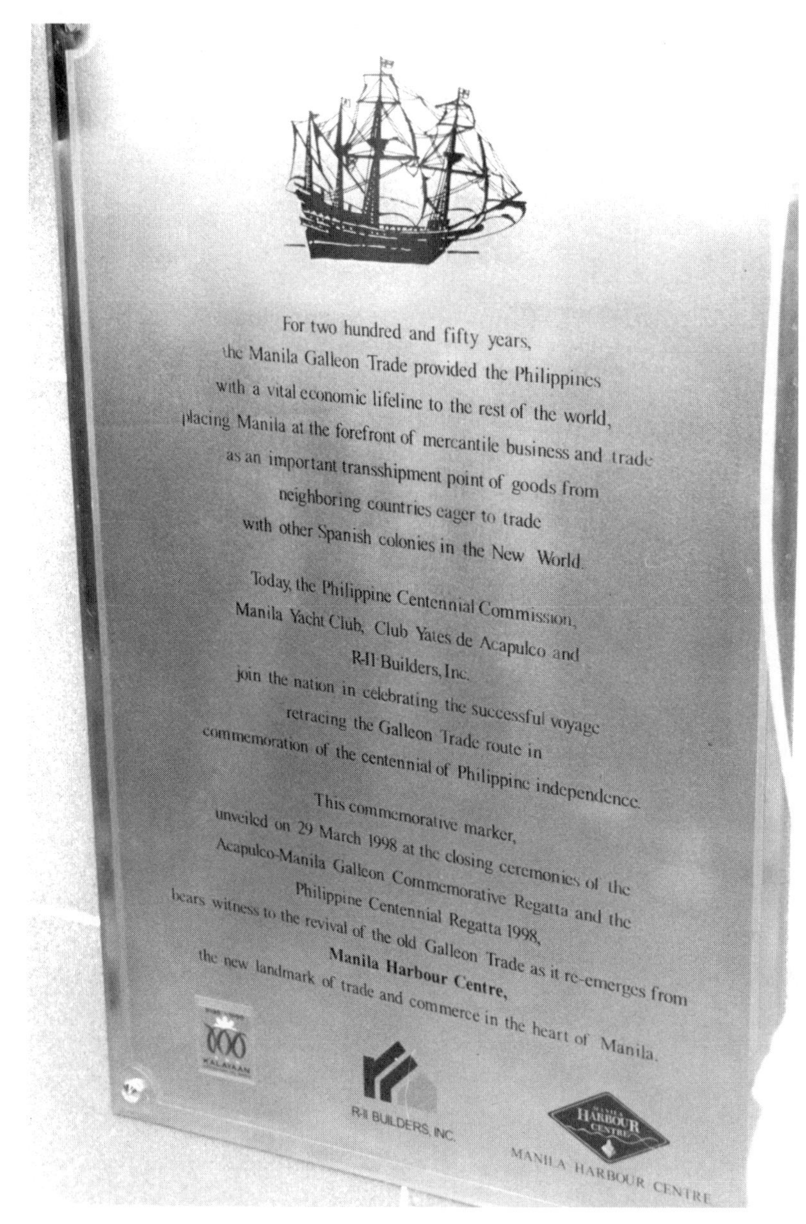

Historical marker commemorating Manila galleon trade and regatta, 1998.

Manila-Acapulco Galleons." Ambassador Michel, for instance, talks about the cargo exchanged between the two colonies and how the galleon trade would forever tie Mexico and the Philippines. Later, Ambassador Michel unveils a historical marker that commemorates the regatta and the Manila–Acapulco trade route. More photos are snapped.

The Race of the Century (Manila–Acapulco Commemorative Regatta), sponsored by R-II Builders Incorporated, a private company building the Manila Harbour Centre, is coorganized by the Manila Yacht Club and the Club Yates de Acapulco, under the auspices of the National Centennial Commission, a Philippine government-sponsored commission that organizes centennial events in the Philippines. The Chairman and Chief Executive Officer (CEO) of R-II Builders Incorporated, Reghis M. Romero, is next on the program. His task is to introduce the Manila Harbour Centre, the new port facility and free trade zone, where the postregatta festivities are being held. The Manila Harbour Centre, described by corporate sponsors through their press packets, is supposed to be an "ultramodern port city" with port facilities, assembly plants, and a financial center. The Manila Harbour Centre is also a free trade zone and a significant project of Philippines 2000. Chairman and CEO Romero speaks to the regatta participants and attendees:

> This is the area that came from what you see across—the Smokey Mountain, where since 1952, the whole of Manila was dumping its garbage. . . . With much resolve, His Excellency, President Fidel V. Ramos pursued the transformation of Smokey Mountain into what you see now. Thirty residential buildings, where 3,500 families who were former residents of Smokey Mountain live. This area where we are all standing on now is envisioned to be the showcase of the vision of the Philippines 2000. It has three zones, the 15 hectare port, the 32 hectare industrial park and 32 hectare central business district.
>
> It is therefore easy to see that in the same way the galleon trade made Manila the hub for trade and commerce in the 15th century *[sic]*, in this area along the Manila Bay, shall also rise this generation's prestigious business address.
>
> However, the vision for Manila Harbour Centre is not the main reason for its being. *Its underlying purpose really is to create this bridge between the affluent and the underprivileged; to create a venue where investments can flourish and where employment can be generated.*
>
> As we work toward the fulfillment of our dream for Smokey Mountain and the Manila Harbour Centre, our strategy now is to

> make this facility available for significant events like this regatta. Consider it our humble gesture to bring it closer to the people who are the ultimate beneficiaries of this development. [emphasis added]

During his remarks to the regatta crowd, Chairman and CEO Romero uses the Race of the Century and Manila–Acapulco galleon trade histories to articulate and signify neoliberal capitalist hopes and free-trade desires. Romero's speech marks a clear temporal moment in which the Manila–Acapulco galleon trade history is evoked, not only because of the obvious historical and geographical transpacific connection that the regatta retraced, but to emphasize Manila's place and the Manila Harbour Centre's place in regional and global economies, in the past, present, and future.

In both Ambassador Michel's and Chairman and CEO Romero's speeches, Manila–Acapulco galleon trade histories were used to celebrate Manila's strategic location in the context of Asia/Pacific and global economies, the legacy of the Manila–Acapulco maritime trade, and the potential of neoliberal free trade and corporate globalization at the new port and free trade zone, the Manila Harbour Centre. In the celebrated special economic zone (another euphemism for free trade zone), multinationals will receive many of the benefits previously outlined. In addition, because assembly plants will be housed at the maritime port/new free trade zone, multinationals will also have easy access to cheap Filipino/a laborers who can manufacture goods such as electronics or garments at the site's assembly plants.

Ambassador Michel and Chairman and CEO Romero both deployed a particular narrative of the Manila–Acapulco galleon trade history; namely one that emphasizes historical and cultural rationales, which they believe will attract foreign capital and capitalists, both needed to spur capitalist commerce. Through a superficial account of the Manila–Acapulco galleons that ignored social inequalities that constituted the maritime trade (e.g., the concentration of wealth generated in elite Spanish, Chinese, and mestizo/a economic classes and that the galleons were often products of virtual or actual Filipino enslaved labor), state officials and corporate leaders recycled maritime history for their particular elite neoliberal free trade agenda.

In addition, the ambassador's and Chairman and CEO's use of the commemorative regatta and Manila–Acapulco galleon trade histories provided an opportunity for them to stress Manila's role and position in *contemporary* regional and global maritime trade, underscoring the ways that Manila not only was a key port city in the past but also is a major port city player in the present. In other words, state and corporate officials (and here I am reading Ambassador Michel as a diplomatic collaborator of the

Philippine state) evoked Manila–Acapulco galleon imaginaries and histories to stress Manila's and the Philippines's importance in maritime trade and the global economy centuries ago, but just as significant, to emphasize Manila's and the Philippines's contemporary importance to regional and global economies.

Global City Desires

Taking the regional context of Southeast Asia into consideration, we can read state and corporate narratives of Manila–Acapulco galleon trade histories performed at the regatta and free trade zone as a move that sought to demonstrate Manila's past maritime and cosmopolitan glories, while also signifying Manila's present and future economic and cultural sensibilities in a dynamic part of the world. The version of the Manila–Acapulco galleon narrative participants heard and witnessed at the postregatta festivities, in particular, suggests to capitalist investors, the business community, and the general public that if historic Manila was "global" *back then*, it means that Manila is or must be a *global city today.* For elite state and corporate figures in Manila, achieving global city status at this particular historical juncture was especially important because many nation-states in Asia, along with their respective political leaders and major cities had for decades been competing as each attempted to attract foreign or multinational capital investments to their particular global city and nation. This intraregional competition intensified in the 1990s as neoliberal economics expanded in Southeast Asia, and it continued at the end of the decade even as the Asian Financial Crisis escalated.

In the closing decade of the twentieth century, cities such as Hong Kong, Bangkok, Kuala Lumpur, Jakarta, Manila, and Singapore were discursively competing with one another in the public relations realm and also competing to become or reinforce the image of being the premiere "hub city," "world city," or "global city" in Southeast Asia. According to geographer Dean Forbes, Singapore had been particularly successful in promoting itself as a hub city. In turn, Singapore's developed financial infrastructures were also critical to Singapore's acquiring its new status as a world city.[34] The Singapore Ministry of Information and the Arts, which plays a prominent role in the city-state's public relations, in its mission statement, for example, states that its goal is "to help inform, educate and entertain, as part of the *national goal to make Singapore a hub city of the world*" [emphasis added]. This public relations battle among cities and nation-states is a critical aspect of the competition for capital in Asia, Southeast Asia, and the broader Asia and the Pacific region. That is, to attract capital investments a city must be *perceived* as a "hub" or "global," while also housing the necessary infrastructure or "high service functions" to attract and keep investors. Subsequently, Southeast Asian cities were competing with one another to develop the premier centers for air, surface, and sea transport; telecommunications linkages; and financial services.

Singapore had succeeded in promoting itself as a hub city with a "global city image" and also offered the prerequisite high service functions. For example, Singapore has established financial centers and corporate headquarters, excellent telecommunications systems, and access to cheap labor and natural resources. Forbes, therefore, suggests that Singapore was or is the city (and state) to beat in Southeast Asia. Although Singapore does not actually have ultra-cheap labor or significant natural resources, Singapore collaborated with Malaysia and Indonesia to provide what the city-state lacks. The governments of these three countries worked together to create a "growth triangle," which connected "Singapore's capital, technology, and managerial talent with the land and labor resources of southern Malaysia and island/coastal Sumatra."[35]

The Ramos administration, economic elites, and corporate representatives in the Philippines aimed to challenge Singapore's dominance in Southeast Asia by offering a Philippine or Filipino version of what it means to be a global city, namely that Manila is global precisely because of Manila–Acapulco galleon trade histories and because state and corporate elites sought to further develop high service functions, such as the those offered at the new Manila Harbour Centre. To challenge Singapore and the growth triangle, Manila and the Philippines (through state and private [or corporate] partnerships such as the Manila Harbour Centre) aimed to offer local and foreign investors free trade zone incentives and benefits, cheaper rents for corporate offices, cheap and abundant labor, shipping facilities and improved interisland transportation, a large English-speaking and educated citizenry, and an eager consumer population funded in large part by overseas Filipinos dollar remittances.

Manning Capital of the (Shipping) World

A connected aspect of global cities phenomena and discourse involves the role of or access to different forms of labor. Although sociologist Saskia Sassen and geographer James A. Tyner assert that labor in global cities (or in globalization) is often marginalized in globalization studies, low-cost labor is important to Manila's global city image and is an important component of what the city and state seek to "offer" the world. Migrant global Filipino/a laborers are also important sources of foreign currency remittances, which are used to support migrant workers' families and communities but are also badly needed by the Philippine state to finance IMF-World Bank-Asian Development Bank debts and other expenditures. Tyner writes, "a key component of globalization for *indebted states* is the drive for export oriented, hard-currency earnings; in the case of the Philippines, however, this has been augmented and indeed, *largely generated* by labor export" [emphasis added].[36]

Labor in globalization studies can involve highly specialized "professional" financial workers such as corporate executives, fund managers, and stockbrokers who are typically associated with financial capitals such as New York, Tokyo, or Singapore, but it may also involve lower cost, or underpaid and undervalued, forms of service and migrant labor, embodied, for example, by factory workers, construction workers, domestic helpers, and seafarers and seamen who work on what journalist Alecks Pabico calls "sweatships."[37]

Thus, to more fully interpret the Race of the Century/Manila–Acapulco Commemorative Regatta that was celebrated at the Manila Harbour Centre and free trade zone and Philippine state and corporate elite global city desires, addressing a connected narrative, the manning capital of the (shipping) world narrative, is necessary. Philippine state officials and private manning agencies (employment agencies) promoted this second narrative during the same time frame that state and corporate officials celebrated Manila–Acapulco galleon narratives at the Manila Harbour Centre. For example, just six months before the Race of the Century, in a speech delivered by then-President Ramos at the 2nd National Seafarers' Day Celebration held on August 18, 1997, at the Philippine Coast Guard Compound in the port area of Manila, Ramos exclaimed,

> For more than a decade now, the Philippines has been leading the world in producing and deploying highly qualified seafarers in the international maritime industry. This development has earned for our country the title "manning capital of the world." . . . The government, in cooperation with the private sector, has put in place a *manpower* development system that is geared towards improving the quality of Filipino seafarers.[38] [emphasis added]

In his speech Ramos praised Filipino seamen for their economic and social contributions to the nation, implicitly echoing the notion that overseas Filipino/a workers (OFWs) are "bagong bayani" (new heroes).[39] Moreover, Ramos tried to reassure the sea-based migrant/maritime community that his administration was trying to support Filipino seamen in their professional endeavors, for example, through educational reforms and "radical structural reforms" in "licensure and certification," that would help to maintain Filipino seafarers' competitiveness in the international labor market, which would in turn ensure that the large sums of foreign currency, remitted by Filipino seamen, continue to flow into the Philippine economy.

Not surprisingly, Philippine Labor Secretary, Leonardo A. Quisumbing, also used the manning capital of the (shipping) world discourse and went even further by connecting it to Ramos's Philippines 2000 economic development scheme. In an interview with journalist Rodney J. Jaleco (reporting for *Philippine Magazine*) Quisumbing asserted,

> The Philippine ship manning industry is a vital component of our vision of attaining the status of a Newly Industrializing Country beyond the year 2000. . . . The Philippines has been the world's top supplier of seafarers since 1987. About 20 percent of the total 1.2 million seafarers world-wide aboard ocean-going vessels are Filipinos. . . . We can serve as the next maritime hub in Asia by the turn of the century, considering that we are an archipelago and dubbed the manning capital of the world.[40]

Quisumbing's comments illustrate his faith in a holy trinity of Philippine state and corporate neoliberal economics: Philippines 2000 with its foundational philosophy of free trade and privatization; the divinity of the Philippines continuing to export Filipino/a migrant labor worldwide (to continue financing state indebtedness); and a steadfast belief in privatizing transportation/maritime infrastructures for Manila/the Philippines to become the next or leading maritime hub. Ramos and Quisumbing fundamentally stress that Manila's strategic role in the global economy, or Manila's "competitive advantage" as a global city, is its surplus of labor. For the Philippine state, this "surplus," of course, generates significant revenue for the national economy in the form of "hard currency" or foreign exchange remittances, sent back to the Philippines by OFWs or Filipino/a immigrants. Within this neoliberal capitalist logic, Ramos and his administration sought to maintain Manila's position as the manning capital of the (shipping) world, by simultaneously advancing Nic-hood and global city desires.

Moreover, by evoking Manila–Acapulco galleon narratives in the manner in which they did at the Manila Harbour Centre, state and corporate elites were able to highlight and celebrate Manila's contributions to past and present global economies as they advanced global city and globalization desires, but just as important, they were also able to promote specific maritime-based Filipino masculinities and constructions of manhood in the context of regional Philippine/Filipino/a feminization through a "Manila as the manning capital of the (shipping) world" discourse. In doing so, state and corporate elites highlighted Filipino male and masculine labor through the figure of the Filipino sailor or seamen in the international labor market and in Southeast Asian public relations battles. In other words, Manila–Acapulco galleon trade histories offer a masculinist pathway for state and corporate elites to "talk back" to regional and international political relationships, political economies, and discourses that seek to portray the Philippines as hyperfeminine or hypervictimized (in heteropatriarchal cultural and economic logics). This anxiety about femininity is a result of the masculinist intraregional competition and broader global competition for capital and corporations, which undervalue and marginalize femininities. And so, although it might (at first) seem like a reasonable anticolonial nationalist strategy, there remain several troubling aspects of the Manila–Acapulco galleon and manning capital of the (shipping) world discourses as deployed by state and corporate elites that need more critical ethnographic analysis and cultural critique.

As briefly addressed in the Introduction, in the last half of the twentieth century, the Philippines, its citizens, and its global migrant labor force (men and women) have been feminized through debt and dependency and gendered and sexualized through orientalism and colonialism by more powerful and wealthier nations such as the United States and Japan.[41] This feminization of the (Philippine) nation and Filipino/a overseas populations was particularly acute because of the 1995 Flor Contemplacion case in Singapore in which Contemplacion, an overseas Filipina working as a domestic helper, was accused of murder and later executed by hanging by the Singaporean state. When the Ramos administration was unable to diplomatically intervene in what many considered to be an unfair trial and stop the execution, Filipino/as in the Philippines and around the world were outraged by the injustice, the Singapore's state violent actions, and the inaction and sense of powerlessness of the Philippine state. In addition, as noted in the Introduction, Filipino migrant men and their labor have also been feminized; for example, sociologist Yen Le Espiritu and historian Linda España-Maram both, respectively, document that Filipino men working in the U.S. Navy and in California-based domestic service industries were also feminized through gendered and sexualized orientalist and U.S. colonial cultural logics and political economies.

Thus, if we read and culturally interpret Manila–Acapulco galleon histories and the manning capital of the (shipping) world narrative alongside these kinds of misogynistic, racist, classist, and (neo)colonial discourses of Filipino/a feminization, which regularly circulate, it becomes clearer that Manila–Acapulco galleon trade histories and the manning capital of the (shipping) world discourse provide expanded opportunities for state and corporate elites to emphasize the masculinities of Filipino males or men laboring in (past and present) transpacific maritime trade, in the contemporary global shipping industry, and in the project of nation-building. In heteropatriarchal and normative nationalist cultural logics, males or men are usually more important to nation-states because historically, nationalisms that are heroically articulated or valiantly performed through men's stories and men's bodies are privileged and honored (over femininities or marginalized masculinities). Philippine Studies scholar Reynaldo C. Ileto, for example, argues that heroic Christian and Christ-like masculine Filipino ideals have been crucial to the development of a Filipino nationalist "pantheon" of nationalist heroes or imagined heroes (e.g., Rizal, Bonifacio, [B.] Aquino, and Marcos).[42] Ileto argues that tropes of dominant masculine and nationalist heroism have become integral to Philippine historiography, local Philippine politics, and notions of Philippine national identity.

Furthermore, in a regional and international context in which the Philippines has been historically, economically, and socially constructed as "feminine" through IMF–World Bank–Asian Development Bank debt and dependency, as well as through the cultural logics of U.S. heteropatriarchal, misogynistic, racist, classist orientalisms, and (neo)colonialisms, Manila–Acapulco galleon histories and Filipino sailors or seamen become increasingly compelling narratives and figures for state and corporate elites who are competing with their counterparts in other countries in trying to attract capital investments, while also trying to naturalize global city-ness through public relations efforts. An event or spectacle such as the Race of the Century therefore created spaces for state and corporate elites to articulate the contributions of Filipino (sea)men, subsequently creating places through which to celebrate and naturalize dominant state- and corporate-created Filipino maritime-based masculinities. In other words, the masculinities of Indio-cum-Filipino seamen who risked their lives in the transpacific voyage during the Manila–Acapulco galleon trade, once marginalized masculinities have now been co-opted by late twentieth century state and corporate elites.

In the heteropatriarchal and normative cultural logics of state and corporate elites, Native/Filipino sailors or seamen provide a compelling masculinist counterdiscourse to the types of discourses Tadiar analyzes. (discussed in the Introduction): child, ward, mistress, and hooker, as well as the well-known Flor Contemplacion story. (Remember, these feminine imaginaries and discourses become particularly disempowering if misogynistic, racist, classist, and (neo)colonial cultural logics are privileged. Feminine subjects need not be interpreted through a lens of victimhood or disempowerment.[43]) Ironically, by deploying state- and corporate-sanctioned dominant narratives of Filipino seafaring and "masculine industries" such as sea-based transport and shipping, what was actually being materially advanced in Manila at the Manila Harbour Centre were low-wage manufacturing jobs that Filipinas will probably occupy in greater numbers at the Manila Harbour Centre's free trade zone.[44]

Remembering the Asian Financial Crisis

In addition to the other regional contexts I have already addressed, it is also crucial to keep in mind that at the time of the Race of the Century, several countries in Southeast Asia—Thailand, Indonesia, the Philippines, and Malaysia (plus Korea, considered an East Asian nation)—were experiencing financial crises that brought about "capital flight." Currencies throughout the region, beginning with Thailand's *baht,* were devalued as currency speculators from around the world unloaded huge amounts of local monies in their search for "safer" currencies. This financial flight destabilized economies in Southeast Asia. Bello asserts that at the time, "crony capitalism" had become an "all purpose" explanation for the economic collapse in Asia. However, Bello argues that the biggest culprit in the crisis was the unregulated flows of capital in a capitalist world system.[45]

Bello writes that during the mid-1980s to early 1990s, a massive influx of capital from Japan flowed to Association of Southeast Asian Nations (ASEAN) countries. This emerged because of the Plaza Accord of 1985, in which the (Japanese) yen was forced to appreciate relative to the U.S. dollar, as a result of U.S. pressure. The United States sought to reduce its enormous trade deficit with Japan by lowering prices of U.S. exports to Japan while making Japanese imports to the United States more expensive for U.S. consumers. With the yen devaluation, production costs in Japan increased, so Japanese corporations and multinationals moved the more labor-intensive phases of their production to cheap labor locations, primarily to Southeast Asia. Bello suggests that this was the fastest and largest movement of capital into the developing world in recent times.[46] He cites one conservative estimate that between 1985 and 1990, $15 billion worth of Japanese investment flowed into Southeast Asia. By 1996, ASEAN countries (Indonesia, Singapore, Malaysia, Thailand, and the Philippines) had received $48 billion from Japanese investors.

This was a significant shift in Japanese strategy. Previously, Japan primarily focused on extracting resources from Southeast Asia. However, now the goal was to turn Southeast Asia into a production base for corporations that manufactured goods for export to the United States and Europe.[47] Japanese economic elites also saw Southeast Asian middle classes as important consumers for Japanese products.

With Japan's investments in Southeast and East Asia, the region experienced high growth rates, which attracted currency speculators from the North who were looking for higher returns on their investments. In particular, mutual and hedge funds from the United States were steered to the "emerging markets" of Asia. According to Bello, prior to this massive influx of Japanese capital, the Philippines was largely excluded from Japan's earlier investments in the 1980s, primarily because of the political instability during the U.S.-Marcos dictatorship, the political unrest during Marcos's overthrow, and the instability of the newly elected (Corazon) Aquino administration. In this context, U.S. portfolio investments were seen as a potential way for the Philippines to catch up with its East and Southeast Asian neighbors. Thus, the Philippine government and other ASEAN nations took policy steps to attract portfolio investments; for example, foreign exchange restrictions were eased or abolished, interests rates were kept high, and central monetary authorities intervened in local economies to maintain stable exchange rates. This resulted in significant capital flowing into the Philippines and the rest of the region.

Similar to the U.S. American-led and -developed financial crisis that intensified in 2008, investors saw Southeast Asian real estate sectors, where mutual hedge funds could be directed to, as sites for high returns. Soon a real estate glut in Bangkok, Manila, and Kuala Lumpur developed. With this oversaturation, developers were stuck with large numbers of unsold real estate, which translated into defaulted mortgages. This created the potential for a volatile domino effect. Thailand was the first country to economically destabilize as currency speculators quickly withdrew their capital. Anticipating a similar situation in other countries, capital flight occurred in Indonesia, the Philippines, Malaysia, and Korea.

Despite this failure in neoliberal free trade and the financial crisis that emerged in Southeast Asia in 1997 and 1998, many Philippine state officials, corporate leaders, and economic elites continued to believe in the promises of neoliberal free trade and corporate globalization. As such, they used events such as the Race of the Century and the Manila Harbour Centre free trade zone launch to continue promoting the same tired social and economic policies that played a role in precipitating the crisis in the first place. In other words, state and corporate economic elites continued to tout neoliberal free trade and corporate globalization as sensible cures for social and economic ills such as poverty and poor health conditions in poor countries such as the Philippines even as the 1998 crisis of capitalism continued to intensify. As the 2008 U.S. American subprime mortgage meltdown and ensuing economic recession indicates, this capitalist free fall repeated again, but this time it began in North America, not Southeast Asia. In 1998, Manila, this on-going celebration of neoliberal economics may have continued because economic elites may not have felt the effects of the financial crisis as severely as the poor, working poor, and working classes who immediately felt the effects on their already limited resources. It was these more marginalized socioeconomic groups that felt the pain and violence of larger macroeconomic and social policies as the price of basic commodities and services soared. Putting things in broader and longer historical perspective, it is critical to remember that for the millions of Filipinos (and other Asians) who lived in poverty *prior to* 1998, their social and economic situations were already extremely dire. The Asian Financial Crisis simply provided a contemporary name and perpetrator for long-standing national and regional economic and social inequalities.

A few years after my initial fieldwork in Manila, I was working at Global Exchange (GX) (a San Francisco, California-based nonprofit organization that organizes local/global social and economic justice activist campaigns), conducting fieldwork in Oakland, and revising this first chapter (then in the context of my dissertation) when a Philippine state official and member of then-President Joseph Estrada's administration (Estrada followed Ramos), a Mr. J. M. Lamorena, visited GX's office in the Mission District. During a conversation with GX staff about economic/corporate globalization, Lamorena admonished, "You have to ride the boat. You can't miss the boat. There's only one boat."[47] When he made this rhetorical move, I could not help but think of the Race of the Century and the Manila Harbour Centre and how the crowd waited for the *Karakoa-MHC* to arrive at the postrace celebration. Race of the Century organizers, Manila Harbour Centre promoters, the Ramos administration, and now Mr. Lamorena, a representative of Estrada's administration, were all collaborating, creating a "fantasy-production"[49] of galleons, corporate globalization, and gallant migrant seamen who would continue to help repay state debts. I imagined state and corporate elites sailing their shiny new neoliberal yacht into a dazzling Manila Bay sunset, with global city–manning capital of the world Manila steadfast on the shore.

As this chapter demonstrates, the winners at the Race of the Century celebrated at the Manila Harbour Centre were not really the *Karakoa-MHC* sailors who won several legs of the regatta across the Pacific. Rather, the winners of the Race of the Century, ultimately a race to accumulate capital and surplus profits, are multinational corporations, their executives, and other economic elites, including those who work in the top echelons of the Philippine state. These are the people who substantially and unjustly benefit from riding the boat Lamorena seemed to be enamored with. As such, neoliberal policies such as Philippines 2000 and privatized free trade zones such as the Manila Harbour Centre will not bring the fabled riches of the Manila–Acapulco galleon trade to the Philippines or to ordinary Filipinos, especially the poor, working poor, and working classes. Lamorena's admonishment was amiss. There are actually many kinds of "boats" for Filipinos and others to ride. Indeed, in choosing "karakoa," a precolonial indigenous boat that once traveled the seas of Mindanao and the Moluccas in the sixteenth century, the Manila Harbour Centre and Race of the Century organizers unintentionally or ironically illustrated that in a crosscurrents space such as the Philippines, there are definitely other boats to sail, which can help steer Filipino/as into more sustainable economic waters.[50] And, for sure, there are other stories to tell besides state- and corporate-sanctioned dominant narratives of glorious galleons and global cities or heroic Filipino sailors and seamen who simply sail for the state.

CHAPTER TWO

Ashore and Away

Filipino Seamen as Heroes and Deserters

The Captain-General leaped into the water.
I jumped in. . . ,
The water was thigh-deep.

CÁRLOS CORTÉS, *Longitude*

Ashore in Manila: Filipino Seamen as Bagong Bayani

The "OFWs as bagong bayani" (overseas Filipino/a workers as new heroes or heroines) is a persistent and dominant narrative in the Philippines and in some parts of the diaspora. An illustrative example of this discourse is presented in the video *Tagumpay Nating Lahat (The Success, Prosperity, or Victory of All of Us)*, shown as an audiovisual tribute to Filipino seafarers at the Philippine Manning Convention in Manila, November 12–13, 2007. The film depicts a young Filipino boy staring in contemplation at Manila Bay (near Roxas Boulevard) with two industrial container ships in the distance. Sensual piano music begins to stream in the audio as the boy is shown while a Filipina with a gripping high octave voice sings a Tagalog song; English subtitles appear below the video's images. Two Filipino seamen approach and welcome the boy. One wears orange coveralls or a jumpsuit that Filipino seamen commonly wear while working on ships (particularly on deck); the other seaman wears a merchant marine's khaki officer uniform.[1] To indicate Filipino seamen's "bayani-ness" (patriotic heroism), Filipino men are shown participating in valiant hypermasculine action on land, at sea, and on ships. The lyrics (which are slightly modified and repeated throughout the video) support the masculine heroic imagery. The opening English subtitles read: "I have a simple dream.

For my beloved country. With one united effort. Together we can reach our goals. I come from a land of heroes. A place where you can find the finest Filipino seafarers. Bring pride to the whole Nation." As the video continues, the music shifts, becoming more fast-paced and exciting; drums roll. Images of Filipino cadets and merchant marines marching in unison flash on the screen. A young seaman proudly waves the Philippine red, white, and blue flag with yellow sun and stars. Another seaman intensely embraces a woman (his wife? girlfriend? lover? sister? friend?) during a heartfelt homecoming. Other Filipino seamen are shown handling paperwork, answering telephones, calculating navigational maneuvers, fixing equipment on ships, working together as friends, sharing bottled water, and putting their arms around each other, sometimes linking arms and appearing in groups, holding their index fingers up high to declare, "We're number one!" A Filipino seaman sits on his bed in his shipboard cabin praying, making the sign of the cross. Another cooks in the galley. Other seamen, wearing cold weather gear, stand tall at attention proudly in a straight line on the deck of a ship. The almost seven-minute long video comes to a close with multiple shots of Filipinos (the majority are men) who are presumably executives or staff of manning agencies and shipping companies (given the venue of the tribute). One noteworthy shot shows President Gloria Macapagal Arroyo smiling and shaking hands with a manning agency or shipping company official. A closing message appears on the screen: "We salute the Filipino Seafarers for bringing honor to our country. One noble purpose. One united industry. One proud nation. Mabuhay ang marinong Pilipino (Long Live Filipino Seafarers or Seamen)."

In addition to being a audiovisual tribute, the video also appears to be a potential recruitment tool that attempts to attract viewers, especially young Filipino men and boys, through images that highlight Filipino seamen as hypermasculine and adventurous sea-based patriots, always heroic and hyper-heteromanly, always responsible and loyal subjects in the project of Philippine nation-building. In this way, the video is similar to television advertisements shown in the United States that are produced and distributed by the U.S. Navy, Army, Air Force, and Marines in the their efforts to recruit young people, often young working-class men (of color), to join the U.S. military.

The other intended audience is clearly those employed in or affiliated with manning agencies and shipping companies (companies based in the Philippines and beyond that recruit and hire seamen) because the video was initially shown at a Philippine Manning Convention. The video visually celebrates manning agencies' social and economic contributions in the Philippines and symbolically seals their partnership with the Philippine state through a handshake with Macapagal Arroyo, granted with her trademark smile. Ultimately, the video highlights the male workers that manning agencies (especially companies that work with shipping companies) target and deploy: Filipino seamen.

In short, through the video, Filipino seamen's masculinities and manhoods are imagined and constructed as hypermasculine and macho, heterosexual and heteronormative, responsible and hard-working, cooperative and devoutly Catholic, and heroically patriotic. Through the cinematic strategies deployed, I read the video as a dominant visual representation of Filipino seamen's masculinities that seeks to highlight the quasi-military orientation of seafaring and thus its docility. This latter reading (docility) is possible because the video shows the little boy being interpellated[2] ("hailed" in the Althusserian sense) by the older seamen (wearing the orange jumpsuit and merchant marine's khaki), as well as representatives or partners of the state (maritime schools and academies, manning agencies, Philippine Overseas Employment Agency [POEA] officials, and political leaders), in the end attempting to visualize seamen-citizens as faithful and docile state subjects (along with the other facets of masculinity previously outlined).

Through its representational strategies and political/economic agenda, the video tribute powerfully taps into broader images and discourses of OFWs as bagong bayani. Several key Philippine Studies/Filipino/a Studies scholars, including Vicente L. Rafael, Neferti X. Tadiar, Rhacel Salazar Parreñas, Robin Rodriguez, and Steven C. McKay, among others, have commented on this well-established and dominant discourse, trope, and imaginary in the Philippines, critically analyzing some of the term's ideological, racial, class, gender, and sexual implications.[3] Building on this scholarship, in this chapter, I elaborate on several points that have not been exhausted in academic dialogue, particularly from an ethnographic and masculinity studies perspective. In this chapter, I clarify gendered aspects of the bagong bayani term, image, and discourse that have not been fully engaged in recent Filipino/a Studies scholarship, and I elaborate on how the psychosociocultural concept or sensibility of "utang na loob" (translated in various texts and historical moments as "gratitude/solidarity/spiritual-social debt"), an important element of Filipino/a notions of bayani-ness, is used and manipulated by the state in its efforts to try to interpellate Filipino/a citizens and migrants into its system of Filipino/a global migration as a key long-term economic development strategy. I also illustrate how and why the Philippine state engages a conservative neocolonial and nationalist conceptualization of utang na loob (conservatively defined here as "social debt"), which the state stresses in its desire to create loyal, hard-working, nonconfrontational, and/or docile subjects, including Filipino seamen, as illustrated in *Tagumpay Nating Lahat*. Showing resistance to this dominant discourse and image of Filipino masculinity (i.e., OFW/seamen's heroism embodied through bayani-ness and conservative notions of utang na loob), in the second half of this chapter, I analyze a different but related psycho-socialcultural concept or sensibility called "lakas ng loob" (guts), which is expressed, embodied, and enacted through oppositional masculinities, specifically, the masculinities of Filipino seamen who jump ship.

Instead of interpreting the entrenched and gendered discourse of OFWs as bagong bayani solely from the perspectives of the Philippine state and manning agencies, both of which are geographically centralized or situated in Manila, I culturally interpret the discourse and counterdiscourse of bagong bayani from two key vantage points: first, from Manila/Philippines and second, from Oakland/United States, through two different figures and positionalities, Filipino seamen who the Philippine state culturally constructs as bayanis or heroes and Filipino seamen who are seen as "deserters" (those who "jump ship" in ports outside of the Philippines). In the context of neoliberal "manning capital of the (shipping) world" Manila (discussed in chapter 1) and sociologist R. W. Connell's theoretical framework on masculinities, Filipino seamen constructed as bayanis or heroes can be understood as a dominant form and discourse of masculinity, especially as conceptualized through hegemonic (Philippine) state cultural and ideological logics, whereas masculinities that fall outside normative seamen's heroism, that is, the masculinities of Filipino seamen who jump ship, can be read as "marginal or subordinate masculinities"[4] (Connell's terms) since they "jump out of" or exit dominant currents (notions/practices) of Filipino masculinities. My hope is that this chapter contributes to dialogue about how marginal and subordinate masculinities culturally work in opposition to dominant Philippine state, manning agency, and shipping company discourses such as the bagong bayani narrative. Filipino seamen as deserters may be marginalized or forgotten figures in Philippine cultural politics or underexplored in Philippine Studies, Filipino/a / Filipino/a American Studies, Asian American Studies, American Studies, gender/masculinity studies, and anthropology, but they provide a different perspective and alternative performance and practice of maritime masculinity through which to understand the crosscurrents of Filipino seafaring, masculinities, and globalization.

To gain a deeper understanding of the concept of bagong bayani, let us first consider its composite parts. The University of the Philippines *Diksiyonaryong Filipino* (Filipino dictionary), defines "bago" as "iba sa dati"[5] (different than before) or "iba sa nakita o nalaman na"[6] (different from what was seen or previously known). The first definition for "bayani" is "tao na may kahanga-hangang katapangan at abilidad" (person with admirable courage and abilities); "hero" is included in the definition as a synonym. Definition 3 for bayani is "pangunahing tauhang lalaki sa dula, kuwento, pelikula, at katulad" (the leading man in drama, stories, films, and the like); the synonyms "bida" (star/hero/heroine), "hero," and "protagonist" (among others) follow this definition. The marker "ng" notes that two words are in relationship, in this case, bago and bayani; however, the "marker also indicates that the word that follows it is *not* the focus of the sentence."[7] Subsequently, "bago-ness" (newness) is the focus, not necessarily bayani. Combined, bagong bayani translated in English can be understood as a new hero or heroine, a star who is different from what has been previously seen or known. Although in its English translation "bayani" has often been narrowly or incompletely defined as simply "hero," that is, *without "heroine,"* recall that Filipino is a more gender-neutral or inclusive language. That is, to indicate this neutrality or inclusiveness, there are no masculine or feminine pronouns and the University of the Philippines dictionary (in its definition 1) begins to describe "bayani" through the gender-neutral and inclusive term "tao" (human, person).

Steven C. McKay addresses what he calls the "gendered ambiguity"[8] of the term "(new) heroes." That is, hero or heroes is often used by the Philippine state and manning agency representatives to evoke heroic men or "exemplary masculinities" but are the same terms used to describe the large and growing populations of Filipin*a* (women/female identified) migrants around the world. The gendered ambiguity that McKay refers to is a result of the feminine component of bayani's Filipino definition being lost or left behind in English translation. If the linguistic/cultural logics of the Filipino language and its more gender-inclusive, gender-neutral, and gender-ambiguous orientation is emphasized, a more culturally expansive and precise understanding of bagong bayani emerges because the indigenous understanding of tao has space for people or humans of many genders, not just males or men. As Filipino/a overseas migration has been feminized (i.e., more Filipinas work overseas than Filipinos), this global economic and social situation has created some clear and vexing "gender trouble"[9] for the Philippine state, and thus the state seeks to promote patriarchal, heteronormative, and conservative masculinities embodied precisely through particular narratives, images, and imaginaries of Filipino seamen. That is, part of the trouble is that gender inclusivity and fluidity exist in multiple Philippine and diasporic cultural/linguistic contexts, and, as many scholars have analyzed, OFW communities and populations have become increasingly female or feminized (including some migrant men).

These are critical issues and factors that begin to explain why, in particular local/national Philippine contexts, Filipino seamen are inscribed or depicted as new heroes and have emerged as important cultural, economic, and social figures in state, corporate, manning agency, and shipping company discourses and imaginaries. The discourse and image of Filipino seamen as new heroes, depicted, for example, in the video tribute enables private manning agencies who work closely with the Philippine state to highlight hyper–merchant marine masculinities, which further enable them to circumvent or sideline the troubling *gender contradiction* of "feminization" in the context of regional and global cultural politics and political economies (discussed in the introduction and chapter 1). At a minimum, these social actors attempt to discursively and visually circumvent or sideline the gender trouble of expanding feminization through an emphasis on masculinities.

In evoking "iba sa dati" (different than what came before or "new"), bagong bayani as a national or nationalist discourse operates on multiple axes and levels of meaning, including a horizontally imagined ethnic, racial, kinship, and geographic community and a temporally imagined community, especially through notions of national(ist) history.[10] Historian Lawrence Meir Friedman, for example, writes about horizontality and nationalisms in this way: "there is usually a sense of oneness—a sense that everyone is in the same boat, that everyone shares a common allegiance. And this requires, of course, the technologies of the horizontal society—without these the oneness cannot be sustained; indeed, it cannot even be created."[11] In the Philippines, this sense of nationalist "oneness" has been historically forged, created, and embodied in large part through the struggle against Spanish, U.S. American, and Japanese colonialisms. The narrative implies that as Natives of the archipelago now known as the Philippines, Filipino/as involved in nationalist anticolonial movements imagined themselves to be in the "same boat" of colonialism(s) and as a result, Filipino/as were imagined to be working with one another in anticolonial resistance, especially through imagined "horizontal" relations of ethnic/racial kinship/brotherhood or sisterhood. In sum, historians and other scholars, as well as leaders of the Philippine nation-state and its citizens, considered and acknowledged the Filipino/as who worked as imagined or "real life" "equals" in anticolonial, nationalist, or revolutionary struggles as true bayanis (heroes and heroines) of the nation or the republic.

Rafael and Tadiar address the temporal axis or historical dimension of bagong bayani, suggesting that bagong bayani broadly recalls a dominant, but not static, genealogy of what another scholar, Reynaldo C. Ileto, theorizes as a "pantheon" of Filipino/a heroes and heroines. This genealogy or pantheon usually begins with historical figures and patriots such as Dr. Jose Rizal, martyred (executed) author of *Noli Me Tangere* and the Philippines's national hero, and Andres Bonifacio, Supremo and cofounder of the Kataastaasan Kagalang-galang Na Katipunan Nang Manga Anak Nang Bayan (KKK or Katipunan for short; the full translation in English [in gender-neutral terms] is "Supreme and Venerable Society of the Children of the Nation"[12]). The genealogy or pantheon also includes twentieth century Philippine heroes and heroines such as Senator Benigno "Ninoy" Aquino, Jr. (whose assassination is widely believed to have been directed by the Marcos regime in 1983) and President Corazon Aquino (cocredited with People Power I, which toppled the Marcoses and the dictatorship in 1986).

Philippine Studies scholar Maria Jovita Zarate addresses how the concept of bayani-ness is emphasized and solidified through education and other discursive practices:

> Nang maitatag na republika ang Pilipinas, lalong mamumuo ang konsepto ng bayani at gagamitin ng estado ang sistema ng edukasyon para palaganapin ang diskursong ito. Sa pagpapakilala ng buhay ni Jose Rizal, Andres Bonifacio, Emilio Jacinto at Gabriela Silang sa mga kabataan, at sa pagtatayo ng mga monumento at estatwang pamplasa ng mga bayaning ito, maitatak sa kamalayang pambayan ang angking *gravitas* ng mga inituring na bayani.[13]
>
> (When the republic of the Philippines was founded, the concept of bayanis solidified even more as the state used education to expand this discourse. With youth becoming exposed to and acquainted with the lives of Jose Rizal, Andres Bonifacio, Emilio Jacinto and Gabriela Silang, and also with the establishment of monuments and plaza statues of these bayanis, the national consciousness was marked by a naturalized gravitas in its attitude toward bayanis.)

Here, Zarate indicates how state-driven notions of national(ist) history and bayani-ness are inscribed, emphasized, and naturalized in the national consciousness through the educational system and also through localized spatial and iconographic practices (e.g., monuments and statues in plazas). Subsequently, through institutions and everyday practice, the Philippine state is able to conjure up expansive cultural meanings of bayani-ness without having to elaborate or explain in great detail what (bagong) bayani means. In this way, we might understand bagong bayani as operating imagistically, attempting to evoke or succeeding in evoking images and feelings among readers or addressees, for example, the Philippine general public, OFWs, seamen, manning agency employees, etc. The state's deployment of bayani and bagong bayani discourse, therefore, is able to trigger, or potentially trigger, quick mental images and emotions among OFWs and Filipino/as more broadly and Filipino seamen and maritime recruits more specifically as they recall and remember the political and social contributions, deep personal and collective sacrifices that past bayanis have made, including death, in various nationalist struggles. Subsequently, by creating or showing bayanis who work diligently on land, at sea, and on ships, and by highlighting sea-based (hyper-)masculine bayani-ness, the manning agency convention video tribute seeks to create and establish a strong association and link between contemporary Filipino seamen working in the global shipping industry and past Philippine bayanis such as Rizal and Bonifacio.

At the close of the twentieth century, what made bayanis "new" was the fact that Filipinas who work(ed) as domestic helpers more specifically and OFWs more generally were embraced as bayanis by the state. Through declarations, proclamations, and speeches, state officials and manning agency representatives have addressed or referred to OFWs as bagong bayanis in brief and frequently repeated references that have been deployed at the upper echelons of the Philippine state, but which have also filtered down to mid and lower-level officials. For example, in a well-known speech in Hong Kong in 1988, President Corazon Aquino addressed an audience of Filipinas who were working as domestic helpers in Hong Kong. Cited and translated by Vicente Rafael, President Aquino proclaimed, "Kayo po ang bagong bayani" ("You are the new heroes *[sic]*").[14] As a result of death and "martyrdom," specific contemporary OFWs such as Flor Contemplacion, a Filipina working as a domestic helper in Singapore who was unfairly tried and later executed by the Singaporean state, has also been incorporated into the pantheon of Filipino/a bayanis. More recently in 2005, deploying a gendered variation of the bagong bayani trope, President Gloria Macapagal Arroyo proclaimed Angelo dela Cruz the "Filipino Everyday Man,"[15] similarly recalling the millions of Filipino/as who migrate overseas in search of work. At the time of Macapagal Arroyo's declaration, dela Cruz was a 46-year-old Filipino man working as a truck driver in Iraq when he was captured and held hostage by Iraqi nationalists and fundamentalists in the context of the U.S. invasion of Iraq. Because of intense domestic pressure and massive protests in the Philippines, Macapagal Arroyo was pushed to withdraw Philippine troops in Iraq, a key demand of dela Cruz's captors. The Filipino Everyday Man narrative is another example of how the Philippine state makes attempts to emphasize OFW masculinities in the context of the feminization of Philippine global migration and labor. In another twenty-first century variation of bagong bayani, in the same year, Macapagal Arroyo also called OFWs "heroes of the New Millennium" at a meeting with Filipino/as in Malaysia.[16]

Like OFWs more broadly and domestic helpers more specifically, recent Philippine presidents have made official declarations of seamen's bayani-ness. In addition to President Macapagal Arroyo who was shown in the manning agency convention video tribute honoring Filipino seamen as bayanis, through Presidential Decree No. 828, on August 18, 1996, President Ramos established "National Seafarers' Day," now celebrated on the last Sunday of September (a result of Presidential Decree No. 1094). A year later, at the 2nd National Seafarers' Day Celebration, President Ramos, like President Aquino, delivered a speech, but this time it was directed to the Philippine maritime/seafaring community in Manila. Ramos exclaimed, "The National Seafarers' Day celebration . . . is but a simple gesture of gratitude and recognition of the country to our modern heroes—the Filipino seafarers."[17] Through the state-institutionalized National Seafarers' Day, Ramos inscribed the Filipino seafarers/seamen as bagong bayani through state-sanctioned temporality; that is, Filipino seafarers and seamen were granted a national day, through which they are guaranteed an official twenty-four hours where their bayani-ness is acknowledged and celebrated by the state and the seafaring/maritime community in Manila.

Numerous mid- and low-level state officials I met during fieldwork also evoked the discourse of Filipino seamen as bagong bayanis. For instance, during a lunchtime conversation with me in a cafeteria near the POEA office, Mr. "Oscar Villanueva" a man in his forties who was working at the POEA in a middle-management position (like past and present Philippine presidents) repeated the discourse of Filipino seamen as bagong bayani:

> Filipino seamen contributed billions of dollars to the Philippine economy in 1996. The figures have not yet been calculated for 1997, but I'm sure it will be as big, if not bigger. That is why our President Ramos calls the Filipino/as who work overseas—the OFWs—"mga bagong bayani"—the new heroes. Talagang "heroic" ang trabaho nila sa dagat, at siempre "heroic" din ang pera nila. Kaya nga hindi lumulubog ang ekonomiya ng Pilipinas. (Their work/labor at sea is truly heroic, and, of course, their money is also heroic. That is why the Philippine economy is not sinking.)

Here, Villanueva emphasizes the substantial and therefore heroic (or epic) economic contributions that Filipino seamen have made to the nation-state (relatively new in historical terms). The national struggle this time is not Spanish, U.S. American, or Japanese colonialisms, nor the United States–Marcos dictatorship, but rather, the Philippines's poverty and high debt burden (discussed in chapter 1) and the Philippine state's subsequent need for foreign currency that goes to paying Philippine international debts.

Philippine State Notions of Utang Na Loob

Utang na loob (as stated above, variously defined as "social debt" or "gratitude/solidarity") was not a new concept to me when I began fieldwork in the late 1990s. As an immigrant Filipino American raised by two Tagalog parents, both from Malolos, Bulakan, in a bilingual (English-Tagalog) household in Oregon, utang na loob was a concept and term that I was familiar with because it was something my parents discussed, and I witnessed them expressing and enacting utang na loob (as gratitude or solidarity) with their family members and friends, most notably with both of my grandmothers who came to live with us during their extreme old age (during my childhood). Throughout their lives, both of my grandmothers made heroic sacrifices as they came of age during the U.S. colonial era and matured during World War II and in postwar Philippines. In particular, they made profound personal sacrifices to provide educational opportunities for my parents. Although my maternal grandmother was illiterate, she labored through most of her adult life as a mostly-single mother market woman who sold meat at the local palengke (market) in Malolos so that my mother could earn a degree from Far Eastern University, which my grandmother believed would provide her with more socioeconomic opportunities. Similarly, my paternal grandmother raised seven children (along with my paternal grandfather) and worked as cook in a food stall at the local cockfighting arena (also in Malolos) to help my father earn a degree at the University of the Philippines, Diliman. (As noted in the preface, my paternal grandfather was a fisherman.) Showing their gratitude to these courageous and hard-working women, upon immigrating to the United States, my parents financially supported them with remittances and later took care of them in our home in Oregon for many years. (Both of my grandfathers passed away before they could migrate to the United States.) And so as I conducted fieldwork in Manila and Oakland, I drew from these important life experiences of utang na loob in action.

During fieldwork I also observed utang na loob as a form of gratitude when I saw first hand the financial and material help that Filipino seamen shared with their parents, relatives, and friends. Utang na loob literally "concretized" in people's homes as I spent time with parents of Filipino seamen or OFWs on the islands of Luzon and Panay. A mother or father of a seaman would give me a tour of his or her home, showing me a new roof or kitchen or bathroom or landscaping or sometimes a completely brand new house paid for by their seamen sons. "Donding Rodriguez," the father of "Esteban" (a former seaman I discuss at length later in this chapter) was one of these parents who proudly showed me multiple additions and renovations to his house, structures and home improvements that Esteban generously financed as a way to express gratitude for the love, care, and help his parents gave him throughout his boyhood and early adulthood. Although these personal and collective acts show utang na loob expressed as gratitude and solidarity, this chapter will also show how utang na loob can shift, depending on context, taking on different meanings and implications.

Utang na loob plays a significant role in the bagong bayani discourse and imaginary, but has multiple meanings and possible effects. Therefore, to more fully understand how the bagong bayani discourse and imaginary work culturally, psychologically, and economically (and why they are so powerful) as well as how the Philippine state deploys or activates the narrative for conservative and neoliberal purposes, we must continue to address the indigenous psychosociocultural concept of utang na loob in detail, particularly through a genealogy of Philippine or Filipino/a Studies, which to date, has not been synthesized, but remains a key site for understanding this often misused and misunderstood term and concept. By understanding how utang na loob has been misread or deployed by neocolonial/U.S. American researchers, we gain an improved understanding of the relationship between knowledge production, culture, and power.

As mentioned previously, utang na loob can be defined in different ways, namely "gratitude or solidarity" and "social debt," among other nuanced understandings that I will elaborate on shortly. Utang na loob, in particular its conservative definition as social debt, is critical to the efforts of the Philippine state's manning agencies and shipping companies to create docile and loyal subjects and OFWs who enact bayani-ness and subjecthood through patriotic hard overseas or migrant work, respect for authority and hierarchy, and notions or practices of deep personal sacrifice or martyrdom.

According to psychologist Virgilio G. Enriquez, founder of the field of Sikolohiyang Pilipino ([indigenous] Filipino psychology), in a *decolonizing* framework, utang na loob refers powerfully to a sense of "gratitude/solidarity" or "appreciation of kapwa solidarity,"[18] where kapwa refers to the "unity of the 'self' and 'others'" and the "recognition of shared identity, an inner self shared with others."[19] That is, in Philippine or Filipino/a psychosociocultural logics (especially among Christianized lowlanders; note that Enriquez does not consistently address the heterogeneity of ethnolinguistic traditions in Filipino/a or Philippine contexts) an individuated sense of self of personhood is *not* what is emphasized, but rather it is the sensory/*inner awareness of relationships of unity between oneself and other people* that is critically important. In Enriquez's indigenous psychological and decolonizing framework, kapwa is the "core value" of sikolohiyang Pilipino, *not* utang na loob as some U.S. American scholars have emphasized. As such, it is through kapwa that other psychosocialcultural sensibilities and orientations emerge.

Enriquez explains kapwa further by stating that "the concept of *kapwa* as a shared inner self [is] very important, psychologically and philosophically. . . . A person starts having *kapwa* not so much because of a recognition of status given him *[sic]* by others but more because of his *[sic] awareness* of shared identity" [emphasis added]. This means that kapwa originates in a person through her or his personal/interpersonal "sensory" awareness of a shared identity with others. In this way, kapwa or a sense of unity is not achieved or created through a dynamic that comes from the outside, for example, through hierarchy, social status, or top-down approaches. As a consequence, if kapwa exists at a core psychological level then relationships or dynamics of utang na loob (gratitude/solidarity) emerge because of a realization, "reading" (Vicente Rafael's term), or consciousness of a shared identity or sense of unity between "selves" and "others" who are ultimately united. By understanding and emphasizing kapwa, Enriquez theorizes and offers an anticolonial or decolonized understanding of utang na loob, a significantly different understanding compared with Euro-American colonial conceptualizations.

According to Enriquez, Ileto, and Rafael, utang na loob has a history of being mistranslated or appropriated, especially by colonial authorities, institutions, and scholars, for conservative colonial or neocolonial agendas. Rather than stressing gratitude or solidarity, neocolonial knowledge production has stressed notions of indebtedness, hierarchy, and inequality. Enriquez, for one, shows how the concept was misunderstood and misused by U.S. American researchers who were unfamiliar with Philippine languages and cultural concepts.[20] He argues that utang na loob was problematically overemphasized in scholarship, especially by white U.S. American researchers, for example, Charles Kaut, who mistranslated and narrowly defined utang na loob as a "debt of gratitude." Enriquez argues that this narrow definition reinforces neocolonial power dynamics and a more "accommodative," that is, a conservative neocolonial understanding of Filipino/a psychocultural dynamics. Enriquez explains the negative epistemological and psychological impacts of U.S. American colonial scholarship related to the concept of utang na loob. I quote Enriquez's important analysis at length because he was the scholar who developed an early postcolonial or decolonized critique of utang na loob:

> The problems with the token use of Filipino psychological concepts in the context of a Western analysis that relies on the English language and English categories of analysis are many. It no doubt can lead to the distortion of Philippine social reality and the furtherance of the mis-education of the Filipinos. It is no coincidence that Kaut (1961) hit upon *utang na loob* (debt of "gratitude") as a key concept for the analysis of Tagalog interpersonal relations, considering that *utang na loob* is just one among many psychosocial concepts that relate to the theoretically fertile concept of *loob*. We have *sama ng loob* ("resentment"), *kusang loob* ("initiative"), *lakas ng loob* ("guts") and many others. Samonte (1973) needed no less than three pages just to list down such concepts. In addition, Kaut admitted that "debt of gratitude" is not altogether unknown in Washington, D.C. Even Americans [*sic*] recognize *utang na loob*, they just happen to prefer *kaliwaan* or immediate payoffs whenever possible. To argue that *utang na loob* is a Filipino value is therefore misleading to say the least, and dangerous at best. *Utang na loob* would be convenient in perpetuating the colonial status of the Filipino mind.[21]

Here, Enriquez indicates in this insightful scholarship how the narrow focus or emphasis on utang na loob as "debt" and the marginalization or exclusion of other Filipino/a psychosocial concepts may be used to perpetuate or further a neocolonial Filipino/a psychology or mentality where the person who is "in debt" or in a state of indebtedness perpetually owes something to the person or figure who has made the unrequested social "loan" or "gift," which in turn subsequently reinforces a specific power dynamic or mode of inequality in which the receiver of a loan or gift is in a more disempowered social status or situation than the giver. Substantiating this viewpoint, Rafael writes, "Studies of Tagalog reciprocity have stressed the *inequality built into debt transactions*" [emphasis added].[22] As a result, if we engage this limited "mercantile" understanding of utang na loob in the context of a (neo)colonial United States–Philippines relationship, then the Philippines stands in for the "indebted," whereas the United States is the benevolent benefactor or patron, in a neocolonially predictable relationship of inequality; that is, the neocolonial nation of the United States has more social power and cultural/economic capital, while the Philippines is in a more disadvantaged and unequal position.

Offering a related postcolonial critique, Ileto criticizes the role of U.S. American social scientists, especially anthropologists, and their overemphasis of utang na loob, especially through conservative and neocolonial definitions of social debt, which he suggests has created problematic caricatures or stereotypes of "the Filipino." Ileto writes,

> When behavioral scientists today speak of social values like *utang na loob* (lifelong debt to another for some favored bestowed), *hiya* (shame), SIR (smooth interpersonal relations) and *pakikisama* (mutual cooperation), they give the impression that these values make Philippine society naturally tend toward stasis and equilibrium. . . . If we accept most current definitions of the Filipino, we come up with something like the image of the smiling, peace-loving religious, deferential, hard-working, family-bound and hospitable native.[23]

In this passage, Ileto exposes the relationship between neocolonial knowledge production and notions of Filipino/a identities, showing in particular how U.S. American social sciences are implicated in perpetuating colonial dynamics, "passivity and reconciliation rather than conflict,"[24] and conservative/colonial notions of Filipino/a subservience. Ileto's historical and political analysis in *Pasyon and Revolution* demonstrates how popular mass social movements in the Philippines (1840–1910) engaged the cracks and fissures of closed colonial definitions or translations of utang na loob by engaging utang na loob's more *revolutionary* meanings and dynamics. This remains an important critical intervention. In this chapter, however, I focus more on utang na loob's conservative and neocolonial-now-nationalist meanings and implications.

Ileto's late 1970s discussion of the implications of U.S. American neocolonial ideas about utang na loob and how they contributed to popular descriptions of the Filipino as a "smiling, peace-loving religious, deferential, hard-working, family-bound and hospitable native" is regrettably similar to the contemporary Philippine state's expectations of how Filipino seamen are supposed to behave and represent the nation. One Filipino seaman I spoke with in Manila, "Mark Jacob" (thirty-five years old from Bacolod City), elaborated on this point:

> The government, the POEA, and manning agencies don't want us to cause trouble while we're working at sea. No way! No strikes, no complaining, no bad-mouthing, no fighting, nothing. It's like what the

> government wants is for us to work hard and provide service with a smile. It's like we're at "McDo" (McDonald's fast food), but I don't even work as a cook or steward! I work on deck! It's hard to smile sometimes because our life is difficult. Sometimes I want to punch the white officers [on my ship] because they mistreat Filipinos and are arrogant. But we're not supposed to cause any trouble. We're supposed to work hard, earn money, send it home, and we're not supposed to complain. Otherwise, we're "blacklisted" (i.e., blocked from employment). And then we start the cycle again. Return to a ship, work again, send it home. Return to a ship, work again, send it home.

Mark Jacob's comments first point to the legacies and present-day realities of colonialism and neocolonialism that help to produce a racialized and classed hierarchy of masculinities on board ships, which, in turn, makes "serving with smile" extremely difficult and deeply problematic for many Filipino seamen. (In Mark Jacob's case, this difficulty was expressed in his anger and resentment toward "arrogant" white officers.) Second, his comments reveal how the Philippine state still wants Filipino seamen who work in an industrialized shipboard setting to provide a stereotypical (indeed racist) Native brand of hospitality, providing maritime labor with a smile, just like other service workers in the "new global economy" who are not supposed to organize or resist capitalist or state oppression. And finally, Mark Jacob's comments reveal how the Philippine state must contend with shipping companies that operate in an international/global labor market that desires a more accommodating Filipino face or performance of labor. However, as the video tribute to Filipino seamen also showed, when the state or state partners (manning agencies) address local Philippine audiences, seamen's hypermasculinities are highlighted, but they are masculinities that must ultimately remain docile to the state (and capital), which precisely means that seamen are not supposed to create, embody, and/or perform oppositional masculinities. (Again, the state and its manning agency partners emphasize masculine Filipino seafaring and OFW honor, duty, and obligation, which can all be interpreted as contributing to docility.)

Similar to neocolonial U.S. social sciences and the neocolonial U.S. state, which relied on neocolonial knowledge production to maintain neocolonial rule, the Philippine state engages and deploys a more conservative understanding of utang na loob, that is, notions of social indebtedness, *not the progressive or radical notions of solidarity* analyzed by Ileto, in its attempts to continue expanding and naturalizing Filipino/a global overseas migration as a key long-term economic development strategy for the Philippines. Philippine state leaders and officials, manning agencies, and shipping companies seek to activate this emotional and social affect through notions of nationalist heroism or heroineism, as well as through the conservative or normative familial components of utang na loob where the state performs parenthood, more specifically motherhood or "Inangbayan"[25] ("Mother Nation") and OFWs are supposed to perform childhood, and thus as children, they are supposedly indebted to the nation-state in perpetuity.

Relationships between parents and children, especially relationships between mothers and their children, according to Rafael, are exemplary relationships that illustrate and embody conservative, accommodative, or neocolonial notions or dynamics of utang na loob. Since mothers give the "gift of life," Filipino/a children are in an enduring relation of utang na loob with their mothers, due to a "debt" that can never be paid back in full. As a consequence, Rafael writes, "the child. . . accumulates a burden of indebtedness, and even after one enters adulthood one never stops owing one's parents. . . ."[26] In the same way, the (Philippine) nation-state as mother gives its citizens and subjects (including OFWs and seamen) "life" through imagined national kinship; cultural, historical, and political affinities and a sense of national identity. In this set of logics, citizens and OFWs, as children, are supposed to be indebted and beholden to the nation-state for the long-term. Because of a super-burden of debt, Rafael suggests that partial or token "payments" are often key strategies used by those wishing to manage utang na loob relationships because the ongoing tokens of appreciation or (social debt) payments minimize or deny the space or possibility of "hiya" (shame). In this way and through neocolonial-now-nationalist cultural logics, infantilized as children of the Philippine nation-state, OFWs (including seamen) in this heteronormative familial-state model are supposed to manage the unequal utang na loob relationship with the Philippine state by making ongoing payments in the form of social obedience and monetary remittances that provide the foreign currency needed by the national government for the purposes of debt repayments to United States–backed financial institutions such as the World Bank, International Monetary Fund (IMF), and Asian Development Bank (discussed in chapter 1).

At the same time, a perplexing slight of hand is operating, particularly in terms of how the Philippine state attempts to stimulate accommodative or conservative notions and affects of utang na loob. On the one hand, citizens and migrants are infantilized and so must behave deferentially and obediently in relation to the more powerful Philippine state, but on the other hand, as bagong bayani in the Philippine state's "fantasy-production," OFWs are elevated and respected through "words of deference" such as "ho" and "po," which *appear to reverse* the utang na loob dynamic because ho and po are terms that people who are of or in a "lower social status" are supposed to use when addressing someone occupying a higher social status, for example, one's mother, another parental figure, one's landlord supervisor, or a political leader or official. Rafael writes,

> These terms ["ho" and "po"] are usually attached to the words directed to the figure of authority. . . . Only when they are inserted between words directed to one's parents or elders do they take on significance, and then they signal respect. To this extent, they are also the signs of *utang na loob* ties that would otherwise remain unarticulated.[27]

In this passage, Rafael stresses how terms of deference help to identify or call out unspoken bonds of utang na loob as conservative social debt.

As discussed earlier, in 1988 President Aquino addressed a domestic helpers' audience in Hong Kong in this manner: "*Kayo po* ang bagong bayani," and in 1997, the year I began my fieldwork in Manila, President Ramos addressed a maritime audience with the statement, "The National Seafarers' Day celebration. . . is but a simple gesture of *gratitude* and recognition of the country to our modern heroes—the Filipino seafarers."[28] In these two examples, Philippine state leaders use rhetoric of respect and deference, which creates an illusion that the social positions of indebtedness and inequality have been inverted. That is, the Philippine state appears to be in a less advantaged position, supposedly behaving deferentially and respectfully toward OFWs more broadly and domestic helpers and seafarers/seamen more specifically. However, OFWs, domestic helpers, and seafarers/seamen (among other kinds of migrants) are the people, many of whom come from poor or working-class backgrounds, who are perpetually making economic and social payments to the Philippine state, while the state and its many elite representatives remain largely ineffectual in combating the poverty, landlessness, national indebtedness, underemployment, and unemployment that are the social and economic conditions significantly pushing or propelling much of the Philippines's overseas/global migration in the first place. Indeed, Walden Bello calls the Philippine state "the anti-development state" because of the multiple ways it impedes radical social and economic change and justice in the Philippines.[29]

In short, the Philippine state and its manning agency and shipping company partners do the bare minimum to protect or advocate for social and economic justice on behalf of OFWs, making minor gestures[30] to appear as if they care about global Filipino/a migrants, but millions of Filipino/as believe otherwise. The consistent massive outrage and protests against the

Philippine state ranging from the Flor Contemplacion case to the Angelo dela Cruz situation to hundreds of thousands of other cases of OFW injustices reported daily in Philippine and diaspora news outlets are evidence of the Philippine state's poor track record of protecting human rights, including those of land and sea-based OFWs.

To conclude this section, if one sees through the discursive and historical maneuvers of the Philippine state, it is reasonable then to analyze the state-sanctioned bagong bayani narrative and the state's tactics of a reverse and dubiously performed utang na loob as a kind of Philippine state magic,[31] discursive and historical "smoke and mirrors" that are critical to the state's efforts to continue expanding Philippine global migration for the purposes of accumulating the foreign currency needed to pay back IMF, World Bank, and Asian Development Bank loans that past regimes and administrations have incurred. In the context of the feminization of Filipino/a global migration and labor, the state engages powerful and compelling discourses of bayani-ness, hypermasculinities, and conservative notions of utang na loob in its official role and capacity as a key recruiter or national "broker"[32] (to use sociologist Robyn Rodriguez's term) in the Philippines's "warm body export"[33] of Filipino/a migrants around the world. These discursive strategies of masculinization, especially in a local/Philippine contexts, enable the Philippine state, manning agencies, and shipping companies to continue recruiting Filipino men into the seafaring and shipping industries by interpellating Filipino seamen or sea-based migrants through dominant notions of heroic Filipino seamen's masculinities and a conservative pattern of utang na loob, not solidarity, that kapwa and more progressive or radical notions of utang na loob suggest. Moreover, discourses of bagong bayani, seafaring hypermasculinities, and utang na loob are also tropes and psychologies that assist the Philippine state, manning agencies, and shipping companies in processes of "subject-making"; that is, the discourse ultimately hopes or helps to create heteronormative Filipino masculinities and "(sea/)men" who in the logics of the state, nationalism, and capitalism are supposed to be subservient and loyal to the Philippine state and local/global corporate power (manning agencies and shipping companies).

Away (at Sea and in Oakland): Filipino Seamen as Deserters or Men with Lakas ng Loob (Guts)?

After observing that the Philippine state discourse of Filipino seamen as bagong bayani had emerged as dominant during fieldwork in Manila, I traveled to the Western Visayas, specifically to "Rosca,"[34] a small town on the island of Panay, to learn other perspectives on seafaring, masculinities, and globalization from those situated outside of Metro Manila. I was familiar with Rosca and Panay because I had been traveling to Rosca since the late 1980s. My family has relatives there and during fieldwork one of my uncles graciously invited me to visit again. When I arrived, my uncle's friend, "Donding Rodriguez," a Visayan man in his mid-sixties wanted to help with my research because his son "Esteban" had worked as a seaman for nine years (1984–1992). Esteban jumped ship in Oakland, California (United States) and for two years was living as an undocumented immigrant or migrant—sometimes called "TNT" in Filipino/a communities. (TNT is an acronym for "Tago Ng Tago," which can be literally translated as "always hiding" in English.) During conversations with Donding in Rosca, he stressed a "father's perspective" on seafaring and im/migration, as well as the importance of local roots, place, and affiliations in his understanding of Filipino identity and manhood.[35] Donding also put me in touch with Esteban in the San Francisco Bay Area, who provided important perspectives on seafaring, utang na loob, lakas ng loob, transnationalism, and the politics of location.

Through my conversations with Esteban in Oakland (2000), I learned that in many ways Esteban had experiences in the global shipping industry that were similar to other Filipino seamen's experiences told to me during fieldwork in both Manila and Oakland. For example, his career (overall) followed a standard path and narrative where social, geographic, sexual, and economic mobilities were central to his seafaring experiences and notions of sea-based migrant manhood. In short, Esteban's life story indicated that he was seen as a "good son" in the context of his family and an exemplary migrant man and citizen in the context of nation building. Throughout his seafaring career, he expressed key components of the exemplary "heroic" OFW masculinity, enacted through utang na loob, as discussed previously. At the end of his career, however, Esteban experienced a major personal and social crisis, which contributed to his decision to jump ship. In this section of this chapter, I elaborate on Esteban's specific journey, but rather than staying at the level of the individual, I also address some of the broader historical, cultural, political, and economic meanings and implications of his seafaring journey and his jumping ship in California.

In particular, I analyze how Filipino seamen who engage lakas ng loob (guts) and jump ship are literally "jumping out of" or withdrawing from dominant Philippine state "currents" or ideologies of bagong bayani masculinities and conservative notions and practices of utang na loob (i.e., utang na loob as social debt). In addition to resisting state narratives and practices, Filipino seamen who jump ship also potentially resist unequal interpersonal-familial hierarchies and power dynamics enacted or performed through utang na loob, which in turn potentially disrupt conservative heteronormative family and psychosocialcultural dynamics that are critical to the Philippine state's strategy of global Filipino/a migration as a long-term development plan. Finally, by contextualizing Esteban's story and biography in a larger and more collective historical, cultural, and economic context, we can also better understand how and why Filipino seamen's "marginalized 'deserter' masculinities" (in the cultural logics of the Philippine state) become sites to develop oppositional masculinities.

As a son of a Tagalog mother and Visayan father, Esteban chose seafaring as profession because several of his older cousins in Rosca were working as seamen. Other seamen during my fieldwork similarly revealed that family histories and connections with seafaring were important factors that inspired or pushed them into the profession. For instance, Esteban was impressed with how his cousins' lives improved after they began working as seamen and how people in Rosca respected his cousins more as a result of their global line of work and higher socioeconomic standing. Esteban also admired the high(er) salaries of seamen, especially when compared with local positions that are compensated in Philippine pesos, the gifts and luxuries seamen brought home after being away at sea, the parties seamen threw (or were thrown for them) while in the Philippines, and the opportunities for global travel that seafaring provides. Since Rosca is by the sea, Esteban also admitted that the close proximity and familiarity with the ocean was another factor that attracted him to seafaring.

After completing a two-year Maritime Engineering course from a maritime school in Manila, Esteban secured an entry-level position through a family contact. This was and remains a common employment practice; other seamen in Manila and Oakland discussed the importance of family or personal connections when trying to find employment in the shipping industry in Manila. In Esteban's case, his father knew a Norwegian seaman who lived in Rosca part time and who was married to a local Roscan woman. The Norwegian seaman told his Norwegian shipping company that Esteban was a relative and, as a result, the company hired Esteban. Through this Norwegian connection, Esteban worked primarily on Norwegian-owned ships during his career. Steven C. McKay writes that, "in the 1980s, [the] recruit[ment] [of Filipino seamen] took [a] big leap; in a single year, Filipinos on European-owned ships went from 2,900 to 17,057 and by the end of the decade, there were more than 57,000 Filipinos aboard some 4,000 ships."[36] It is highly likely then that in addition to the personal/family connection, Esteban was hired as a result of this shift in recruiting and labor patterns.

Like other Filipino seamen I met during fieldwork, Esteban began his career at the lowest rank(s). Beginning first as an engine cadet (the lowest position in the engine room), he then moved up in rank and worked as an oiler. His first ships were "car ships" that transported automobiles from Japan to the United States, for example, to the ports of Long View, Washington; Long Beach, California; Oakland, California; and Ketchikan, Alaska. His ships also stopped in Canadian ports such as the Port of Vancouver in British Columbia. In addition to car ships, Esteban also worked for "trampers," cargo vessels that do not sail regularly between fixed ports, but rather transport cargo wherever shippers desire. Esteban recalled a typical list of major ports and port cities where his ships docked:

> Besides Oakland/San Francisco, I've been to Longview and Seattle, Washington; Long Beach and San Diego, California; North Carolina; South Carolina; Philadelphia; Galveston and Corpus Christi, Texas; Mobile, Alabama; a small town in Florida; New Orleans, Louisiana. In Europe, I've been to Norway, Sweden, Germany, Italy, Greece, and Portugal. I can't remember them all. I've also been to Canada—St. John, Canada, past Boston, Massachusetts, and to Nigeria. My longest voyage was twenty-five days or twenty-six days. We went from San Diego to Africa, to Nigeria. We passed through the Panama Canal and then we went up to Africa. We loaded crude oil in Kabon, Nigeria. We went to a big river. That voyage took us on "the highway" (open sea) for about twenty-seven days.

This recollection was only a partial itinerary; Esteban, for example, does not mention Asian ports of call. Through inference and follow-up conversations, Esteban elaborated that he had traveled to several Asian ports, including ports in Japan, Hong Kong (when the city was under the British), South Korea, and Singapore. He also clarified that his ships had sailed to multiple ports/cities in Europe and western Africa but was unable to recall all specific port names at the time of our interview.

In addition to this kind of geographic mobility, Esteban also relayed conventional stories of heterosexual mobility and "adventures" that resulted from his work and travels as a seaman. This was another typical narrative I heard during fieldwork. During one of our conversations, he described his social-sexual journey while at sea and in ports. In the beginning of his career, he described himself as "hungry," a young seaman who frequented "bargirls" and "ladies" (usually women who work in bars providing companionship and conversation and/or women who work in prostitution or sex work). However, with the global HIV/AIDS pandemic that developed in the 1980s, Esteban became more cautious about having sex with people he did not know well or having sex with multiple partners. He went to bars less frequently when in port to lower his risks of HIV/AIDS exposure and to save money. Esteban described this period in his career:

> In the evenings we went out. That was normal for a sailor. We had to go out, we had to go to the bars! That's what we did every night. All the money you saved, you lost in port! Even your watch! Sailors did that. Sometimes they would fall in love with a bargirl. This happened to one of my friends and also to me. Seamen give ladies presents. My friend had just bought a nice TV and he was going to bring it home to his family, but he fell in love with this lady and he wanted to give the TV to her. He even gave her his watch.

Esteban expresses here the heterosexual masculine excitement he felt as young seaman who was away from home for the first time, extra cash in hand, time off from his duties on board his ship(s), enjoying friendship, love, and sex with ladies and bargirls in portside spaces.

As he gained more experience, Esteban changed his behavior and outlook and described his sociosexual orientation in different terms:

> The new sailor. . . when they first arrive in other countries, they're hungry. . . . They go to the bars to meet ladies, but after that, they learn how to calm down. You have to take it easy. You have to learn how to do this because what if you get a disease? It's scary. The word "AIDS" was spreading at the time. I still went to the bars, but I no longer got together with women. I just stayed there and chitchatted and drank.

Here, Esteban conveys how his attitudes towards sexual mobility started to shift as a result of "calming down" and the new sociosexual context of HIV/AIDS in the 1980s.

Esteban's comments reveal how heterosexual practices are key components of how seamen create and perform their masculinities. The heterosexual mobility he experienced early in his career, however, runs counter to established constructions of Philippine state patriarchal, heteronormative, exemplary, and heroic masculinities. Recall, for example, that the manning agency video tribute included shots of Filipino seamen embracing their wives or girlfriends during homecomings and the importance placed on family or families in Philippine state discourse and policies. That is, to be a good Filipino, good OFW, or good seaman, one has to be a good husband, father, son, and provider, what sociologist McKay calls "breadwinner" masculinities. At the same time, it is important to note there are contradictions in how this exemplary masculinity is understood and constructed. So, although heterosexual breadwinner masculinities are held in high esteem by the state, they are not always constructed or experienced as monogamous. That is, hyperheterosexual or "macho" behavior such as "having a girl in every port" or frequenting bars and bargirls is simultaneously naturalized by some Philippine state officials and the seamen themselves. Esteban, for example, described such behavior as "common," and several Philippine state officials also commented on the hyperheterosexualities of Filipino seamen, even expressing moments of vicarious masculine pride or envy in seamen's sexual mobilities. One POEA staff member, "Rey Diaz," commented, "Naku, machong macho sila! Ang daming babae! Pero 'good husbands' naman sila. Magaling silang mag-provide sa mga familya nila. Minsan, nakaka inggit." (My goodness, they're [Filipino seamen] super macho; they have so many women! But they are still 'good husbands.' They are good/effective in providing for their families. Sometimes it creates envy [in me].)

Early in his seafaring career, Esteban behaved in these hyperheterosexual and macho ways, but like the dozens of Filipino seamen I spoke with, he also clearly and successfully performed breadwinner seaman-hood. Over the course of his career, Esteban's salary ranged from $700 to $1,000. It was mandatory for him to send back 80 percent of this salary to the Philippines (Esteban recalled sending home "$500 to $600 each month"), as this policy enables Philippine banks and the Philippine state access to the foreign currency needed to make debt repayments and pay other budgetary expenses. At the same time, families, loved ones, and communities in the Philippines are assured of steady financial support. In Esteban's case, his remittances significantly subsidized his parents' and older brother's daily living expenses and occasionally those of his extended family or friends. Note that Esteban's family was not destitute; his father was employed as a manager at a governmental agency, his mother worked at home, and his brother worked a number of odd jobs primarily in journalism and clerical services.

Esteban also paid for major renovations of his family's one-story, three-bedroom concrete bungalow-type home in Rosca; the renovations included a new ceiling, roof, and kitchen; structural improvements to the interior and exterior of the house; interior and exterior painting and enhanced landscaping; and a nipa hut "rest house." Improvements on an existing home or the purchasing of a new one became common during the 1980s and 1990s when Esteban was working as a seaman. This phenomenon has only increased and expanded through the years as the demand for real estate has increased, as more Filipino/as live and work abroad, as real estate "bubbles" have developed in the Philippines and around the world, and as OFWs have improved access to capital and housing loans. Indeed, during fieldwork and more recent trips back to the Philippines, it has become everyday practice for locals to identify homes and places by saying, "Bahay 'yan ng seaman" ("That's a house of a seaman") or "OFW ang owner" ("The owner [of that house] is an OFW"). The homes are usually quite grand compared with other local housing options.

Esteban's seafaring trajectory and everyday practices suggest that throughout his career he embodied many of the significant elements that constitute Philippine state constructions of exemplary seamen's masculinities or normative bagong bayani masculinities. He worked hard during his career, he made personal sacrifices along the way (most notably through remittances and his success at meeting the challenges of a seafaring and migrant life), and he always followed Philippine state rules and family expectations by making regular "partial payments" to the state and his family, which helped to fulfill his responsibilities or obligations of utang na loob (as social debt) with the nation-state and kin.

After nine years of working as a seaman, a breech occurred in Esteban's personal and professional life. It was a family incident that greatly shocked him, yet the experience also went beyond "the personal"; that is, if we probe a little further, we see there are larger social, cultural, psychological, and economic implications to Esteban's story. Esteban recalled that since their family house in Rosca had been significantly renovated, he no longer wanted to send money back home to his family, but rather, he wanted to start saving money in case he "met a lady" and wanted to get married. Esteban's mother agreed this was a good course of action, so he established a different bank account for his personal savings. As in the past, over the next ten months (the length of his particular contract), Esteban deposited $500 to $600 into his bank account. However, when he returned to the Philippines, he asked to see his savings "account book," but his older brother would not show it to him; something was wrong. Esteban described the situation in his own words:

> He [my older brother] said he forgot my account book at the office, and tomorrow he'd bring it. That first day, I wasn't really concerned. I had only been in Manila for one day, and since I just arrived, I was jet lagging. I was sleeping a lot and sitting around watching TV. The next

> day though, I felt refreshed, so I said to my brother, "Please go get the money now. I don't have any pesos." He said again, "Oh, I forgot (the book)." I said, "What's going on?" I already suspected that something was wrong. On the third day, he said, "There's no money in the book." I said, "What?!!" "There's no money, I spent it," he said. I said, "You're crazy!" That day my mind was going crazy. I went to the airport, bought a ticket and flew to the Visayas and told my dad and mom what happened. My father was angry, but my mother was trying to calm me down.
>
> That month my brother planned on having a big reunion. My dad knew I was supposed to help by providing some money for this, but my dad told me, "Don't even spend a centavo. Just cancel this reunion." But my mom cried. She said to me, "You only have one brother, so forget it. It's only money." "Yes, yes," I said. "I'm forgetting it but it was my ass working on the ship. He doesn't even know what it's like to work on the ship. I wish you could see how hard it is. I wish you could see for yourselves how hard it was." I was so angry! I got tired of all this. On my last ship, I decided, "Okay, forget you guys, I'm going to start my life here in the United States."

To Esteban's consternation, although throughout his seafaring career he had been a good and dutiful son and brother, from Esteban's perspective, his mother ultimately sided with his older brother, which greatly disappointed him. His father expressed anger and frustration at the older brother, but in the end, there were still no repercussions for his brother's behavior and misuse of Esteban's savings ($4,000). The quarrel appeared to be resolved as his mother basically asked Esteban to be more patient and forgive the family, especially his brother. He replied to his mother that yes, he would "forget" the money and his brother's trespasses, but he reminded her that it was his "ass working hard on the ship." For Esteban, the situation was not fully resolved. Rather than continue with an utang na loob dynamic and relationship with his family, he instead engaged lakas ng loob (guts) and decided to jump ship in California to begin a new life in the United States.Esteban lived as TNT for two years, working in housing construction and renovations with other undocumented im/migrants, including another former seaman who had also jumped ship, and eventually began a more permanent position as a janitor in an East Bay hospital. In 1994, Esteban married a white U.S. American woman he met at a karaoke bar, but he was detained at an INS facility for a month in the same year because he was arrested by INS officials (This occurred at a court hearing where Esteban was trying to help his seaman friend who had gotten into some legal trouble.) In time, Esteban was eventually released because he was married to a U.S. citizen and he had already applied for a green card (permanent residency in the United States). In 2000 he was naturalized as a U.S. American citizen and at the time of our interviews, Esteban was exploring ways to return to a life at sea (e.g., he hoped to find work on a tugboat).

How does Esteban and other (former) seamen's engagement of lakas ng loob figure into Filipino seafaring, masculinities, and globalization? Psychologist Virgilio G. Enriquez defines "lakas ng loob" as "guts," an "inner resource for change."[37] In contrast to utang na loob, which Enriquez has argued is a "colonial or accommodative" psychosociocultural orientation, he suggests that lakas ng loob is "confrontat[ional]," in other words, a more actively resistant, radical, and/or revolutionary positioning. Enriquez writes,

> *Lakas ng loob* is a key ingredient in the realization of *pagbabagong-dangal* [the process of changing one's dignity or honor], enabling one to face difficulty, even death, to vindicate the *dangal* (dignity/honor) in one's being. *Lakas ng loob* [guts] is a *damdamin* (internal feel *[sic]*/ attribute/trait) necessary for actualizing the good not only in one's self but also in one's fellow man (*kapwa* [shared identity]), in one's *loob* [shared inner self], and in facilitating the "social good" in *kapwa*.[38]

Here, Enriquez continues to develop theories of indigenous Filipino/a psychologies. Although past neocolonial knowledge producers "misused" utang na loob to emphasize Filipino/a docilities, Enriquez counters by emphasizing and elaborating on the more oppositional positioning of lakas ng loob.

To further develop this epistemological and political intervention, Enriquez substantiates his theory with historical examples that demonstrate Filipino/a lakas ng loob, including Lapu-Lapu's defeat of Ferdinand Magellan and his (supposedly) "superior [fire]arms" in 1521 and the 1986 People Power I movement where "businessmen and professionals in Makati joined ranks with the urban poor and protesting laborers from Tondo. . . in a united move to bring about *pagbabagong-dangal*," which eventually "dislodge[d] a dictator." These *collective acts of resistance* illustrate lakas ng loob, and they also emphasize and reveal the core Filipino/a psychosociocultural value of kapwa (where kapwa refers to the "unity of the 'self' and 'others'" or the "recognition of shared identity, an inner self shared with others"[39]).

Keeping kapwa and notions of solidarity in mind, one must understand that Esteban's "individual biography" (one way to read his story) and his decision to jump ship are not exclusively individualistic. Rather, through the act of jumping ship Esteban jumps out of normative social, economic, and psychological structures, flows, and currents, for example, Philippine state–sanctioned overseas migration, state ideologies of bagong bayaniness, seamen's hypermasculinities, and utang na loob, which emphasize an ongoing cycle of social debts and perpetual repayments, and he jumps into a much larger collective crosscurrent or historical and contemporary counterflow of marginalized and oppressed people jumping ship, including, for example, enslaved Asians and Africans, as well as marginalized working-class sailors. Indeed, there is another way to interpret Esteban's story. Rather than simply understanding Esteban's journey as an individual biography, his desertion and act of jumping ship have historical dimensions and cultural and political implications where desertion can be read as both a personal, but perhaps, more importantly, a collective strategy to escape different forms of oppression, violence, and danger.

An important historical event of a precolonial native, Indio, or Malay from the archipelago region deserting or jumping ship is the case of "Enrique de Malacca," a Malay enslaved by Ferdinand Magellan who also worked as the language interpreter during Magellan's attempted circumnavigation (1519–1522). de Malacca jumped ship in the Visayas in 1521 in the present-day Philippines. Although it is difficult to ascertain de Malacca's birthplace and ethnic identity, some historians and writers in contemporary Philippines, Indonesia, and Malaysia claim de Malacca as a Malay maritime ancestor because his origins are somewhere in the Malay archipelago.[40] Historian Tim Joyner suggests that Magellan "acquired" de Malacca in Malacca (present-day Malaysia) in 1511–1512.[41] As Magellan's enslaved language translator, de Malacca participated in the infamous voyage around the earth that began and ended in Seville, Spain. Antonio Pigafetta chronicled this voyage in a travelogue/proto-ethnography first published in Italian in 1522, entitled, *The First Voyage Around the World: An Account of Magellan's Expedition*.[42] From Sanlúcar de Barrameda, an outport of Seville, Magellan's armada sailed across the Atlantic Ocean to present-day South America, and from present-day Brazil, the armada sailed south, following the South American coast to a strait that connected to the Pacific, an ocean named by the conquistador (Magellan). In the Pacific, Magellan and his crews sailed to the present-day Mariana Islands where Magellan's crews were met with strong resistance and next to the Visayas in present-day Philippines.

According to Pigafetta, in Mactan, de Malacca played a key role in a native act of resistance against the invading Europeans.[43] At the time of this resistance, Magellan had already died on a Mactan beach during a battle against Lapu-Lapu, a local "datu" (leader) who refused to bow down to Spanish/European authority. Pigafetta writes that de Malacca was wounded in the battle and so was resting, "always beneath a heavy blanket." Duarte Barbosa (the new commander of the flagship) yelled and threatened de Malacca with "flogg[ing]" because he would not go ashore to "attend [to their] necessary affairs." Pigafetta writes, "Duarte . . . cried out to [de Malacca] and told him that although his master the captain was dead, he was not therefore free; on the contrary he (Barbosa) would see to it that when we should reach Spain, he should still be the slave of Dona Beatrice, the wife of the captain-general."[44] De Malacca "feign[ed]" as if he was following Barbosa's orders. However, rather than obey, with "presumptuosness" or "cunning," and I would add with lakas na loob, de Malacca worked with Visayan natives to ambush and kill the encroaching Europeans. He went ashore with European officers and sailors to a morning meeting and meal where the local "king" was supposed to give "jewels" to the "king of Spain." However, during the gathering native men killed at least twenty-two European crewmembers. João Serrão, a crewmember who ran to the beach after the attack, cried to the ships, requesting that his shipmates not fire [their canons] because the natives would kill him. Serrão also reported, "All [were] dead except the interpreter [de Malacca]." Twenty-four crewmembers went to shore that morning, but Serrão and de Malacca were the lone survivors. At this point, de Malacca vanishes from Pigafetta's account of the voyage, as the Europeans quickly fled after the natives repelled them. It is clear, though, that de Malacca did not continue with the circumnavigation, which Juan Sebastián Elcano eventually completed. (Elcano is often cocredited with Magellan for the first circumnavigation of the earth.) So, rather than face bodily violence (flogging) from Europeans and a lifetime of planned enslavement at the hands of Magellan's wife, de Malacca deserted the Magellan-Elcano crew by jumping ship in the Visayas. In doing so, he also escaped near certain retaliation at the hands of his former shipmates and on-going or future acts of European colonial violence and brutality against other indigenous peoples (e.g., Asians and Africans) during the remaining segments of the voyage.

De Malacca's jumping ship in Cebu foreshadowed other cases of Indio or Native seamen jumping ship in the context of colonialism. As discussed in the introduction and in chapter 1, subsequent waves of Indio or Native seamen jumped ship in North America during the Manila–Acapulco galleon trade (1565–1815). Historian Marina E. Espina writes that Spaniards in the Philippines maintained a colonial policy of "Christianization. . . and exploitation of native labor."[45] In this context, "Filipinos were forced to become woodcutters, shipbuilders, crewmen and munition workers." As a result of "stringent"

Spanish control, like Enrique de Malacca in Cebu, other Filipino seafarers sought to escape the harsh realities of laboring on Spanish ships, but this time they jumped ship in Mexico, territory in the Americas similarly occupied by the Spanish Empire. Espina writes,

> Always excellent seamen, the Filipinos were forced into service in the galleon trade with Mexico as well as other parts of the New World. Each year, however, some of the Filipino seamen jumped ship in Mexico to escape the brutality of the Spaniards, and many of these later migrated eastward across Mexico to gulf ports. Louisiana became a haven for the fugitive Filipino seamen as they created settlements in the coastal bayous and marshes.[46]

This passage and Espina's larger historical project illustrate the important role of significant numbers of Native seamen from the Philippines (also called Manila-men) who resisted and circumvented Spanish maritime colonial control by jumping ship, subsequently contributing to the collective efforts, which eventually developed land-based communities in present-day Louisiana such as "Manila Village," "the home of Filipino seamen and fishermen for more than a century"[47] (located in Jefferson Parish), and "St. Malo," the "first Filipino colony established in the mid-eighteenth century"[48] with "houses built on stilts in Manila-esque style"[49] and where people spoke "Spanish, Cebuano and Tagalog"[50] (situated near Bayou St. Malo near the mouth of Lake Borgne).

In a broader eighteenth century slave trade and seafaring context, like de Malacca and Manila-men sailors who jumped ship during the Manila–Acapulco galleon trade, African sailors who were enslaved or working as "free blacks" jumped ship to escape slavery and shipboard oppression. Many officers and specialists on board slave ships, for example, on "Rhode Island ships," had special privileges that allowed them to bring people whom they had enslaved (much like Magellan). The Royal Africa Company, to give another example, allowed a captain "the right of two slaves free of freight for every hundred whom he carried." As a result of the blurring lines between "slave" and "sailor" and the harsh disciplining of both, Thomas writes, "[The captain] had to have the presence of mind to deal with difficult crews who might jump ship. . . ."[51] Offering a different gendered perspective on Africans who were enslaved by Europeans and who jumped ship, literacy studies scholar Elaine Richardson documents that "Equiano's *The Interesting Narrative of the Life of Olaudah Equiano* tells of captured African women who jump ship during the middle passage when they find out they are pregnant by White sailors."[52] (Olaudah Equiano was an enslaved African [Igbo] who bought his freedom and who later worked in the abolition movement.) Richardson and Equiano show that enslaved Africans were brutalized in highly racialized and gendered ways in the context of the slave trade. That is, they speak to how African women were brutalized through racialized and gendered sexual violence (rape), which African women sought to courageously escape by jumping ship or resistance by suicide.

Writing about working class seamen in an eighteenth century "Anglo-American maritime world," historian Marcus Rediker argues that working-class seamen also jumped ship to escape "devil(s)" and the "deep blue sea" (oppressive captains and the dangerous oceanic world of maritime labor).[53] As described previously, the isolated "wooden world(s)" that seamen worked on were often dangerous, brutal, and overly disciplined. As such, the seamen Rediker studied "thwarted" their captains and the British imperial maritime labor market through desertion or by jumping ship. Although Rediker argues that working-class European seamen were among the most socially and economically marginalized workers of the world, like de Malacca and Indio sailors of the Spanish galleon trade, they deserted or jumped ship to resist social and economic injustices and create other opportunities.

For example, seamen threatened desertion as a way of creating "advantage" on board ships, to increase their pay, and/or to improve their working conditions. They jumped ship(s) when weather was bad or to play off the competition between the Royal Navy and merchant services, both of which were competing for maritime labor. Many seamen also jumped ship in maritime markets where seafarers were scarce or where there were other social and economic opportunities, such as other forms of employment. In so doing, they were able to increase their wages (because of the lower supply of sailors) or tap into other forms of livelihood. Rediker concludes that in the context of international maritime labor and the British empire, "desertion was extremely attractive."[54] That is, because the British Empire was so vast, seamen could escape the brutalities of the devil and the harshness of the deep blue sea by moving across nonexistent colonial borders in relative ease (compared with today), choosing to desert or jump ship in imperial geographies such as British Caribbean or American colonies, which offered a wide array of social or economic possibilities, especially for seamen of European descent who could take advantage of the colonial situation.

Contemporary Filipino seamen who jump ship do so for reasons that are often similar to those of their historical counterparts. Indeed, during interviews at the Port of Manila and Port of Oakland, Filipino seamen *regularly* reported that they found working at sea extremely challenging and difficult and would rather stay and live and work in the Philippines. Sometimes mistaking me for a labor organizer when on board their ships, Filipino seamen volunteered to talk with me because they wanted me to record the difficulties they faced. (Upon finding out that I was actually a graduate student-ethnographer, they still wanted to discuss some of the problems of their shipboard lives and working conditions.) Their accounts often described working conditions in which their employers (shipping companies) were paying them substandard wages or they were owed back pay, their non-Filipino or non-Asian supervisors were racist and/or classist, they were being treated with disrespect or hostility on the job, they were frustrated by the bad food and general unhygienic conditions of their ships, and/or they felt depressed owing to the loneliness and extreme isolation of their work.

Virgel C. Binghay, a researcher of labor and industrial relations, concurs with the Filipino seamen I met during fieldwork. Binghay documents and argues that "Filipino seafarers. . . [usually] handle mostly 3d (dirty, dangerous, and demeaning) jobs onboard foreign vessels."[55] Journalist Alecks Pabico, writing for the Philippine Center for Investigative Journalism, concurs. Pabico writes that "FOC (flag of convenience) ships are often marked by poor onboard conditions, extended periods of work, low and unpaid wages, and crew abandonment (in ports)."[56] As a result of the "dirty, dangerous, and demeaning" working environments that thousands of Filipino seamen face in the global shipping industry, many jump ship as a way to escape the deplorable working conditions. However, because of the poverty and limited economic and social opportunities in the Philippines, many Filipino seamen I encountered preferred to work in a land-based job, but they felt this was not a reasonable or accessible option, so they worked at sea.

And then there are the Filipino seamen who jump ship because they are dissatisfied with the national economic and social context of the Philippines, disgusted by the exploitative and duplicitous state practices and policies, and/or ambivalent about or mistrustful of national/familial obligations resulting from conservative notions of masculinity and utang na loob. Indeed, at another point during my interview with Esteban, he exclaimed, "It's like the government and my family just wanted money from me. Ano ba ako, ATM? (What am I, an ATM?) I couldn't handle it anymore and the time and conditions were right, so I decided to jump ship and now here I am [in Oakland]." "Gino", another former (Filipino) seaman who also jumped ship and was a friend and co-worker of Esteban's, recalled, "I was tired of paying all of the required fees in Manila just to renew my (seafaring) contracts. Racket lang iyan sa Maynila. (It's just a 'racket' in Manila.) I got sick of the scene and thought I could make a new life in the U.S." Concurring with Esteban and Gino, a chief mate in McKay's study commented, "We should be called *Gagong Bayani* [Stupid Heroes] because even if we contribute significantly to the country, the government fails to help unemployed sea men. . . . I pity my fellow seafarers."[57] These seamen offer a insightful cultural critique of Philippine state–sanctioned global migration as a long-term development strategy for the Philippines and notions of social debt to the state, especially in light of the state's ineffectualness in providing local social and economic opportunities or "antidevelopment" tendencies.

Although it appears as if Esteban utilized the more confrontational psychosociocultural sensibility of lakas na loob as a way to simply disrupt a more conservative dynamic of utang na loob *in his family,* where his mother and older brother in many ways had more social and familial power during the unsettling family quarrel, even as Esteban had more economic power, it is also relevant and productive to engage this family crisis as a metaphor that similarly illuminates how Esteban's decision to jump ship was also an expression of lakas na loob that potentially confronts Philippine state power. In other words, if the nation-state relies on notions of heteronormative families and genders and conservative psychosociocultural formations in which the nation-state is constructed as mother, while citizens and subjects, including overseas migrants, are called upon as children and so are perpetually indebted and paying ongoing payments like an "ATM," Esteban as an OFW, sea-based migrant, and seaman, not only engages lakas na loob to simply disrupt a "personal family drama" but he also simultaneously and just as importantly acts in opposition to the Philippine state, which seeks to infantilize OFWs.

Given the multitude of compelling reasons for Filipino seamen or seafarers to jump ship, how many actually do? It is difficult to calculate how many have jumped ship(s) in ports around the world as a way to thwart devilish captains, escape the deep blue sea, resist state and corporate power, reject family or interpersonal dynamics, and/or access other opportunities and forms of livelihood in different locations. Currently, Philippine state agencies and institutions that manage "legal" forms of overseas Filipino/a migration (including seafaring) "have lost count of how many Filipino seamen have 'jumped ship' while abroad. . . ."[58] This is probably not a statistic that the Philippine state and manning agencies want to publicize as it runs counter to the image of the responsible, loyal, and docile Filipino seafarer/seamen that they seek to promote in the international maritime labor market. Despite not having clear statistics of how many Filipino seamen or seafarers have jumped ship in the United States or other countries, it is sometimes done openly as reported by passengers on board the superliner *Queen Mary 2*. A 2004 newspaper article, for example, reports that *Filipina* seafarers also jump ship (similarly expressing lakas na loob):

> Travellers disembarking this weekend at Rio de Janiero, Brazil where the QM2 [*Queen Mary 2*] has docked for the start of the city's world-famous carnival, reported that 40 crew had walked out during a stopover at St. Thomas in the Caribbean. Up to 18 crew had left the ship at its first port of call—Fort Lauderdale in Florida—while others were stepping down at Rio. Those most unhappy appear to be Filipino, Portuguese, Chinese, Indian, and Polish workers in low-paid cleaning and catering jobs.

Jumping ship also appears to be a common enough practice that Philippine consulates in the United States address the specific needs of Filipino seafarers or seamen for a legal form of identification, precisely resulting from the act of jumping ship. Because seamen do not generally hold their passports while working on board ships and because officers or captains usually hold or secure all crewmembers' passports, when seafarers jump ship they usually "lose" or relinquish their passports. To meet the needs of Filipino seafarers or seamen who have jumped ship, the Los Angeles, California–based Philippine Consulate's Web site, for example, includes this FAQ (frequently asked question): "How does the Consulate deal with cases involving assumed names, or in the case of seamen who jump ship?"[59] The consulate's answer is "Cases involving assumed names, and cases involving seamen who jump ship, are treated in the same way as lost passport."[60] In other words, the consulate will help a seaman who has jumped ship replace his "lost passport." Moreover, because this question and answer are included in the consulate's public Web site, it acknowledges that Filipino seafarers or seamen must be asking this question on a regular basis, which further suggests that jumping ship is an ongoing phenomenon in the United States and more specifically in California.

To conclude, although the Philippine state constructs particular ideologies, imaginaries, and narratives around "true bayani-ness" and although the (Philippine) state may see Filipino seamen and seafarers who jump ship as "deserters," if we look from a different vantage point and prioritize different figures and experiences, we can understand Filipino seafaring, masculinities, and globalization in a less normative way. By taking this tack, we learn that seamen and seafarers who jump ship often do so as a personal and collective strategy that enables historically marginalized peoples to resist and escape oppression, inequality, and different kinds of violence, including discursive, economic, and social violence. In the contemporary context of neoliberal manning capital of the (shipping) world, Manila and the Philippine state's insatiable need for IMF, World Bank, and Asian Development Bank debt/repayments (discussed in chapter 1), Filipino/as who jump ship are also removing themselves from the Philippine state–sanctioned system of Filipino/a global migration as a long-term development plan. In addition, by engaging the oppositional affect and psychology of lakas ng loob instead of conservative hierarchies of utang na loob, Filipino seamen who jump ship also simultaneously critique and resist Philippine state ideologies, narratives, and imaginaries of exemplary OFWs and exemplary seamen's hypermasculinities. In doing so, these courageous Filipino/as do not maintain the status quo, merely going with the flow, but rather they join a sea of subaltern (and sub/marine?) people who have historically and contemporaneously jumped ship(s) as a strategy to restore personal and collective dignities and reestablish lost or stolen dreams.

CHAPTER THREE

Ethnography in Blue

Navigating Time-Space in the Global Economy

Filipino Seamen at Rizal Park, Manila

During fieldwork in Manila in 1998, I traveled by jeep or taxi from Quezon City (where I lived) to Rizal Park in Ermita (district), to the Teodoro M. Kalaw Street side of the park, near the National Library. There on T. M. Kalaw, Filipino seamen or those aspiring to become seamen gathered, in search of employment on board ships. Rizal Park, formerly known as "Luneta" ("small moon" in Spanish, which describes the area's shape) or "Bagumbayan" (evoking "new community" in Tagalog) was a location I visited regularly during fieldwork in Manila. Through participant-observation research at the park I learned that "the scene" repeated during the weekdays and months and would continue to repeat in the coming years.

Once when I was at the park, at least thirty Filipino seamen were gathered.[1] They stood in multiple small groups of eight to ten, sometimes sitting on an available plastic chair or wooden bench, sometimes leaning against a tree. This was the scene on one of the late mornings I visited the park: a short balding man with a clipboard shared information with a half dozen attentive seamen. The man with the clipboard read off the names of manning agencies (employment agencies) that he said were currently recruiting seafarers for different shipping companies and ships. He told them that the companies were looking for able-bodied seamen, cooks, and officers with experience. After this general listing, he talked to the seamen individually or in smaller groupings, asking them about their credentials and past experience, and he told them which manning agency they should contact. I asked a few of the seamen who were standing on the outside circle of the main group how often they came to the park and how they felt about looking for work. "Reggie," age twenty-three, said he had been coming to the park for almost six months. He is from Cotobato City on Mindanao. Fortunately for him, he said, he has relatives in Manila with whom he stays while he is looking for work. Although he is concerned that the job search is going slowly he tries to stay hopeful. Based on conversations with other seamen, it appears there is a range of time that they have been coming to the park, from a few weeks to eight months. An older Filipino seaman who had been searching for work for approximately seven months disagreed with Reggie's more positive outlook. Describing the long process that he's been involved with, he said, "Nakaka depress" (the situation makes me depressed). After the lunch hour, a Japanese journalist and his cameraman came to the park and captured the seamen on video. The journalist said that because of the high numbers of Filipino seamen on Japanese ships, television audiences in Japan are curious about them. He was in Manila reporting on their situation. Unlike the Japanese journalists, local Filipino/as (e.g., students, office workers, vendors, and police officers) who pass by the large group of Filipino seamen looking for work at the park did not pay attention to them. To seasoned Manileños, Filipino seamen are a common sight at the park and street in Ermita.

In 2009, when I visited Rizal Park again (something I tried to do during visits after my initial fieldwork year), the scene was similar, but some things had noticeably changed. The seamen's spot had moved even closer to the National Library building at the intersection of T. M. Kalaw and Marin Orosa, and where previously the Filipino seamen had simply gathered in an area right on or close to T. M. Kalaw Street, but still definitely in Rizal Park, there were now two rows of large white canopies stretched out across a section of the city block, similar to what one might find at a local farmer's market or informational booths at city fairs in public places in the United States. In addition, there was now a small seafarer's center with a small dormitory and a computer room, which is available for seamen transiting in and out of Manila. A historical marker explains the new structure and "waiting area," both created in 2006:

> Constructed as part of the Buhayin ang Maynila Program of the City Government of Manila as it responds to the needs of seafarers by providing them a clean, well-lighted and comfortable waiting area along Teodoro M. Kalaw Street. This area by practice developed into a recruitment place for maritime employment. The city government

> recognizes and honors our seafarers as the country's unsung modern heroes. (Gloria Macapagal Arroyo, President and Captain Gregorio S. Oga, President Associated Marine Officers and Seamen's Union of the Philippines [AMOSUP])

This means that after many years of literally gathering on the street searching for maritime employment (described as "practice"), city and national leaders constructed the new waiting area in Rizal Park, a park famous for celebrating and monumentalizing national heroes, most notably Dr. Jose Rizal, whose monument sits and is protected 24/7 (twenty-four hours, seven days of the week) by a military guard on the Roxas Boulevard side of the park. Several years ago, Rizal Park was a site of nationalist controversy, as then-Tourism Secretary Richard Gordon erected and unveiled a thirty-foot bronze statue of Lapu-Lapu (a gift from South Korea) at the park on February 5, 2004. (Recall from chapter 2 that Lapu-Lapu was a Visayan datu [leader] who killed the commander-cum-invader Ferdinand Magellan.) Through the statue, Gordon aimed to celebrate and monumentalize Lapu-Lapu's anticolonial actions and legacy. In the same year, because of protests by the National Historical Institute (NHI), governmental authorities removed the Lapu-Lapu statue. According to an account by journalist Bobit S. Avila, reporting for the *Cebu Star*, "NHI officials said only the monuments of heroes of the Philippine Revolution could stand at the Agrifina Circle in Rizal Park."[2] In the end, (then) President Macapagal Arroyo allowed the Lapu-Lapu statue to be reinstalled and it was re-inaugurated on April 27, 2005.[3]

Another interesting feature that I noticed was a long, horizontal row of multiple round silver clocks that hung in the front of the seafarer's center. The clocks tell the time of several major cities and regions across the globe, starting on the left side with London, then Rome, Paris, Athens, Dubai, Moscow, Beijing, and finally Manila. Although an incomplete representation of every time zone of the world, the row of clocks signify how Filipino seafarers/seamen work 24/7 in global or globalized time-space through their labor in local, regional, transoceanic, and global maritime shipping and transportation. In other words, as Filipino seamen wait and search for work at Rizal Park, in Manila-time(-space), at any given moment, other Filipino seamen are living and working in varied time-spaces on the planet.

These introductory reflections based on participant-observation at Rizal Park in 1998 and more recently in 2009 reveal how multiple cultural constructions, experiences, and everyday practices of time-space intersect or converge in the waiting area and the broader context of Rizal

Park. First, there are the actual time-space experiences and practices of Filipino seamen like Reggie who literally wait for hours, days, months, years(?), trying to find employment in domestic, regional, and global shipping industries. Although it is now common to hear of "time-space compression" in globalization (I will elaborate on this idea later in the chapter as it is an important concept), for the Filipino seamen at Rizal Park, their job searches are not "fast" or "instantaneous," common descriptors of temporality in contemporary economic and cultural globalization, and the unemployed seamen do not currently occupy traditional sites or circuits of global maritime space, that is, ships transporting goods across the world.

Second, the Filipino seamen (in 1998 and 2009) are also situated in the local/national temporal-spatial context of Manila and the nation-state. Rizal Park is literally a contested national or nationalist time-space where gendered notions of Filipino national identity and history, mostly masculine, male, or masculinist subjects, are "settled" or unsettled in the park, such as in the case of Lapu-Lapu (and the statue). Stated differently, Filipino seamen occupy or take up time and space at Rizal Park, a unique and important local/national time-space where the crosscurrents of Filipino nationalist masculinities are reinforced or contested (e.g., the Rizal monument, the Lapu-Lapu statue, and the historical marker honoring Filipino seamen as heroes, as well as the seamen's relatively new recruitment area and building).

Third, I read the row of clocks hanging on the wall as representations and signs of "global" or "globalized" time-space (compression?) in the context of economic and cultural globalization, or what geographer David Harvey calls "flexible accumulation"[4] produced through capitalism. The clocks tell the times of global cities and various time zones around the world, subsequently evoking the times and spaces of "the global," which Filipino seamen occupy and move through as they labor on ships that transport goods and commodities locally/nationally in the archipelago, regionally in Southeast Asia or Asia and the Pacific, and around the world, or in the case of unemployed seamen, as they search out available positions and unemployment in Manila (which was one of the cities/time zones represented in the row of clocks).

Using these fieldwork reflections as opening examples, in this chapter I address how Filipino seamen working in the global shipping industry navigate time-space as they move through different locations and moments of the global economy. Rather than universalizing dominant understandings of contemporary economic and cultural globalization (see the introduction), in this chapter, I argue that if we orient our analytical and ethnographic optics towards Filipino seafaring and the experiences of Filipino seamen in the global shipping industry, then we will be better able to understand economic and cultural globalization, particularly from the "sea up" (rather than "ground up"), revealing other implications and consequences of the crosscurrents of seafaring, masculinities, and globalization in the context of late twentieth and early twenty-first centuries. Rather than conceiving of the Philippines or Filipino/a subjects as passive subjects of globalization, being affected by a "single global trajectory" or as part of the "backwaters" of modernity, in this chapter I illustrate how we can understand and imagine these local/global processes differently if the sea, maritime space/place, and Filipino seamen are remembered and centered, not marginalized. This line of ethnographic inquiry follows anthropologist Anna L. Tsing's lead, as Tsing suggests that instead of assuming a "single global trajectory," anthropologists should consider attending to "varied globalist claims and perspectives."[5] To contextualize the ethnographic material and stories that are central to this chapter, I first address relevant theoretical debates about globalization and everyday implications for Filipino seamen, in particular, discussing key theoretical considerations related to time-space, culture, and globalization from anthropological perspectives, as well as theoretical interventions developed in Philippine Studies, Filipino/a American Studies, and queer studies.

Time-Space Considerations for the Crosscurrents of Seafaring, Masculinities, and Globalization

Cultural anthropologists Jonathan X. Inda and Renato Rosaldo synthesize key time-space and cultural considerations for the "anthropology of globalization" by discussing key theoretical frameworks that they suggest are critical to theoretically and ethnographically understanding and interpreting cultural phenomena in the context of contemporary economic and cultural globalization. Their discussion in the introduction of *Anthropology of Globalization* includes a discussion of a number of insightful frameworks on globalization, but here I focus more specifically on geographer David Harvey's notions of time-space compression in modernity/postmodernity because several experiences and everyday practices of Filipino seamen that I observed and learned from during fieldwork run counter to some of Harvey's theoretical insights.

Harvey suggests that time-space compression where "space appears to shrink to a 'global village' of telecommunications and a 'spaceship earth' of economic and ecological interdependencies. . . and [where] time horizons [have shorten[ed] to the point where the present is all there. . . ."[6] has become the norm in the contexts of modernism and postmodernism, especially in "the European case" (Harvey acknowledges his "somewhat" ethnocentric focus[7]) but also in other parts of the world as capitalist modes of production have expanded to other regions. Since the 1970s, a period he describes as post-Fordism and postmodernism, Harvey suggests that time-space compression has increasingly intensified compared with that in previous historical periods (note that for Harvey modernism begins during European "Enlightenment") because technological innovations in the areas of production, transportation, communication, finance, and consumption have expanded in the context of global capitalism. For example, he suggests that Fordist assembly plants enable and create faster manufacturing processes, although more flexible and disciplining forms of labor control, and devaluation, including, for example, "off-shoring" (moving production to "zones of easier labour control"[8]), outsourcing, subcontracting, putting-out, "home work" strategies, and the hiring of increasingly higher numbers of temporary, part-time, and seasonal workers, enable capital to occupy and control multiple geographies and temporalities.

Moreover, time-space compression in a capitalist world system has developed because of improved transportation systems and services, including, for example, improved rail and trucking, containerization, and mechanization in shipping, expanded air travel and freight systems, and "just in time" inventory and distribution, ultimately creating more efficient commodity chains. International finance systems based on the U.S. dollar, not gold, as well as "fictitious capital" (debts) have also contributed to a more interconnected and integrated capitalist world system in which more flexible accumulation of capital can occur. Last but not least (since all of these phenomena and issues are interconnected), new regimes of consumption have also developed due to new technological enhancements in communications and information technologies. Mass media such as television and film (Harvey does not discuss the Internet and the World Wide Web because these technologies and infrastructures were not fully formed or accessible yet) improved the marketing and distribution of products, which contributed to higher rates of consumption. Moreover, mass media and advertising significantly shaped, influenced, and/or created consumer desires, habits, and behaviors in international markets. Improved access to "around the clock" financial services also added to higher rates of consumption and wealth for some classes of people. Increases in consumption have also resulted (especially in the last century, in the Global North, but increasingly so in "newly industrialized economies"), as more "disposable products" were produced, distributed, and purchased, and as product trends and designs changed quickly, a result of the interconnected processes and technological changes I have just summarized based on Harvey's theoretical framework.

Although Harvey provocatively develops a general theory of the transition from modernism to postmodernism (especially in Europe and the United States), the specific causes and effects of "flexible accumulation" in capitalist systems, the relationship between aesthetics and production (in architecture, art, cinema, and popular culture), and the effects on ideologies and discourse of time-space in postmodernism and through flexible accumulation, he inadequately addresses the specificities of these phenomena in Global South contexts and their effects on Global South labor migrants, either those in the Global South or those situated in diasporas. In sum, Harvey only discusses how capital predictably shifts production to "zones of easier labour control"[9] to produce desired surplus (profits) through brief discussions. Moreover, he makes similar kinds of brief gestures when it comes to discussing the innovations in maritime transportation, but, again, he does not fully engage the global maritime shipping industry or how Global South/Filipino migrant laborers might experience time-space in new regimes of production and transportation. Although it is clear that these kinds of issues fall outside the parameters of his study, based on the major thrust of his arguments, Harvey appears to suggest that maritime transportation workers (e.g., Filipino seamen) must ultimately experience time-space compression because time-space compression is far-reaching and nearly universal in Harvey's account.

Anthropologist Anna L. Tsing raises several important critiques and questions related to Harvey's general theories of postmodernism and flexible accumulation in a capitalist world system and their implications for an anthropology of globalization. Tsing writes,

> For me the space and time section is the least satisfying of the book. Harvey describes categories for understanding human encounters with space and time, representations of space and time in the arts and letters. . . and anecdotes about space and time in the capitalist workplace. *No ethnographic sources for understanding spatial and temporal texture or diversity are consulted.*[10] [emphasis added]

Tsing critiques Harvey here for the lack of ethnographic basis for his social theories and in a different part of the essay also critiques anthropologists of globalization who make universal cultural claims as a result of their particular reading or application of Harvey's text. To further develop and extend her critical interventions, Tsing makes several recommendations for future anthropological and ethnographic research on globalization; one is particularly useful for this chapter's purposes. She continues,

> We might learn to investigate new developments without assuming either their universal extension or their fantastic ability to draw all-world making activities into their grasp. International finance, for example, has surely undergone striking and distinctive transformations [since the early 1970s]. Certainly this has effects everywhere, but what these effects are is unclear. It seems unlikely to me that a single logic of transformation is being produced—or a singular moment of rupture.[11]

Here Tsing makes a broader call for anthropologists to conduct ethnographic research on the impacts of economic and cultural globalization, and she also makes a case in her essay for different "reading practice[s]" to appreciate "multiple, overlapping, and sometimes contradictory globalisms," citing for example, Ulf Hannerz, Michael Kearney, and Arjun Appadurai's critical scholarship on modernity and globalizations as counterpoints to Harvey's influential general theory.[12] Agreeing with Tsing, I suggest that in addition to doing the ethnographic research as Tsing suggests, if we also extend or diversify our reading practices and engage additional interdisciplinary scholarship on time-space and seafaring, migration, gender, and globalization, we will be better equipped to culturally interpret and engage more specific discourses, imaginaries, and everyday practices of time-space in the context of Filipino seafaring, masculinities, and globalization.

Thus, if we return once a again to the ethnographic scenes at Rizal Park in Manila, for the unemployed Filipino seamen searching for work in the waiting area, time is not necessarily moving or feeling faster as Harvey theorizes. In fact, their wait to become employed seamen is often long, protracted, and arduous.[13] Upon completing their training at two- to four-year maritime schools or colleges they must complete numerous bureaucratic procedures, for example, securing a Seaman's Identification and Record Book (SIRB) at the Maritime Industry Authority (MARINA). Before acquiring a SIRB, however, many seamen must often find and bribe a "fixer," someone who works at MARINA who can potentially help to facilitate (or grease) the process. Next, seamen must go to the Technical Education and Skills Development Authority (TESDA) to be certified that they have completed the appropriate training courses. After certification at TESDA, they can then proceed to the Philippine Overseas Employment Authority (POEA) to apply for a Seaman's Registration Card. After fulfilling the necessary accreditation and acquiring the required documents at these multiple agencies (and if necessary, paying the appropriate fixers at each one), a seaman can finally go to manning agencies (or speak with their representatives at Rizal Park) to find a position on board a ship. However, seamen are still not employable until they complete all the required training courses at a training center associated with the particular manning agency they are working with. The training lasts five to ten days and costs P3,000 to P5,000 (U.S.$60 to $100) for basic safety courses, while officer training costs P23,000 to P47,000 (U.S.$460 to $940)[14] (This is another way that manning agencies generate profits.)

What we therefore see on the ground are the everyday state and private bureaucratic practices of MARINA, TESDA, POEA, and privately owned manning agencies, which significantly *slow down* the employment process for Filipino seamen, ultimately contributing and creating different time-space scenarios in migration and globalization processes. In addition, with multiple bureaucratic "requirements," which take significant time, energy, and resources to fulfill, the protracted training and hiring system also generates significant revenue for the aforementioned public and private agencies. Furthermore, because there is an oversupply of available Filipino seamen, there is also significant unemployment, which is another reason for the "long wait" (due to local/national competition in the industry). In 2002, journalist Sonny Evangelista, for example, reported that there were more than 300,000 Filipino seafarers unemployed that year. (Evangelista calculates this figure by subtracting the number of employed Filipino seafarers [approximately 180,000 at the time of her writing] from the number of registered Filipino seafarers [500,000].) In other words, because of multiple bureaucratic processes, fees, and an oversupply of labor, for young seaman Reggie and the other seamen searching, waiting, and applying for positions at the old and new waiting areas in Rizal Park, time is protracted and moves slowly, making aspiring seamen "depressed." (Nakaka depress.)

On the other hand, on more macro temporal and spatial levels, for Filipino seamen at Rizal Park, time-space compression (in Harvey's terms) does occur because social and economic phenomena, for example, consumer spending in the United States (on the consumption side) and rising oil prices in the Arab Gulf (on the production side) have an impact on the demand for Filipino seafaring labor. In this way, events or phenomena in other regions of the world (i.e., outside of the Philippines or Southeast Asia) affect the numbers of positions that are ultimately available to Filipino seamen. These interconnected "events" contribute to the kind of time-space compression Harvey theorizes.

On a more micro (personal) level, time-space compression is still relevant, but on a different scale. To give an example of this, while I was conducting fieldwork in Manila in 1998, governmental officials, maritime industry leaders, and seafarers' advocates were concerned with passing Senate Bill Number (SBN) 1816, a legislative act that would update the training requirements of Filipino seafarers. If passed, the legislation would signify Philippine compliance with the International Maritime Organization (IMO) Seafarer's Training, Certification, and Watchkeeping (STCW) Convention of 1995. This 1995 convention established and revised the "baseline" through which seamanship around the world is evaluated. Amendments made in 1995 to the original 1978 STCW Convention generally focused on cargo securing, loading, and unloading on bulk carriers. The 1995 STCW Convention was, therefore, the most recent principal international treaty that sought to establish maritime education and training standards worldwide. The amendments to the old STCW Convention were scheduled to enter into force on February 1, 2002.[15] In 1998, the IMO requested the Philippines and other nations that supply maritime labor to the global shipping industry to communicate how individual governments planned to comply with the new standards. Before the implementation date, the IMO planned to monitor and evaluate each country's progress to verify which countries would make the so-called "IMO White List," a list of countries in compliance with the new STCW standards.

I attended a Philippine Senate hearing in Manila in 1998 related to SBN 1816 and the new IMO STCW standards. The participants at the Senate meeting included approximately a dozen shipping company owners and executives, maritime school officials, manning agency owners, and a seafarers' union leader, along with Senator Nikki Coseteng, who presided over the hearing. One after another, various maritime transportation industry leaders and representatives told Senator Coseteng that it was absolutely critical that the Philippines complied with IMO STCW to make the desired IMO White List. Maritime school officials told her that they were assessing their programs and schools and would do their best to cooperate with the government. Manning agency owners told the senator that the Philippines must make the list or they would not be able to find work for seafarers, whereas the lone seafarers' trade union leader emphasized the importance of assuring that qualified individuals would be responsible for assessing the maritime education and training in the Philippines. In sum, these men suggested that if the Philippine Senate did not pass the proposed bill and comply with the updated IMO STCW Convention, Filipino seamen would lose their advantage in the labor market and ultimately their livelihoods.[16]

This information gathered at the Philippine Senate, as well as the ethnographic vignettes from Rizal Park, suggests that although working-class Filipino seamen are aware of international and global contexts and they are indeed "connected" to people in the archipelago and to other parts of the world via telecommunications media, for those who are still searching for work or who are currently still living in the Philippines, the time-space compression (on a micro level) may be happening at a more local or national level. Thus, a young seaman like Reggie, unemployed and living in Manila and looking for work at Rizal Park, is better able to maintain connections with family and friends in Cotobato City in Mindanao as a result of improved telecommunications (which fits into Harvey's framework). However, although cognizant of and affected by global events and politics (such as the 1995 IMO STCW Convention or the 1998 Asian Financial Crisis), local/national politics related to Filipino labor, seafaring and overseas migration, such as SBN 1816, may have a more immediate effect on those looking for work, as well as those currently employed, suggesting that a different scale of time-space compression may be relevant or in play.

My point here is that clearly there are moments and contexts when Filipino seamen experience time-space compression (in the sense described by Harvey), but it is important to document and ethnographically interpret other or alternative time-space constructs, experiences, or everyday practices through fieldwork. By doing so, we are then able to see ethnographic counterexamples of how time-space is understood, constructed, and experienced in the context of contemporary globalization. Moreover, by attending to different scales and different notions and experiences of time-space, we avoid universalizing dominant theories of globalization as Tsing advocates.

In the following section, I move away from local/national Philippine contexts and address how *employed* Filipino seamen experience time-space while working on ships that move through oceans and seas and transport goods and commodities to different ports. The ethnographic/travel vignette that follows is based on fieldwork experiences on board an industrial container ship that sailed from the Port of Oakland (California, United States) to the Port of Hong Kong (China) during the summer of 2006.

Transpacific Voyaging, 2006

My fieldwork voyage officially begins for me when I leave my old apartment where I was temporarily staying, located in the Lake Merrit area of Oakland. I am taking a taxi to Berth 55/56 at the Hanjin Terminal at the Port of Oakland (in West Oakland) where I will board the "*Penang Prince*," a German flagged container ship that is en route from Long Beach, California, to Hamburg, Germany. The *Prince*'s regular route is to travel back and forth between Western Europe and Southern California, stopping in ports in the Mediterranean, Red Sea, and Indian Ocean and Southeast and East Asia and then crossing the Northern Pacific Ocean to North America, docking in California's two major ports (Oakland and Long Beach). I will be joining the ship as a passenger-ethnographer for approximately two weeks (the approximate time it takes to cross the Pacific by large industrial container ship).

The Port of Oakland where I am heading is the third largest and busiest container port on the U.S. west coast, following the Port of Los Angeles and Port of Long Beach.[17] The port has twenty deepwater berths and thirty gantry container cranes for large industrial container ships like the *Prince,* which transport goods and commodities from around the world. Connected to four freeways, Interstate 80 (north and eastbound), 880 (southbound), 580 (eastbound), and 980 (eastbound), as well as rail systems operated by the Burlington Northern Santa Fe and Union Pacific railroad companies, the Port of Oakland is a key node in a complex and far-reaching transportation system. According to the Port of Oakland, in 1998, 58.9 percent of Oakland's trade was with Asia; 10.3 percent with Europe; 4.7 percent with Australia, New Zealand, and other South Pacific Islands; 8.8 percent with other nations; and 17.3 percent was "domestic" (more accurately, "colonial," i.e., Guam and Hawai'i, plus military cargo).[18] Key exports from the Port of Oakland include fruits, nuts, vegetables, wastepaper, beef and poultry, resins, chemicals, animal feed, raw cotton, wood and lumber, crude fertilizers or minerals, industrial machinery, and cereal or cereal preparations. Key imports include auto parts, computer equipment, apparel, toys or games, plastic materials, processed fruits or vegetables, household metal products, beef, pottery, glassware, ceramics, iron and steel, beverages, and lumber products.[19]

The *Prince* will transport an assortment of goods and commodities from the previous list[20] and will follow the Northern Pacific Rim, traveling north from the San Francisco Bay Area up the U.S. west coast and off of the coast of Vancouver, British Columbia (Canada), and west toward Asia, passing through the Gulf of Alaska, past the Aleutian Islands, and into the Bering Sea. From there, the *Prince* will sail south toward East Asia eventually dock at the Ports of Tokyo and Osaka in Japan and Kiaoshung in Taiwan. Afterwards, the *Prince* will travel to Hong Kong (China) where I will disembark, while the ship continues with its regular itinerary.

I get off on the wrong foot with my taxi driver, a Nigerian man, because I am too impatient and aggressive, insisting that I show him where the Hanjin terminal is on a map that the shipping agent (a woman named "Joy") sent to me. The driver is annoyed with me and says that he knows exactly where Hanjin terminal is; he doesn't need to see any map, he'll be able to take me there fine. We approach the outskirts of the port area in West Oakland, and we see the gigantic robotic "arms" of the port's white container cranes, which mark part of the perimeter around the Oakland Harbor. Daily commuters crossing the Bay Bridge between San Francisco and Oakland see these large container structures from a distance as they drive back and forth across the bay, but rarely see the port from a closer vantage point. From the Bay Bridge, coastal areas, and hills throughout the Bay Area, local residents can also see the large container ships that move in and out of the bay and the Port of Oakland, but again, rarely do they see or interact with the ships, the seamen, or dockers. As Allan Sekula documents, maritime ports around the United States have been established in or relocated to marginalized urban areas. This geographic marginalization of ports is part of why Sekula suggests that "the sea has been forgotten"[21] in the United States.

As the taxi passes by different terminals, the driver and I can see containers waiting to be loaded onto different ships. China Ocean Shipping Company, Hanjin Shipping Company, Hyundai Merchant Marine, "K" Line, Maersk Line, Sea-Land Service, and Star Shipping are some of the shipping lines that pass through the port. The container ships are massive, and their capacities range from 1,500 to 6,000 TEUs.[22] The bulky and generic ships (generic except for the shipping company line names found on their hulls) are stacked with numerous differently colored containers that are similarly generic. The containers repeat over and over and over again on ships being loaded and unloaded; they repeat and wait in terminals, and move on trucks and trains—white, maroon, red, blue, green, black in color, contents unknown. The taxi driver is correct; he knows exactly where Hanjin Terminal, Berth 55/56, is.

I try to shift the tone of my conversation with the taxi driver so that my ride closes (and my voyage begins) on a friendlier note. Trying to engage in small talk, I tell the driver I am going to travel across the Pacific Ocean by ship for the first time. He seems open to the chit-chat and asks me if I work on a ship. "No," I say, "I'm a researcher writing a book about Filipino seamen and other issues related to the sea." "Well, you'll have a lot of time to learn about it while you're out there. Where are you going and how long will it take?" he asks. "Hong Kong. Fifteen days," I say. "Anything past twelve hours, I can't take," he declares. "I want to go to Hong Kong, but I'll be flying!" he says proudly, smiling.

He tells me that he is not allowed beyond the gate, so he plans on dropping me off as close as he can to the security guard. I'll be in an area where there is a long line of eighteen-wheeler trucks. We arrive and I pay the driver and he wishes me luck. I walk the rest of the way to a security booth. An African American security guard looks at my passport and calls the shuttle service to pick me up. A few minutes later a shuttle van arrives. I carry my baggage into the vehicle and we head for the *Penang Prince*. After I get out of the van I immediately see some men of color in orange, khaki, and navy blue coveralls or jumpsuits at the top of the gangway standing on the deck of the *Prince*. They wave and walk down the gangway.

Eventually two large brown men who I suspect are from Kiribati and not the Philippines offer to carry my bags up the gangway. (Joy, the shipping agent, told me that it was likely that the crew would comprise seamen from Kiribati, the Philippines, and Germany. When I bought my ticket she could not say for sure what the crew composition would be, but based on past experience she tried to give me a rough idea of the racial/national breakdown of the crew.) The two Kiribati seamen and I reach the top of the gangway. Another seaman (from Kiribati) requests to see my passport and then a Filipino seaman wearing a yellow safety hat speaks to me in Tag-lish (Tagalog and English). "Oh, we almost left you behind," he jokes. "Dito ka ba galing? Dito ba ang magulang mo?" he asks. (Is this where you're from? Is this where your parents are?) Filipino language specialist Teresita V. Ramos argues that this kind of questioning is common and not intrusive in Filipino/a contexts. Ramos writes, "Filipinos are usually not inhibited about initiating conversations because talking to a stranger is generally not considered intrusive. If thrown together for almost any reason, someone will break the ice. A common conversation opener is *Tagasaan ka*? 'Where are you from?'"[23]

Although I have been living in Minneapolis, Minnesota, for one year, I still feel like Oakland/Northern California is home (since I lived in California for fifteen years before moving to the Upper Great Lakes Region), so I say, "O ho" (Yes, sir [I'm from here]). I get the feeling that the older seaman thinks I am still in my youth and that he's also trying to figure out if I am a Philippine national or "Fil-Am" (Filipino American), so I elaborate: "Matagal ho ako dito sa California—fifteen years—pero ngayon na sa Minneapolis, Minnesota ako, doon ho ang trabaho ko. Lumaki ho ako sa Portland, Oregon; nandoon ang magulang ko, pero sa Malolos ako pinaganak. (I lived in California for a long time, sir—fifteen years—but now I live in Minneapolis, Minnesota, that is where my work is, sir. I grew up, sir, in Portland, Oregon; my parents are there, but I was born in Malolos.) Although I am in my late thirties at the time of this fieldwork-voyage, I have a history of people thinking that I am a twenty-something-year-old person, or sometimes I am mistaken for a teenager. As a result of this kind of "reading," strangers often initially interact with me as if I am significantly younger. My usual response (with most, but not all, people) is to be open to sharing parts of my biography, as a way to respond to Filipino/as' culturally appropriate line of questioning and their inquisitiveness, but also to indicate that I am an older, independent adult.

I follow the Pacific Islander seamen who are carrying my bags and we enter a room where they introduce me to the (German) master (it is maritime/merchant marines tradition to call the captain "Master"). He is an older, small-framed man with grey hair and a mustache, probably in his late fifties or early sixties. We briefly introduce ourselves, and then he requests that I hand over my passport and fill out some nonliability forms. After meeting the captain, I follow the Pacific Islander seamen to the "E deck" where my cabin is located. A tall, large German man (the first mate) shows me around my cabin (which includes a small bedroom and bathroom) and tells me he lives next door. His name is "Boris." The cabin is similar to a standard motel or hotel room, in terms of amenities offered, only smaller. The top-level officers on the ship have similar one-bedroom cabins, other officers have studios, and lower-ranked seamen have to share a room. I look around the cabin, my temporary home base during the voyage. I unpack and make last-minute phone calls to significant others, as cell phones will not work beyond the coastline or in the open sea. After making my calls, I planned to go out on deck, but the captain sees me coming up the stairs and asks if I want to see the bridge. I say yes to his invitation.

As we are walking up to the bridge I ask the captain how long he has been working at sea. "Forty-one years," he counts. He started as an apprentice and worked his way to the top of the command structure. I express awe at his long career and congratulate him. When we get to the bridge, there is an amazing view of the city of San Francisco, the Bay Bridge, blue skies, and bay water. As we are both admiring the scene, the captain tells me that twenty-two men (including him) live and work on board the *Prince*.[24] Six are German (master, chief mate, chief engineer, second engineer; and two engineering apprentices); five are Filipino (second mate, third mate, third engineer, electrician, and chief cook). The remaining eleven seamen are from Kiribati (bosun, steward, four able-bodied seamen, three machinist mates, and two ordinary seamen).[25] Two other passengers are also on board: an older, retired heterosexual German couple in their late sixties or seventies; the man ["Helmut"] is listed as the purser on the crew list and the woman ["Maritza"] is listed as a stewardess. I am listed as a cook. The captain explains that he has listed all three of the passengers as crew members to make sure that things go smoothly for us when we want to go on shore leave.

After spending some time on the bridge, I walk around on deck and take photographs of the Oakland hills, San Francisco skyline, *Penang Prince*, Port of Oakland (e.g., containers and trucks), and bay. Afterwards, I go to the galley, which from previous fieldwork on board ships in ports I know is usually one of the most important, if not the most important, center of social activity and conversation on board ships. There I meet "Yoyoy Villyami,"[25a] the Filipino chief cook, a chubby, gregarious, and comical fellow in his late thirties. Yoyoy is from a small town in Western Mindanao. He easily makes small talk with people who stop in the galley. Eventually the second mate whom the Filipinos call "Segundo" ("second" in Spanish to signify he is the second mate) who Yoyoy later names "Max Alvarado Perez" (for the purposes of my book) enters the galley. Max is a handsome and muscular man and he looks dapper in his navy blue coveralls. He is the most serious of the Filipinos I have met on the ship so far, and he doesn't joke with me like the other two Filipino seamen I have encountered on the ship. Max tells me he is from a small town (Hagonoy) in Bulakan Province. We begin asking each other if we know this person or that family. We bond on both being Bulakeños (Malolos City, my hometown, and Hagonoy are adjacent in Bulakan province).

After this introductory conversation Max asks me some blunt questions and shares a provocative observation: "Why are you on board this ship? Why not sail on ship that has more passengers? *Walang buhay dito.*" [*There is no life here.*] I respond to his queries by explaining that I am writing a book about Filipino seafaring and other maritime issues, so I'm on the ship hoping to learn more about their shipboard lives and work and their experiences in ports. I also try to explain that I did some research at the Port of Manila and Oakland, but this is my first time going out to the open sea. He listens patiently, but after a few moments, he critically observes, "Kulang ang horas mo" (You don't have enough time or you aren't spending enough time [on board]). I have no problem with his criticism and say that I know my time on the *Prince* is inadequate, but I still want to learn as much as I can and I wish I had received more research grants in the past, so that I could have gone to sea more often. He says he knows that sailing as a passenger is expensive and that not everyone would want to go out to sea for long periods of time on this kind of ship. Seemingly satisfied with our exchange, Max grabs a Red Delicious apple, smiles at me, says he has to work, but that he will be around later, and then he exits the galley.

Sailing at approximately ten knots, the *Prince* finally leaves the Port of Oakland and the San Francisco Bay.[26] For the first two days in the open sea, I try to physically adjust to the constant rocking motion of the sea. Although I have previous sailing experience on the San Francisco Bay (on yachts and a schooner) and I have raced Native Hawaiian outrigger canoes in Monterey Bay and the San Francisco Bay, in addition to a past job on a docked educational "tall ship" operated by the National Maritime Museum Association in San Francisco, voyaging on a container ship on the open Pacific still takes some getting used to. During the first few days I don't feel well and I spend significant energy dealing with my minor (yet definitely noticeable) seasickness. Trying to calm my stomach, I eat saltines and suck on dried ginger candy I've brought along. Although I feel nauseous and could stay in my cabin all day and it's difficult to be social under these conditions, I have conversations with some of the German and Filipino officers, the master, and the German couple during our three meal times (where I eat minimally), plus our afternoon "coffee breaks." All of us eat in the officer's mess hall, but the seamen from Kiribati eat in a separate dining area, segregated by rank and occupation but also ultimately by nationality, race, and class. After the meals, I type up field notes on my laptop and I reread Antonio Pigafetta's *The First Voyage Around the World* (about Ferdinand Magellan's attempted circumnavigation of Earth, 1519–1521) in my cabin when I can focus on something besides my nausea.

Through the regularly scheduled meals I meet the remaining two Filipino seamen. "Emilio Nario," the electrician from Cebu, a good-looking fellow in his early thirties, is tall, lanky, dark brown in complexion, with eyes that sparkle when he speaks. Like Max, he asks me why I am on the ship and also asks in jest if I know this isn't a cruise ship. Emilio is married and has a small child, both of whom live in Cebu. He says that the primary reason he works at sea is the money; he can't earn a decent salary in the Philippines. He also asks me if I know that the POEA requires them to send 80 percent of their salaries back to the Philippines. "The Philippines needs the dollars," he explains. Emilio describes the captain as "mabait" (nice), especially if you do your job well, but if not then he's not too nice, in fact, he's "very stricto" (strict). I also meet "Rufo Alvarez," the third engineer, also from Cebu. Rufo is in his mid-forties, but looks younger because he is "baby-faced." He is smaller in stature and seems to be shy. Both of the Visayans seem open to having conversations with me, but later, Emilio tells me he doesn't want to be in any of the photos.

During meal times, I also have my first substantial conversations with the third mate, "Gogong Arroyo" (the first Filipino I met who greeted me when I arrived, the one wearing the yellow safety hat). He is in his late forties or early fifties and has been a seaman for approximately twenty years. One of the things Gogong emphasizes is how difficult it is to be a seaman. "Being a seaman is hard. It's for 'binata' (young single men), not those who are married," he tells me. In other words, he suggests that seafaring is for young men who have fewer family ties and responsibilities. Significantly, although his seventeen-year-old "bunso" (youngest child) is attracted to seafaring as a profession because of his father, Gogong continually discourages him, directing him *not* to become a seaman.

After breakfast on day two, Gogong looks at an empty chair in front of him in the dining room (where we are alone having a conversation) and speaks as if he is talking directly to his son. "Me, I am a seaman and I am OK because I know you are going to school—so the *sacrifice* is OK. You are going to an exclusive high school, so why do you want to be a seaman? Why don't you become a nurse and then you can move to America, England, Germany, or Canada. You will make even more money than me. Being a seaman is hard" [emphasis added]. Through this narrative, Gogong wants to make it clear to me that seamen's lives are truly challenging and that in undertaking this line of work, they give up a lot socially and culturally, especially face-to-face contact with their families and the abilities to participate in larger local/national Philippine cultural contexts. (This was a common narrative I heard during fieldwork. As I discussed in the previous chapter, many Filipino seamen desire other forms of employment in the Philippines and many find seafaring difficult, but their economic opportunities are limited in the archipelago.) From Gogong's perspective, if his son has other opportunities, then he should pursue them, not seafaring, because the required sacrifices are too great.

On the second day, I planned on visiting Max (the second mate) on the bridge because he mentioned earlier that he would be on duty from 1200 to 1600, but I am still feeling nauseous, so I don't make it to the bridge. By early evening I am feeling better, so I go to the galley to see if anyone is there. Max appears after his shift, wanting to continue our conversation. This time, he discusses how maritime schools in the Philippines try to entice young men with advertisements that read, "See the World for Free!" "When they are working as a seaman, yes, [they] see the world 'for free,' but [they] are working and the world is held at a distance." To emphasize this point he sticks his hand way out in front of his face to mark the distance between seamen and the world. A second point that Max makes, which seems to extend his "no life here" analysis from day one is that "life on a container ship is like a *floating prison*." He explains, "You are a prisoner for nine months and then you are on parole (when the contract is done)." Elaborating, he says, "There is no time to go to shore because there is a lot of work that needs to be done once the ship docks. We also have to do things like laundry. If you happened to be working a six-six shift (six hours working, six hours off duty) you are exhausted and you don't want to do anything else, but rest."[27]

The next day my motion sickness is gone, so I visit the bridge from 1200 to 1600 as I previously promised. Max and Oscar are on duty and so is "Iaka," one of the able-bodied seamen from Kiribati. I watch the three of them go about their work. Max and Oscar handle the mostly mechanized navigation of the ship, while Iaka keeps watch, looking through binoculars to make sure there aren't any other container ships or fishing boats in the *Prince*'s path. Everyone, including me, goes about our business, mostly in silence. Oscar is definitely immersed in his duties and doesn't say much throughout the whole time I'm on the bridge. Max, on the other hand, is more open to speaking with me after he finishes his navigational computations and paperwork. He discusses a variety of topics, ranging from stowaways he met when he was on a ship traveling in West Africa, the stowaway policies in Asia, some Cuban refugees he encountered at sea while working on a ship traveling between Honduras and Miami, how "Americans" in port are "slow" and "complain a lot," and how the Japanese work much faster. Max, Iaka,

Able-bodied seaman from Kiribati on look out in the Northern Pacific.

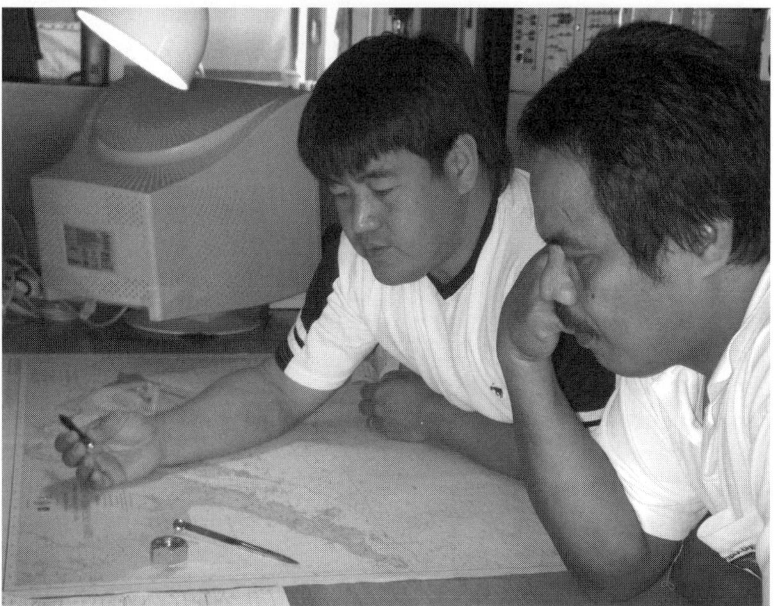

Filipino second mate passes time by showing steward (from Kiribati) the *Penang Prince*'s route after leaving the Port of Oakland.

and I take turns looking through the binoculars. I see a closer view of the mostly royal blue– and stop sign–red colored containers at the bow and a steel grey sea all around. Today there is also mist and rain and the occasional seagull. To me it is a moving and beautiful sight because I love the sea and I find it amazing to be completely surrounded by it, no land in sight. I have also been looking forward to the voyage, and shipboard life in the open sea is still novel to me. During one of the breaks in our long silences, Max shares a different perspective. He concludes, "The four hours on the bridge (the usual length of his shifts) are the slowest four hours ever. Everything is so monotonous." Iaka nods his head gently, suggesting he agrees with the second mate.

Crosscurrents of Time-Space and Masculinities on Ships and at Sea

The *Prince* is not even half way across the Northern Pacific and already the seamen (not to mention the taxi driver who dropped me off at the Port of Oakland) have raised several important questions and have given me a lot to think about. First, what does it mean to go on a journey, or to be more exact, a voyage, that lasts "longer than twelve hours" (the maximum travel time that the taxi driver can handle)? More to the point, what does it mean to Filipino seamen to live and work on board an industrial container ship that transports goods and commodities across the ocean 24/7/9 (twenty-four hours, seven days a week, for nine months), the usual length of Filipino seamen's work contracts? How might we interpret Max's cultural critique when he said, "Walang buhay dito (There is no life here). . . . The world is held at a distance. . . . Life on a container ship is like a floating prison. . . . The four hours on the bridge are the slowest four hours ever. Everything is so monotonous. . ."? Why does Gogong describe seafaring as a "sacrifice" and what are the cultural implications of this trope? How and why are Filipino seamen's cultural critiques of shipboard and portside life, as well as their everyday practices, relevant to the crosscurrents of masculinities created at sea and globalization?

In the crosscurrents that include the *Penang Prince* and our transpacific voyage, Filipino seamen (and other seamen) experience time-space differently from how time-space has been generally constructed or theorized through dominant narratives and imaginaries of globalization. In this way, contemporary industrial container ships operate heterotopically in the Foucauldian sense, as one principle of Foucault's theory suggests that heterotopias represent a break with "traditional time."[28] If traditional [that is, normative] time is imagined and theorized as time-space compression à la David Harvey, then the *Prince* and similar ships in the global shipping industry move within *different* time-space trajectories, ultimately shaping and constituting alternative spaces of contemporary economic and cultural globalization, what I have been theorizing and ethnographically interpreting as "crosscurrents." Thus, although most people who have the economic means can cross the Pacific and other oceanic spaces via air travel, flying over approximately 7,000 miles (the air distance from San Francisco to Manila, to give one example) in a journey that lasts approximately fifteen to sixteen hours and that generally includes four to six meals and snacks (yes, meals are still served on transpacific flights) and three to four movies (depending on airline and cabin class) enabling travel and transportation from one side of the ocean to another in relatively quick fashion (compared with other forms of travel and transportation) and creating what Harvey calls "time-space compression," we must remember that this broadly universalized "everyday experience" is not applicable to all cultural contexts and does not absolutely apply to Filipino seamen (or other seamen) laboring in the global shipping industry.[29]

As the *Prince* moves in an easterly direction away from the North American coastline, near Vancouver, British Columbia, toward the International Date Line (IDL) located at approximately the "180th meridian of longitude but [which] deviates eastward through the Bering Strait to avoid dividing Siberia and then deviates westward to include the Aleutian Islands with Alaska,"[30] the captain, crew, and passengers of the *Prince* set their/our clocks and watches one hour back, producing or resulting in *extended time,* according to the logic, geography, and oceanography of the IDL (a standardized way of time-keeping on Earth). During the voyage, the *Prince* crossed the IDL as it passed the end of Aleutian islands chain, crossing into the Bering Sea, constructing our days into longer ones, but ultimately resulting in a "lost day" as the ship crosses the IDL. (This lost day, of course, also results when one flies over the IDL and so is not exclusive to seafaring, shipping, or sailing.) During the voyage, Max (the second mate) updated me on our location and time by giving me copies of navigational documents that indicated the *Prince*'s position and how long we had been traveling. According to his meticulous record-keeping (part of his job and shipboard responsibilities), the voyage began in San Francisco, located at 37° 45.000 N (latitude) and 122° 40.000 W (longitude), and we reached West Buldir Island in the Aleutian Islands chain, located at 52° 32.000 N (latitude), 175° 20.000 (longitude), 5 longitudinal degrees away from the IDL, on *day* 6. This itinerary and timetable reveals a significantly slower pace of traveling compared with air travel, the Internet, and the World Wide Web, all dominant air- and digital-based imaginaries and phenomena of contemporary globalization.

Like other workers in a capitalist system, for seamen, time is also marked and valued through their labor, but because they work and simultaneously live on a ship, time is measured a little differently. Although most readers are familiar with the concept of "nine to five" hours (9:00 a.m. to 5:00 p.m.) for typical land-based jobs that operate as a result of "business hours," many of the seamen work on a four-four rotation, that is four hours on, then four hours off rotation, the traditional way that nautical time and labor is measured. Since ships travel and operate on a 24/7 basis, crucial functions of the ship must continue throughout an entire twenty-four-hour cycle (e.g., look out and navigation), so seamen share the responsibilities for four-hour shifts. Some positions, like the electrician on board the *Prince,* as well as the engineering crew, work a nine to five schedule. Max described this as "straight day shift." He explained, "They work eight hours during the day and only go down to the engine room if there is an alarm." The cooks and stewards must work according to meal preparation, serving, and cleaning schedules. Some seamen must also work six-six shifts (six hours on duty, six hours off duty). Max worked this type of shift while the *Prince* was docked at the Port of Long Beach for three straight days and by time the ship headed north to Oakland, was completely exhausted. In other words, while my time(s)-space(s) on the *Prince* (as passenger-ethnographer) were marked by meals with the ship's officers (Thursdays and Sundays: "eggs to order for breakfast"; Fridays: fish lunch; Saturdays: pancake breakfasts plus "[German] Saturday soup" for lunch), participant-observation in different spaces of the ship (bridge, galley, dining hall, recreation rooms); and "free time," which I spent socializing and hanging out with the seamen (a topic I elaborate on later in this chapter and also in chapter 4), typing up field notes, walking around on deck, reading, watching videos that were available in the officer's recreation room; Filipino and Kiribati seamen also occasionally loaned me DVDs and CVDs, and exercising in the ship's super-basic gym, the seamen's time(s)-space(s) were marked by nautical time-keeping, work-shifts and their labor in specific spaces of the ship, engaging in work activities and duties required of their rank and position, domestic (personal) chores and upkeep that needed to be done, and off duty/free/recreational time.

Not surprisingly, masculinities on the *Prince* were also marked and shaped in part by time-space, for example, the different length of the labor contracts or the duration of time that Filipino, Kiribati, and German seamen are required to live, work, and remain on board the ship. That is, seamen of each nationality represented on the *Prince* are required to live and work on the ship for different periods of time. Filipino seamen's labor contracts are generally for nine months. The Kiribati seamen's labor contracts usually last twelve months, and the German seamen's contracts are for three months (with two months off with pay). The length of contract, plus their different scales of pay related to nationality, race, and occupation or rank, reveals the "racial and labor segmentation"[31] of the global shipping industry, and also the "queer" ways that working-class seamen (especially those of the Global South) experience time-space in the global economy.

By queer, I am not evoking the sexual aspect of this term, but rather the way that non-normative subjects, such as sea-based migrants, occupy and move through "strange temporalities, imaginative life schedules, and eccentric economic practices," to use the description written by queer studies scholar Jack Halberstam. In other words, different racialized and classed labor, for example, Filipino, Kiribati, or German, must work different lengths of time at different pay scales as the value of their racialized and classed labor/time is hierarchically organized (by nationality, race, rank, or occupation). Moreover, their contracts and their time at sea can be read as queer precisely when their temporal trajectories are compared with how time-space is constructed and experienced in more traditional land-based jobs. It is fair to say, however, that at the same time, especially from the perspective of the Philippines and Filipino/a migrants in diaspora, in many ways, working as a migrant and living away from the Philippines is quite "normative" because millions of Filipino/a migrants and immigrants in diaspora have similar time-space experiences, that is, of living and working outside the Philippines for prolonged periods of time. Retaining this queer reading of maritime time-space is still important, however, because of the way that geographic/land-based experiences are generally seen as more "normal" when compared with maritime/oceanographic existences. Of course, this is a generalization; one still has to pay attention to cultural specificities, geopolitical contexts, and histories, which I have been trying to balance and give attention to in this ethnography.

When I asked the German captain about the hierarchies related to different lengths of labor contracts, he explained, "It is all about costs. It costs too much to renew contracts for Kiribati and Filipinos." By this he means that if Kiribati and Filipino contracts were shorter in duration, their contracts would have to be "renewed" at more regular frequencies. That is, when a seaman's contract runs out and needs to be renewed, shipping companies usually purchase airline tickets for the seaman to fly to a specific port where the seaman can join his assigned ship. (This presumes that the seaman has returned to his home country to reunite with family or vacation.) Since the *Prince* does not make regular stops to Kiribati or the Philippines flying Kiribati seamen from Kiribati to a port in Asia where they can more easily join the ship is expensive. Kiribati seamen on board the *Prince* told me that when they joined the ship, they usually flew from Bonriki International Airport in Tarawa, Kiribati, to Suva, Fiji, and from there, they flew to Auckland, New Zealand, where they caught flights to Hong Kong, which is on the *Prince*'s regular route. For the Filipino seamen, they too must often fly to join their assigned ship(s), but instead of the South Pacific, they fly from Ninoy Aquino International Airport in Manila, an airport that is significantly closer to major Asian maritime ports such as Singapore, Hong Kong, or Tokyo. Since the *Prince* sails regularly to Germany (Hamburg), German seamen are able to join the ship with greater ease and relatively lower costs ("relatively" because although the shipping company does not have to purchase airfare for them, the company does have to pay for their benefits, such as the two months off with pay). I observed the ending and renewing of contracts at the Port of Hong Kong. As I was disembarking the *Prince*, three Kiribati seamen were also leaving because they fulfilled their one-year contracts.

At the same time, three new Kiribati seamen joined the *Prince*'s crew, having flown to Hong Kong from Kiribati (via Fiji and New Zealand). According to Yoyoy (Filipino chief cook), having Kiribati seamen as shipmates was a new phenomenon on the *Prince*. Before Kiribati seamen started contracts on the *Prince* last year, the crew comprised only German and Filipino seamen (with Filipinos in the majority). This "outsourcing" of labor (i.e., shipping companies hiring seamen from countries with cheaper labor, fewer regulations, minimal or no taxes, and fewer labor rights) reveals the economic logics of the "open-ship registry" (or using ships flying "flags of convenience") and the globalization of seafaring labor through capitalism.

Based on fieldwork on board the *Prince*, seamen of different nationalities suggest they were keenly aware of racialized and classed labor (contract) hierarchies. Illustrating this awareness, seamen often talked about seafaring masculinities in relation to labor contract duration. For instance, during another conversation with the captain, he observed:

> The Kiribati men work hard, are friendly, and are good seamen. They must be psychologically prepared because their (one year) contracts are so long and they are away from their homes for a long time. In my opinion, twelve months is too long, but our company needs to keep costs low.

The captain's comments reveal how length of labor contract, mental and physical toughness, and sense of endurance or fortitude inform his empathetic notions of Kiribati seamen's masculinities.

To give another example, Gogong (Filipino third mate) told me two stories, one about a nephew who was unable to handle the life and work of a seaman and another story about the steward's apprentice on board the *Prince*, a young man (nineteen to twenty years of age) from Kiribati who was having great difficulty living and working full-time at sea, away from Kiribati. My field notes record Gogong's reflections and stories:

> "Puro azul ang makita mo, at ang buhay mo—azul."
>
> (Blue is all that you see, and your life is blue too.)
>
> —Gogong, third mate, *Penang Prince*
>
> Gogong told me the story of one of his nephews. He wanted to be a seaman very badly and thought it was going to be an exciting life. He wanted to see the world. He was extremely excited to go to sea. The first week the nephew called Gogong and said he was doing OK. He was in Japan and was still excited about being a seaman. The second week the nephew called again, but this time he was crying. He wanted go home already. He said he felt too lonely. He said he

Able-bodied seaman and bosun from Kiribati kill time as the *Penang Prince* prepares to dock at the Port of Tokyo (Japan).

> was ready to jump ship. The nephew eventually paid for his airfare so that he could return to the Philippines. He also paid the airfare for his replacement. Gogong scolded the nephew, saying, "I told you! The life of a seaman is lonely! I can handle it because I've already tasted it and I am used to hard work. Being a seaman is really hard."
>
> According to Gogong, the steward's apprentice is newly married. Gogong says the young seaman calls home when he can and after each phone call, the apprentice cries. Gogong reports that he's always asking him, "So what do you think of the life of a marino (seaman)?" The young apprentice never replies. Gogogong says he only shakes his head (in disbelief).

Gogong's accounts similarly reveal how issues of time-space intersect with perceptions of differently situated seafaring masculinities, in this case, Filipino and Kiribati. The story about Gogong's nephew illustrates how seafaring masculinities are in part constructed or understood precisely through a seaman's ability to physically, emotionally, and psychologically endure and survive the difficult day-to-day existence of living and working on ships in the sea or in ports, removed and distant from family, friends, and more familiar cultural contexts. In addition, as a seaman gains more experience and years of service, this too informs and helps to construct seafaring masculinities or manhoods. Indeed, part of Gogong's reprimand to his nephew ("I told you!") emerged precisely because Gogong wanted to underscore his nephew's youth, inexperience (or naïveté) and impatience (with seafaring labor and life), which in turn also provided evidence that Gogong's own seafaring masculinity was already tested and proven at sea. ("I've already tasted it and I am used to hard work.") Likewise, Gogong refers to the young Kiribati steward's apprentice to show a parallel current situation where another young seaman was having troubles at sea, being away from his new wife and presumably his other family and friends in the South Pacific. In this way Gogong suggests that the young seamen's masculinities (nephew and apprentice's) have not yet fully matured through time and space away from home(s), through laboring and living at sea, through everyday experiences of "the blues." ("Puro azul ang Makita mo, at ang buyay mo—azul." [Blue is all that you see, and your life is blue too.])

We can also connect and interpret Gogong's critical reflections on the "blue sea" and seamen's blue lives with and alongside Max's critical comments, namely, "Walang buhay dito (There is no life here). . . . The world is held at a distance. . . . Life on a container ship is like a floating prison. . . . The four hours on the bridge are the slowest four hours ever. Everything is so monotonous. . . .", as both seamen's cultural critiques direct

Chief cook, chief steward, and steward's apprentice working in the galley, 2006.

us to consider how laboring and living on board an industrial container ship can be partially understood through the concept of "hyperspace." Citing anthropologist Michael Kearney, researcher Helen Sampson writes that, "hyperspaces are characterized by monotonous and universal features. They are in many senses culturally indeterminate reflecting neither one culture or another."[32] Examples of hyperspaces that Sampson lists include "airports, the offices of multinational corporations. . . franchise enterprises. . . [and] merchant cargo ship[s]."[33] Explaining the hyperspatiality of ships, Sampson writes, "one neither feels in Europe, nor in Asia, nor in the U.S., nor in any other identifiable world region. A feeling accentuated by ships' separation from land. These are not precisely cultural vacuums but they may reflect an occupational rather than a recognizable geo-spatial culture."[34] In other words, based on Kearney and Sampson's interventions, we can partially interpret contemporary industrial container ships as hyperspaces because those owned by large shipping corporations (like the *Prince*) are usually *not* culturally specific sites, but rather, precisely because of corporatization, standardization, and the institutionalization of shipping, industrial container ships are *culturally generic* (or culturally limited) spaces, but not cultural voids. Although different national/cultural groups represented on the *Prince* (and other ships) have some shipboard time and space to perform and enact specific cultural practices (e.g., language, food, recreation, and interpersonal dynamics, I elaborate on some of these points shortly and in chapter 4), seamen's abilities to do so are significantly constrained due precisely to the hyperspatiality of industrial container ships, that is, their corporatization, standardization, and institutionalization, all of which ultimately limit, but not completely eradicate, seamen's cultural differences, practices, and heterogeneities. The limitation of shipboard living and labor, as well as the geographic distance from more familiar cultural phenomena and actors ("back home in the Philippines"), therefore, partially explains why Max said there was "no life" on board the "floating prison" (container ship), why "everything is so monotonous," and why Gogong described seafaring as "blue."

At the same time it is important to consider how power intersects with cultural phenomena on board ships. Although the hyperspatiality of ships emphasizes generic or neutralized cultural spaces, differences, hierarchies, and dynamics of race, class, gender, nationality, and culture exist in crosscurrents spaces/trajectories like ships and I suspect in hyperspaces more generally. In the case of the *Prince,* these hierarchies and relations of power affect differently situated seamen in dissimilar ways (e.g., as I discussed in relation to employment contracts). Thus, while we can understand industrial container ships as monotonous, generic corporate spaces and places, seamen of color on board the *Prince* also observed, experienced, and believed that European, or more specifically German, ways of being, working, and living were dominant compared with Filipino or Kiribati ways of being, which they believed were being marginalized (by European seamen, a European captain, and European-owned shipping company). Other Filipino seamen I spoke with at the Ports of Manila and Oakland also discussed and shared these kinds of perceptions of culture and power. Certainly, it was common during fieldwork for Filipino seamen to discuss the institutional and interpersonal racial, class, gender, national, and cultural tensions and problems that they experienced and witnessed on industrial container ships.

The most obvious site or agent of institutionalized power, of course, is the captain or master. As mentioned previously, in the case of the *Prince*, the master at the time of my fieldwork-voyage was German; as such, he was/is the highest authority at sea, in charge of the entire vessel, including ship, crew, and cargo safety, as well as ship navigation. The captain is also responsible for ensuring that the crew and ship follow all international and local/national laws and that all (shipping) management policies are fully complied with. In this position, the captain is ultimately responsible for the management and discipline of the crew. Although the seamen I spoke with on board the *Prince* respected the captain and found him to be fair and reasonable, the captain's cultural and national background affected the broader culture of the ship because he was the highest ranking official on the ship and could, therefore, implement his particular culturally informed management, communication, and disciplining styles and strategies. This in turn affected the day-to-day working and living conditions on board the *Prince*. (This was another point shared by other Filipino seamen in Manila and Oakland; there was a broad consensus that captains have significant institutionalized powers that affect daily living and working on board ships.) Although the *Prince's* current captain was clearly not tyrannical or abusive (I agree with the Filipino seamen who described him to be "good" and "fair"), Marcus Rediker documents the historical abuse of power that many captains sailing the eighteenth century Atlantic exercised, persuasively arguing that working-class European (and some African) seamen in this historical context were forced to work for and survive the "devil" (the captain), while also contending with the "deep blue sea" (the dangerous environmental conditions of living and working on ships in the ocean).[35] Although the conditions have clearly changed from century to century and although the global/international shipping industry is more regulated compared with the past, those in institutionalized positions of power can still significantly/negatively affect everyday life and work on board ships, and racial, class, gender, national, and cultural tensions and problems still arise in the time-space of ships.

To give an example of how the Filipino seamen understood and experienced cultural politics and the racial, class, gender, and national tensions on board an industrial container ship like the *Prince,* Gogong discussed his past experiences of and critical perspectives on the aforementioned issues. During a postlunch conversation in the officers' mess hall, he tells me that he has experienced "racial discrimination"[36] on the *Prince* and other ships he has worked on: "Sa isip nila, katulong lang kami. (In their [the Europeans'] thinking, we are just servants.) They want to see that you are suffering," he observes. When I pushed him further to explain what he meant by this, he replies, "They [the 'puti' [whites]] are not used to Filipinos being of higher rank [thus, they want to see that we are suffering]." I point out to him that he is fourth in the chain of command—after the master, chief mate, and second mate—and he says he knows this, but he can "still feel this kind of discrimination even though the 'puti' know it is illegal and are scared of legal action."

To give a second example, one night when all of the Filipino seamen were off duty (at least for the next few hours), during a karaoke night and inuman (drinking session) in Yoyoy's cabin, their/our conversation takes a turn toward the topic of food or what I would call the "racialized and classed cultural politics of food." Earlier in the evening, Yoyoy cooked some leftover Spam and beef after dinner. As he entered his cabin a big grin was on his face. He carefully removed a tinfoil package that was previously hidden in the front of his orange jumpsuit, gear that he never usually wore because he works in the galley, not on deck or in the engine room. Yoyoy opened up the tinfoil, showing us the cooked meat as if they were precious jewels. I chuckled at the unfolding scene and asked Yoyoy why he was being so secretive or coy with our "pulutan" (snacks to be eaten while we drank). The electrician, Emilio, jumped in: "The Germans think we [Filipinos] are eating extra/special food, but it's leftover food that they don't really want or like. Some of them get jealous." Yoyoy agrees with Emilio and elaborates further:

> It's not really extra or special food because a lot of times we (Filipinos) and Kiribatis do not want to eat the German food, so we're not taking anything extra since we don't eat as much of their food. Some days we have no choice (but to undertake this strategy). We don't like the German food, so I provide other food for the Filipinos and the Kiribatis. I give the captain some input (on menu planning), but

> basically he tells me the kind of monthly menu he wants and he has the final word, so I must follow his orders, but we also have to eat food that we're used to because the German captain prefers German food.

I had already observed some of these racialized and classed cultural politics of food on the *Prince*; that is, different racial/national groups of working-class seamen have different cuisines and food preferences and all appeared to be in competition and in tension due to the ship's cultural, racial, class, and occupational hierarchies. This became apparent to me during a previous meal on the voyage. In the galley Yoyoy showed me some corned beef and rice that he had cooked especially for the Kiribati seamen. Although the captain had chosen cold cuts and bean soup for everyone's dinner, Yoyoy subverted the menu for the Kiribati seamen because Yoyoy believed the captain's menu choices were unfit for the Kiribatis who worked strenuous and long hours on deck in the cold and wind, cleaning, repairing, and maintaining the ship or in the hot engine or boiler rooms. Yoyoy felt compassion for and solidarity with the Kiribatis and thought they should have more substantial and satisfying food so that they could continue their demanding work. As a result, when he thought it was safe to do so, Yoyoy resisted the captain's menu orders and secretly cooked what he thought was more culturally appropriate and nourishing food for his Kiribati and Filipino shipmates. (Yoyoy acknowledged that rice was not traditional Kiribati food, but he said the Kiribatis liked it and preferred it to the German food.)

The Spam and beef cooked by Yoyoy for our karaoke night and inuman entice Max to think about the next day's breakfast, so he asks Yoyoy, "Why don't you cook 'tapsilog' (e.g., cured beef, fried egg, garlic fried rice—a common Filipino breakfast) in the morning?" "It's not possible," Yoyoy replies. "I have to cook 'mushroom toast' (melted cheese and mushrooms on white bread, a German dish)." Although the mushroom toast sounds fine with me, I agree with Max that tapsilog would be a more delicious breakfast. My response seems to reassure Max and our food discussion encourages him to talk about his other feelings and opinions related to German cuisine. "Imagine taking a piece of bread and putting butter on it, then a cold cut, and then some cheese and then some cream cheese. Imagine what that would taste like?" he asks me with a look of displeasure on his face. Although this does not sound like the most appetizing (or healthy) to me, I resist making negative generalizations about German cuisine because it isn't productive, respectful, or appropriate, especially because I'm inexperienced when it comes to this kind of food and the captain and German officers have been helpful in my shipboard research.

The conversation about the racialized and classed cultural politics of food leads to additional reflections from Max about how he does not really like working on the ship and that he is doing it simply to earn a good living. Max continues with his commentaries about racial hierarchies, rank, and discipline on the ship:

> The Germans are stricter than other officers on other ships. If we were working on an all-Filipino ship (which he says exist) this "food thing" wouldn't be an issue. The Germans come from East Germany and they are very closed—not open like Filipinos. They don't understand how we are. I used to be a third mate on a different ship and I didn't get along with the German second mate. The German would tell me what to do and I would do it, but even after I had already done it, the German would continue to yell at me. I put up with this while we were at sea, but then I filed a complaint against this guy when we got back to Germany. He didn't seem to like Filipinos. Probably, he was racist.

Emilio and I are curious about what happened when Max "complained" to the shipping company. Did the company believe Max? Did management respond appropriately? Max continued:

> Yes, the company believed me, so they did not hire the German back. I had been with the company for nine years and had a good track record. Why would I all of a sudden start being a problem after all of this time? The German second mate was also jealous because his salary was $4,500 per month and (according to the German), he had to pay 50 percent in taxes. At the time, I was making $2,600, but the Philippines doesn't have a high (income) tax. He was jealous of this and didn't like that a Filipino was making more money than he was.

Max's commentary articulates the racial tensions and racism he experienced on a previous ship. His account suggests that a German superior officer treated him harshly, an outcome that Max attributed to the German superior officer's dislike of Filipinos, his racism, and economic frustration that despite Max being positioned in a lower rank, Max earned more net pay.

The ship's European cultural hegemony, robustly expressed through the racial/ethnic/national background and institutionalized authority of the captain, the German shipping company, and other officers; the racialized and classed cultural politics of food; and management/discipline style experienced and described by the Filipino seamen during the voyage have developed in part because of the broader histories of European colonialisms and racism in all regions of the world, and, more specifically, because of specific European colonialisms in the Philippines (e.g., Spanish and U.S. American) and Kiribati (British and U.S. American [the U.S. conducted nuclear testing in the Line islands, which are in Kiribati territory]), but additionally because of how institutionalized power, racism, and whiteness were practiced, embodied, and performed on the ship. That is, because the German shipping company, German master, and German officers institutionalized and interpersonally naturalized European-ness or whiteness as the dominant cultural or racial "norm" (again through figures of authority, food politics, management, and discipline), Filipino and Kiribati ways of being and knowing were marginalized, which subsequently shaped and reinforced inequalities and hierarchies on board the ship.

Moreover, Filipino seamen's analyses of racial discrimination and the racialized and classed cultural politics of food on board ships, including their (and the Kiribati seamen's) regular practice of food resistance and subversion demonstrate that although one way of reading industrial container ships is that they are generic and corporate hyperspaces, on board the *Prince*, from the perspectives of Filipino seamen and Kiribati seamen, European or German ways of being and knowing had emerged as culturally dominant, while Filipino and Kiribati ways of being and knowing were constructed as secondary and/or tertiary sites. As the karaoke night and inuman/drinking conversations revealed, there were clearly moments and opportunities for "other" cultural forms to be practiced on the ship, on the "down-low," to use a queer people of color term, that is, hidden below the surface or in secret.

In conclusion, interconnected issues and coconstitutive axes of race, class, gender, nationality, and occupation shaped and colored the Filipino seamen's experiences and conceptualizations of time-space (i.e., their living and laboring) on the *Prince,* in the context of global shipping. The aforementioned interconnected issues and coconstitutive axes also contribute to creating the blues, and notions of "sacrifice" and "lifelessness" evoked by seamen such as Gogong and Max (discussed in similar terms by other Filipino seamen I met in ports). I purposefully evoke African American cultural practices and expressions of the blues here, described by one scholar as the "complex mingling of sorrow and celebration, erotic ambition and romantic defeat,"[37] as the affects, events, and practices Filipino seamen revealed to me during fieldwork reflect this explanation of the blues. (Although I am not able to address all aspects of the blues, this chapter focuses on some of the challenges or sorrows of seafaring. The next chapter addresses a more celebratory moment.) Filipino seamen get the blues because they labor in and endure long periods of significant social and cultural isolation as they live and work at sea (usually for the duration of their nine-month contracts).

They get the blues because they labor in and endure prolonged confinement, monotony, and maritime "imprisonment," as they work long, unconventional, and non-normative (queer) nautical hours that pass far too slowly, in an occupation that limits their opportunities to leave their ship(s) and experience life elsewhere. And they get the blues because they also labor in and endure the heterotopic and hyperspatial, yet still European dominated, working and living environment that is their ship, the *Prince*.

Indeed, in describing working-class seamen from another era (the eighteenth century) who lived and labored in the deep blue sea, Rediker suggests that "[seamen's] isolation was communal. They could escape neither their loneliness nor each other."[38] Based on participant-observation on the *Prince*, Filipino seamen appear to dialogue with Rediker, suggesting that his historical analysis still resounds with their experiences of temporality, space, and affect in the contemporary global shipping industry. At the same time, Filipino seamen also complicate and build on Rediker's important insight by articulating how their isolation, "azul-ness," (blues) sense of sacrifice and lifelessness were radically coconstituted by race and racism, not only by class or maritime occupation. In addition to Gogong's explicit use of the "kulay" (color)—azul—Filipino seamen's racialized, classed, and gendered experiences and expressions of "sorrow" or the blues were also indicated by Gogong's stories of seamen from the Global South (Philippines and Kiribati) who struggled with the isolation, confinement, hyperspatiality, and loneliness of seafaring, as well as Max's provocative comment: "Walang buhay dito" (There's no life here). Coconstituting forms of oppression expressed through race, gender, class, nationality, temporality, and space surely contributed to Filipino seamen's sea- and ship-based blues.

In addition, consideration of indigenous and precolonial Filipino/a conceptualizations and epistemologies of time-space, as well as Christian Filipino/a notions of "suffering," can also contribute to understanding Filipino seamen's experiences of time-space and this ethnographic chapter in blue. Although indigenous/precolonial Filipino/a and Christian Filipino/a systems of time-space are far too complex to fully address here, several major points related to these systems are relevant. First, if we broadly reflect on indigenous Philippine creation stories, their cosmologies, and epistemologies, discussed by Filipino Philosophy scholar Leonardo N. Mercado, we can further enrich and complicate our understanding of Filipino/a maritime and migrant temporalities and spaces. Interestingly, in Mercado's discussion of Philippine creation myths, what is significant and compelling is that cross-culturally across different ethnic and language groups in the Philippines, the islands and archipelago stand (or is it float?) in an important relationship to the ocean and seas. However, from my reading of Mercado, it appears that although the ocean and seas are important cultural and environmental spaces and places, islands or the (Philippine) archipelago are weighted differently in indigenous cosmologies.

That is, in multiple creation stories from the Tagalog, Northern Luzon, Visayan, and Mindanao regions, evoked by Mercado, in the beginning there was cosmic chaos where "No world existed," or where "the sky was so close to the earth that the sun boiled the rivers and seas," or there were "no people," only "a bottom-less deep and misty world all in confusion," "only boundless sea and space," or there was "no land but only a great body of water flowing from the Upperworld to [the] Underworld." However, as different indigenous deities, gods, and goddesses, as well as spirits and animals, engaged each other in world-altering scenarios and events (again, much too complicated to discuss in detail here), the chaotic worlds shifted, emerging as more harmonious and in balance. As a result of supernatural or extrahuman phenomena, instead of cosmic chaos and boundless seas and space, the "First Man" and "First Woman" appeared, a cooling of the sun occurred, and plants, flowers, rain, moon, stars, thunder, continents, and islands developed. This general outline and theory of Philippine creation stories suggests that although the oceans and seas are definitely important in indigenous precolonial Filipino/a cosmologies and epistemlogies, without the islands or the archipelago, there is a clear lack of spiritual balance or harmony. If we take these indigenous and precolonial cosmologies seriously (which I do), then in addition to racialized, classed, and gendered oppression created through capitalism, globalization, colonialism, neocolonialism, and racism, Filipino seamen working and living at sea for extended periods of time in the global economy also feel intense moments of azul-ness and lifelessness because they are far away and removed from the Philippine islands and archipelago where Filipino seamen seem to suggest is where "life happens."

On a related point, Mercado writes that although "Western" notions of "cosmic time" are linear, that is, time in this system moves from past to present to future, a belief that he suggests is an outcome of how "Indo-European languages. . . stress. . . past, present, and future tenses," Filipino concepts of "cosmic time" are "cyclic. . . spiral and dynamic,"[39] perhaps like oceanic waters and sea currents. According to Mercado, this fluidity in Filipino/a conceptualizations of and behaviors related to temporality is an outcome of Philippine languages "not [being] so time-oriented," but rather, they are more concerned with "modality or aspect."

To explain what modality or aspect means, Mercado cites scholar Paz Ruiz Dorotheo who describes it this way: "English verbs have a well-defined tense system; Cebuano, an aspect system. Tense refers to time of action; aspect deals with *the nature of the action from point of beginning, continuing or concluding*" [emphasis added].[40] To give examples of how this works, Mercado lists several sets of affixes in "Cebuano Visayan," Tagalog, and Ilocano that show the "finished aspect" and "unfinished aspect." Some examples from his list include: "nag" (finished aspect in Visayan and Tagalog) and "mag" or "ag" (unfinished aspects in Tagalog and Ilocano, respectively). He also gives the following sentence as further evidence to support his discussion: "Nagkanta siya sa programa," which Mercado writes can be translated as "He/she sang at the program" or "He/she sings at the program." This sentence and its dual temporal translations illustrate how time is understood, translated, and performed differently and more fluidly in Filipino/a cultural contexts; that is, past, present, and future are not so rigidly defined or translatable compared with European cultural/language tropes or terms. This brief example from Mercado's insightful scholarship also shows temporal fluidities *and* sex/gender fluidities, as Filipino is a gender-neutral/inclusive language, that is, "siya" above, which can be translated at "this person" (emphasizing relationality), is gender-neutral or inclusive. (In the next chapter, I elaborate on sex/gender fluidities and nondualities in Filipino/a contexts.)

With a nonlinear and more fluid notion of time, Mercado writes,

> While the Westerner looks on time in its lineal progress, the Filipino looks at it in its spiral movement. A coil (or a wave?) never returns to the same point. There is progress in spiral motion, for the new cycle is not the old cycle. For the Westerner time wasted is gone forever. But for the Filipino there is always tomorrow.[41] [question added]

Here Mercado stresses how time moves and is understood differently in Filipino/a contexts, where past, present, and future have different creative possibilities, flows, and effects, as a result of time's "spiral motion[s]" or I would add time's watery wave-like construction. However, with the way time is measured and valued through labor in capitalism and with capitalism's emphasis on "efficiencies" (e.g., streamlining time and production), as well as surplus (profits), Filipino (or other non-European or indigenous) temporal fluidities and flows are blocked or marginalized, resulting in more regimented, disciplined, and rigid time(-space), another reason why Filipino seamen working on ships in the global economy can develop the blues.

In seeing and feeling blue, so far away from Philippine islands and archipelago in a capitalist world system that emphasizes speed and productivity,

Filipino seamen additionally stress that their seafaring, migrant lives are "sacrifices" because they give up precious time-space (life experiences) away from their loved ones and extended social networks, as well as broader regional/national Philippine cultural and social contexts (signified, for example, by food on the *Prince*). Although Gogong was the first on the *Prince* to use this noun and verb—sacrifice—many other Filipino seamen I have met during the course of my fieldwork used similar discourse. As I analyzed in chapter 2, the Philippine state also evokes tropes and narratives of sacrifice (particularly, sacrifice for the sake of the family and nation) as the (Philippine) state uses the overseas Filipino worker as "bagong bayani" (new heroes and heroines) narrative in the efforts to maintain and promote overseas migration as a long-term economic development strategy. Although notions of sacrifice play a big part in the (Philippine) state's interpellation narrative, notions of Christian suffering and sacrifice also "color" Filipino seamen's perceptions, experiences, and understandings of seafaring/maritime time-space in the global economy.

In this way, contemporary Filipino seamen echo Filipino male migrants from a previous generation who toiled in agricultural, fishing, domestic service, hotel, and restaurant industries up and down the U.S. west coast, Hawai'i, and Alaska. These early twentieth century hard-working but poorly paid male migrant workers from the Philippines similarly evoked notions and themes of (Christian) sacrifice and suffering as they lived, labored, and endured in a culturally foreign time-space that was "America" (United States).[42] In using this discursive strategy, historian Agusto Fauni Expiritu observes that working-class Filipino male migrants were able to express a sense of dignity in a racially hostile land during a period of U.S. American colonialism in the Philippines and anti-Asian racism in the United States. (Anti-Asian racism was of course, also expressed by U.S. colonial authorities and participants in the geotemporal context of an occupied Philippines.) Likewise, Filipino seamen working as sea-based migrants in the contemporary global shipping industry discuss their lifetimes of sacrifice and suffering, evoking futures with other, more liveable, humane, and just possibilities or outcomes. Many of the Filipino seamen I met expressed this through their future aspirations for their children, whom many hoped would not have to endure or suffer the "life of a seaman." Thus, although aspects of their time-space existence are queer, other aspects fall into a heteronormative time-space trajectory of "reproductive family time,"[43] further revealing the complexities and contradictions of navigating Filipino crosscurrents.

Finally, while keeping indigenous Filipino/a cosmologies, capitalism, and Christian concepts in mind, it is also important to simultaneously stress that the coconstituting forms and axes of oppression and identity related to race, class, gender, nationality, occupation, and cultural differences, which Filipino seamen "endure" or "suffer," *do not* completely diminish or wash away their capacities to celebrate (e.g., drinking partying, and having karaoke nights), create friendships, labor in solidarity with other working-class men of color (e.g., through cooking and sharing nourishing food with Kiribati shipmates), and/or "Filipino-ize" available temporal moments and spatial areas of the ship, which broadly speaking, were incompletely dominated by European (German) ways of being and knowing. This Filipino-ization of time-space on the *Prince* as I have indicated in this chapter was created through Filipino seamen's everyday cultural practices, particularly around language, food, pleasure, performance (such as karaoke and the production and performance of racialized and classed masculinities), as well as "barkadas" (friendship groups). The karaoke night and inuman was a key time-space or event that illustrates this point. In sum, the Filipino seamen waiting and searching for jobs at Rizal Park (discussed earlier in the chapter) and the Filipino seamen who lived and labored on the *Prince* during our transpacific voyage compellingly reveal alternative experiences and conceptualizations of time-space in the context of the global economy and contemporary economic and cultural globalization, which historically have been underanalyzed ethnographically. In further charting the crosscurrents of seafaring, masculinities, and globalization, this chapter illustrates and interprets how Filipino seamen (portside or parkside in Manila and at sea on the *Prince*) navigate time-space as they move through varied sites, moments, and emotions, reflecting the sea's complex hues.

CHAPTER FOUR

Transportation

Seamen and Tomboys in Ports and at Sea

My nation, my body.

NEFERTI X. TADIAR, "Domesticated Bodies"

There is reason to seize the bits and piece of . . . history as they flash up in the randomness of memory. There is a history jeopardized by prevalent understandings of queer identities and tired notions. . . .

RODERICK FERGUSON, "Sissies at the Picnic"

A Transportation Story, Metro Manila, Philippines, 1998

At 5:00 a.m. it is dark and quiet when I wake up, trying to beat the morning rush hour in Metro Manila. The port should only be about a twenty-minute car ride, but with the arteries of the city becoming increasingly clogged, it could take two hours. Other people have similar ideas, so by the time I reach the street corner where the "Quiapo-Pier" jeepney[1] (or jeep) stops to pick up passengers in need of a ride to the other side of the city, the street is already lined with people. (Jeepneys are a form of low cost transportation in the Philippines, typically owned and operated by individuals or families.)

Although I could take a taxi, during fieldwork in Manila, I often rode jeeps to participate in more working-class spaces in the city.[2] I board and take my seat when the jeep arrives, and I stare out the window and begin to watch a clip of the film that is Metro Manila. We pass historical University of Santo Thomas, with its green playing fields and dignified buildings, students waiting at the front gate; 7–11 stores; Jollibees (fast food restaurant chain); residential housing; pawnshops; and dilapidated office buildings.

Eventually, the jeep goes beneath an overpass and enters Quiapo, a historically Chinese or Chinese Mestizo/Filipino area of Old Manila.

I have ridden this route numerous times before during previous stays in the city, for example, when I studied at a local college during my undergraduate days. In Quiapo, I always think about and remember my mother. She completed a bachelor's degree at Far Eastern University (FEU), which I see on my left as the jeep passes through the neighborhood. I think about the stories my mother told me about being young and in college, and I imagine her sitting in a little Quiapo restaurant enjoying a Coke and "hopia" (Chinese bean cakes), her favorite cheap meal, which she said she savored because her "pocket money" was always limited.

After passing FEU, I see Quiapo Church off to the right. The scene is lively, and there is an interesting mixture of people that I observe as the jeep slowly passes the famous church. Believers wearing black buy candles and flowers outside the church doors. Nuns in white, rosaries visible on their chests, approach the church, perhaps to attend morning mass. Vendors sell bottles of oils mixed with herbs for various ailments, teas to heighten fertility, potions to induce miscarriages, and rich coconut oil to soften skin and fortify hair. Young skinny brown boys push wooden carts filled with old newspapers or little brothers through side streets, while middle-class civil servants and Filipina office workers wearing identical grey skirts (uniforms) and white blouses jockey for position as they wait for taxis. A few European tourists wearing safari-wear and sandals with bright magenta backpacks, thirty-five-millimeter cameras and guidebooks in hand wait for local transport.

The jeep crosses the historical Pasig River[3] and continues into Old Manila. U.S. government style buildings, remnants of U.S. colonialism, haunt the landscape. The National Post Office and other governmental buildings with huge columns look worn out, but some are getting new paint jobs in time for the 1998 Centennial Celebrations, which recall the Philippine Revolution against Spain and the establishment of the Philippine Republic, as well as the subsequent Philippine-American war.

Eventually, the jeep gets closer to Intramuros, the Walled City, where Spanish colonial administrators, merchants, and settlers once lived (discussed in chapter 1). Intramuros is architecturally composed of urban poor shanties; medieval structures; a golf course (established during the U.S. American colonial period); several schools; "turo-turos" (low-budget eateries) and corporate fast-food restaurants; upscale Philippine cafes, handicrafts shops, and art galleries; shipping-related offices and seafarers' union buildings; and other anonymous buildings. Intramuros, importantly for my research project, is also adjacent to the Port of Manila. As in any major industrialized port city since the 1970s, large container cranes line the port area, mechanical structures that pick up and move shipping/trucking containers full of all sorts of products and commodities (e.g., electronics, building supplies, food, and apparel).

After passing through the security checkpoint area where my identification and bag are inspected and I am asked the nature of my visit, I walk toward one of the docked ships. There is another security guard by the ship, so I introduce myself, tell him the purpose of my visit, show him my identification, and then ask him (in Tagalog) what kind of crew is on board the ship. He tells me that this one is Pinoy (Filipino). (Some of the other ships, which he points to, in contrast, comprise, for example, all Chinese crews.) The guard asks if I am Japanese. No, I explain to him in Tagalog, I am Filipino, born in Malolos, Bulakan, and raised in the United States, but living in Manila for the year. The security guard says he appreciates my effort to speak with him in Tagalog. He seems pleased that I have not lost my native language and he tells me he pities "balikbayans" (Filipino/as from North America or Filipino/a immigrants) who cannot speak Tagalog. We engage in more small talk (mostly about the port, his daily routine), and then he accompanies me as I board the ship and he introduces me to the crew.

The ship, *Sea Star,* is painted dull gray and is large, but not imposing like other ships I have seen. It is registered in Cambodia and owned by a Singaporean company and mostly transports goods in Southeast Asia. It has just transported rice from Thailand to the Philippines.[4] The crew and dockworkers finished unloading the cargo the day before and soon the ship will depart for Taiwan.

The security guard tells one of the seamen, "Tommy," a man in his mid-thirties, that I am a researcher and that I want to talk to them about seafaring. Tommy nods at me, letting me know it's fine to come aboard. He says that a few of the seamen are eating, but the rest of the crew is sleeping. Tommy then asks me to follow him to the galley and mess hall. Two seamen are eating breakfast. One of them ("Ernesto"), a man who appears to be in his forties, looks up from his plate and asks me if I have eaten. I say yes I have, thanks, but he tells me to eat again. Appreciating his hospitality, I sit down at the table. Another seaman, probably in his late twenties, wearing a bright yellow Los Angeles Lakers baseball cap brings me a plate of scrambled eggs mixed with fried onions, garlic fried rice, and a cup of coffee. The steaming aromas from the onions, garlic, and coffee smell delicious, and I forget that I have already eaten breakfast at home in Quezon City.

As we're all eating they ask me if I work for a trade or transport union. If I do, they say they don't really want to talk; there is nothing to report. The conditions on their ship are fine they say, and the ship owners pay them on time. I tell them I don't work for a union and that I'm a graduate student (at the time), studying anthropology in California, doing research. They appear satisfied with my explanation and want to know where I am from and where I have lived in the United States. I list the places I have lived: Portland/Gladstone, Oregon; Ithaca, New York; and Santa Cruz, California. (This was before I had moved to Oakland and later to Minneapolis, Minnesota, where I currently live.) In turn, they tell me where their immigrant or migrant relatives live. Tommy has a sister who is a nurse in Chicago. Anthony's mother lives in Los Angeles with his older sister. Ernesto does not have family in the United States, but has a younger sister working as a domestic helper in Hong Kong.

We finish eating breakfast, but can't proceed with our discussion because one of the seamen has turned on the television, and the seamen and I are keenly interested in Manila's morning news, the weather report, and local entertainment gossip. We all watch TV and then Tommy and Anthony excuse themselves from the table. I am alone with Ernesto. He pulls out a cigarette and asks me if I want one. I tell him I don't smoke. We watch the TV in silence, but after a while, he, somewhat out of the blue (at least this was my initial reading), says, "Alam mo, mayroon akong kaibigan na tomboy." "You know, I have a friend who is tomboy."[5] "Really? Who?" I ask.

Ernesto begins to tell me about "Percy,"[6] a tomboy he knows through his sister in Hong Kong. Ernesto visits the both of them whenever the *Sea Star* goes to Hong Kong. Percy works in a warehouse and was dating one of his sister's friends. "Percy helped me so much," he tells me. "I was having problems with my wife and kids and I was very depressed. Percy was there for me with advice and told me to be firm with my wife, but also to treat my wife better. Eventually though, my wife left me. I was so depressed during a visit to Hong Kong, so Percy took me out and showed me a good time. We went out drinking, went to some nightclubs, and I tried to forget my wife and my problems. Percy was the one who reminded me that it was over. We were sitting in a nightclub, getting really drunk and Percy just said, 'Tapos na, Pare.' (It's over.) I was so sad, but I knew Percy was right. There was nothing left for me to do."

As he ends his story, Ernesto changes the subject somewhat, asking me if I have a girlfriend or wife. ("Ikaw, me girlfriend o asawa ka ba?" You, do you have a girlfriend or wife?) I tell him I have a girlfriend and that she is currently in the United States. Anthony and Tommy reenter the galley just as I am finishing my sentence. They sit down and want to smoke with Ernesto before they start working. Since they have just overheard the last part of our conversation, they ask me about my girlfriend. They ask if she is white (puti). I tell them she is not, and this begins a conversation about their preferences in women. Our discussion has taken an explicitly heterosexual turn. After a brief discussion about women and sexual and romantic likes and dislikes, like Ernesto, the other two seamen begin to tell me who else they know who is tomboy: a cousin, a high school friend, an older relative. We continue with this conversation for a while. Ernesto eventually realizes they must start working because they are leaving for Taiwan soon. They wish me good luck in my studies, and I thank them for talking and the breakfast and I wish them a safe voyage.

As discussed in previous chapters, during fieldwork in the Philippines I observed a recurring narrative about Filipino seamen often deployed by Philippine state officials and some cultural workers as well as by the seamen themselves. The narrative suggests that Filipino seamen are largely heterosexual, geographically and sexually mobile, heroically nationalistic, simultaneously family-oriented or heteronormative, and usually "macho." Although aspects of this narrative describe some Filipino seamen's experiences and identities, instead of uncritically reinforcing and perpetuating this hetero-patriarchal understanding, imaginary, and discourse of Filipino seamen's masculinities, my ethnographic analysis in *Filipino Crosscurrents* has been to work on developing a cultural critique[7] of dominant narratives about Filipino seamen (see chapters 1 to 3). This cultural critique has developed, in part, through a postcolonial/decolonized and queer Filipino (American) ethnographic focus that seeks to attend to the gaps, contradictions, and contingencies in dominant representations of Filipino seafaring and seamen's masculinities. While I aimed to illustrate the fissures of the dominant neoliberal Philippine state, manning agencies' and globalization studies' representations of Filipino maritime and migrant masculinities in the previous three chapters, in this chapter, I illustrate how other fissures—and crosscurrents—become legible when Filipino seamen's masculinities are engaged through their "intimate relationalities,"[8] that is, through their close social relationships, with Filipino tomboys. (In Filipino [the language] the first "o" in "tomboy" is pronounced with a short "o" sound [shorter than a regular short "o" in English].)

Tomboy here broadly refers to Filipino masculine or male-identified fe/males who generally have sexual/emotional relationships with feminine females. I use the term "fe/male" because some tomboys are female and masculine-identified, whereas others are male and masculine-identified. Tomboys may also identify as "FTM" (female-to-male), indicating a movement or shift in sex/gender identification. This movement or shift may entail medical procedures on the body to change sex (e.g., top/bottom surgeries, hormones, or none of the above). There is indeed a spectrum of tomboy FTM/fe/male masculinities. "Fe/male," to me, indicates this fluidity or range of sex/gender identification among Filipino tomboys. Although historically analyzed as "lesbians" or "women" (I will elaborate on and critique this point later in the chapter), tomboy can also be understood as a form of transgenderism or transexualism where tomboys enact or embody transgressive sex/gender practices and/or identities. This chapter focuses more on the transgender qualities because transsexuality tends to have medical implications (especially in dominant U.S. or "Western" contexts) that are beyond the scope of my focus in this chapter.[9] The chapter highlights sex/gender identifications and cultural phenomena and dynamics related to Filipino seamen and tomboys, rather than primarily focusing on medical models of sex/gender.

As I discussed in the introduction, sex/gender are not seen as distinct terms or embodiments in the Filipino language or in many Filipino contexts. The Filipino language is gender-inclusive or gender-neutral. Indicating this inclusivity and neutrality, the Filipino language, for example, does not have gendered pronouns (e.g., "he" or "she" in English). As such, there is significant fluidity, flow, and nonduality between notions, performances, and embodiments of sex/gender in Filipino/a contexts. Social and interpersonal contexts and self and social identifications are more important than rigid anatomical understandings or biological readings of "the body." These kinds of interpersonal/social and/or self-positioning reveal how notions of personhood or notions of sex/gender are generally more dynamic and definitely less dualistic compared with dominant European notions of distinct sex and gender. To give another brief linguistic/cultural example of how this works, the Filipino word "lalaki" means both "male" *and* "man." This somewhat paradoxical formulation (particularly if you are used to separating sex/gender) reveals again how sex/gender are connected and interdependent and/or in unity with each other, not functioning in a duality.

Like the terms "gay" and "lesbi" in Indonesia (discussed by anthropologist Tom Boellstorff), tomboy can also be understood as a Tagalog-ized or Filipino-ized English word with specific Philippine or Filipino meanings.[10] That is, although "tomboy" as a term might have some similarities with the English word "tomboy," where the word often evokes white female masculinity during childhood or girlhood, I underscore the term's more indigenous and Filipino/a roots, routes, and meanings (not Western or U.S. American understandings). Following Kanaka Maoli Studies scholar and historian Noe Noe Silva's decolonized approach to indigeneity and language, I do not italicize Tagalog or Filipino words (such as "tomboy") in this chapter. Silva states that she does not italicize Hawaiian words in her book, *Aloha Betrayed: Native Hawaiian Resistance to American Colonialism* "to resist making the native tongue appear foreign."[11] This strategy is also important for those in Philippine and Filipino/a American Studies who are interested in decolonizing epistemologies and language(s) in our fields.

As an ethnographer who embodies queer and transgender Filipino (American) tomboy masculinity and lalakiness (maleness/manliness), I learned that upon meeting and getting to know me during fieldwork, Filipino seamen like Ernesto wanted to share commentaries, stories, and memories about tomboys in their past and present lives. As the first vignette shows, Filipino seamen during port visits (and later in other spaces) evoked and remembered tomboys as we talked during meals and as we hung out during their work breaks. Similar interactions occurred when I conducted participant-observation research in Ermita (Manila) and later when I took a transpacific voyage on an industrial container ship.

The following are other examples of this kind of scenario or exchange during fieldwork. (Seamen's commentaries were originally in Tagalog, but I have translated them here in English.) At the Port of Oakland, a Filipino seaman named "Tony" remembered his tomboy cousin, nicknamed "Mel." Tony recalled:

> Mel's mother died when Mel was young, so my mother took care of Mel (plus Mel's two brothers and sister). When the school year started, my mother would buy uniforms and books for my siblings and me. My mother would also buy Mel and my other cousins these things. Mel was close to my age, so we always played together when we were young. Mel is a real guy (tunay na lalaki). Now, Mel has a woman companion. They've been together a long time. When I have extra money, I send some to Mel. Mel has a small business at the market, but I know that Mel still needs the help.

In Ermita (in Manila), retired Filipino captain "Jonas" recalled a story about a tomboy he met early on in his career. Now in his late fifties, Jonas remembers:

> The captain who was a Filipino brought his "anak,"[12] a tomboy who was around twenty years of age, on board the ship for part of our voyage. The captain thought that maybe his anak would meet a man on board the ship and that this would turn her into a "real girl." But none of the men liked the anak. This person was really "guyish" (or boyish or male-ish) (lalaking-lalalaki). When the captain was not around, the anak would be included as part of the group. We would

> talk and tell stories or eat together. But when the captain was around, we acted like this person wasn't part of our group. We didn't want to make the captain mad. The captain eventually sent his anak home because he saw that no one wanted this person (romantically).

And again, at the Port of Oakland, Filipino seaman "Ruben" evoked his tomboy cousin "Lou." Ruben reflects:

> We were close in high school. Lou now works at Mega Mall as a security guard. Lou didn't finish college. When I'm on vacation in Manila, I see Lou and we go out drinking with some others from our group. We're still close.

Since I was not initially expecting these kinds of commentaries of conversations, these ethnographic encounters and narratives strongly suggest that my bodily presence and racialized and classed sex/gender (transgender, tomboy) and performance of lalaki-ness reminded working-class Filipino seamen of tomboys they knew or currently know (Percy, Mel, tomboy anak, and Lou) subsequently, transporting them mentally and emotionally to other times and places (just as I was "transported" when I traveled locally in Manila, recalling, for example, my mother while I rode a jeepney through Quiapo). As a result of being mentally/emotionally/temporally moved, Filipino seamen often shared anecdotes, memories, feelings, and thoughts about tomboy relatives, friends, and shipmates (in the case of Jonas) during conversations. In turn, seamen's narratives and stories about tomboys pushed me to continue exploring how Filipino maritime and migrant masculinities function and are created through everyday practices, in particular, through their social relationships, proximities, friendships, and kinships with Filipino tomboys and what these two overlapping masculinities may mean in terms of understanding broader issues of Filipino masculinities, manhoods, and/or lalaki-ness.

As a result of the kind of fieldwork encounters and conversations discussed previously in this chapter (as well as post-fieldwork reflection and analysis), I show that what at first glance appears to be a heteronormative cultural and economic phenomenon, working-class Filipino seamen laboring in the global shipping industry, when ethnographically analyzed through reflexive and situated ethnographic writing and use of transnational/translocal/transgender cultural logics, scenes in port(s) and at sea actually reveal non-normative, queer, and/or transgender Filipino cultural dynamics; for example, the social, gender, and class affinities between working-class Filipino (sea)men and tomboys and a more expansive, inclusive, and queer understanding of Filipino masculinities/manhoods/lalaki-ness. By critically interpreting the connections, fluidities, and nondualities among and between conventional Filipino masculinities/manhoods/lalaki-ness and alternative (tomboy) masculinities/manhoods/lalaki-ness, this chapter continues to reveal how differently situated Filipinos engage the sea and seafaring to imagine and produce heterogeneous Filipino masculinities, as well as trajectories and spatializations of globalization. The chapter also emphasizes how differently situated Filipino masculinities/manhoods/lalaki-ness, for example, heterosexual male and tomboy, must be understood in relation to, *not* apart from each other (a common tendency in various Filipina lesbian/feminist accounts of tomboys). As such, I suggest that it is productive if more scholars, researchers, activists, and/or cultural workers engage tomboys as fe/male men or "lalaki" in the contexts of masculinity studies, queer studies, transgender studies, Philippine Studies, Filipino/a American Studies, and Asian American Studies. This theoretical and ethnographic move is particularly important if we want to decolonize notions of racialized and classed sexes/genders in Filipino contexts and if we want to "abide"[13] by indigenous Filipino epistemologies and understandings of racialized and classed sex/gender.

In addition to rethinking sex/gender, masculinities/manhoods/lalaki-ness, in this chapter I also ask readers to reconsider and reflect further on the effects and affects of maritime/migrant space and mobility. Although migration studies often begin with the arrival of the migrant or immigrant in the "receiving country," the crosscurrents and transportation frameworks I suggest here include examining the spaces in between and across countries, localities, and spaces (Philippines, United States, and the Pacific Ocean) and how movement and geographic positioning re/configures Filipino identities, masculinities, everyday practice, and life experiences. As in previous chapters, I remain interested in examining crosscurrents and transportation spaces and places such as ports, seas, ships, and different kinds of movement such as seafaring, migration, travel, or sea-based transportation and how mobility reinforces, informs, and/or disrupts cultural meanings, particularly around issues of Filipino masculinities/manhoods/lalaki-ness in local/regional/global contexts.

This understanding of transportation is partially informed by cultural studies scholar James Clifford's cultural theorizing in *Routes: Travel and Translation in the Late Twentieth Century,* particularly his idea that "travel [movement] is constitutive of culture." Clifford elaborates on the importance of movement by saying that "thinking historically is a process of locating oneself in space and time. And a location, in [this] perspective . . . is an *itinerary* rather than a bounded site—a series of encounters and translations" [emphasis added].[14] Inspired by Clifford's understanding of travel, translations, and itineraries, I foreground cultural encounters and translations in ports and at sea and suggest how specific embodied practices of mobility and movement, sea-based transportation, migration, and travel, are constitutive of racialized and classed Filipino masculinities and manhoods. I use the terms *transportation* and *seafaring* to evoke the fact that Filipino seamen are moving through the sea precisely as *sea-based migrant workers,* not as recreational elite travelers, which Clifford acknowledges is what the term "travel" usually connotes. By evoking transportation and not foregrounding travel, I am not suggesting that transportation or seafaring does not involve moments of pleasure or recreation; rather, I do so to underscore that the global shipping industry is a disciplined[15] site of largely Global South migrant male labor.

Moreover, whereas the in-between spaces and places of travel and mobility (e.g., ocean/ships) are clearly important, transportation also involves thinking transnationally, translocally, and transPacific-ly, engaging the multiple, mixed, and/or hybrid cultural logics of two or more places that may be important for mobile and migratory subjects (e.g., seamen, migrants, immigrants, and ethnographers) in the itineraries that they/we create through movement or transportation.[16] For example, in the case of this book and this chapter, it is productive and useful to understand and engage some of the cultural logics at play in the Philippines, the United States, and at sea, as well as the impacts, effects, and affects related to experiences of mobility that inform, create, repeat, and/or resist embodiments and performances of different kinds of Filipino masculinities/manhoods/lalaki-ness (e.g., conventional and tomboy).

Transportation also involves reflecting on how movement (seafaring, transportation [e.g., street-level or sea-level], travel, migration, and immigration) potentially/regularly "moves" subjects to another time and space or place (mentally, emotionally, and/or through cultural memory). In other words, transportation moves us to different geographies or oceanographies, but also to different spaces, places, and moments of temporality, history, affect, and memory. This kind of transportation can take place in (port) city streets, on ocean waves and currents, on rivers and rails, on walking/hiking trails, on road trips, and in other forms of journeying as an act of remembering, reflecting, and meditating.[17] Thus, differently situated ethnographic participants (e.g., ethnographers and the people with whom they/we conduct participant-observation) interact with different people and subjects and move through a variety of places, potentially bringing together a (re)collection of the jetsam and flotsam of personal and collective past life experiences, feelings, and analyses.

Last and certainly not least, transportation also suggests sex/gender fluidities, inclusiveness, and nondualities that the terms "*trans*gender" and "*trans*sexual" suggest because the "trans" in transgender, transsexual, *and* transportation simultaneously evokes movement between and across culturally constructed racialized and classed sex/gender, that is, female/male, manhood/womanhood, masculinities, and femininities. Transportation as a term and framework, therefore, precisely highlights the intersections of embodied movement and migration (seafaring), as well as the fluidities and nondualities of racialized and classed sex/gender formations, identifications, and realities.

Although many middle-class lesbian feminist activists and writers in the Philippines and diaspora regularly use tomboy to describe or evoke Filipina working-class (butch) lesbians, I want to emphasize here that Filipino tomboy formations are akin to other transgender or fe/male masculinities rooted and routed through Southeast Asia, such as tombois in Indonesia and toms in Thailand. Anthropologist Megan J. Sinnott, for example, writes that toms in/from Thailand can be understood as "female 'men'" or "transgendered females,"[18] whereas anthropologist Evelyn Blackwood writes that "*tomboi* is a term used for females acting in the manner of men *(gaya laki-laki)*."[19] In agreement with these ethnographers, as I have been proposing, Filipino tomboys can also be culturally interpreted as a formation of transgendered fe/male masculinity/manhood/lalaki-ness. As a result of centering an indigenous/Filipino understanding of sex/gender in unity, not duality, in this chapter, I aim to push scholarly conversations toward considering tomboys as "males" or "lalaki" because as I have indicated sex and gender are not separated in the Filipino language, and we must seriously consider more deeply the implications of various sex/gender self and social identifications. Indeed, we need to further explore and theorize what it means for tomboys to identify as masculine/males/men/lalaki (a clear gap in academic analyses, as well as literary narratives). Although in this chapter I cannot fully explain (or hope to narratively capture) tomboy masculinities/manhoods/lalaki-ness and tomboy personal and social identifications, my hope is to begin to chart preliminary ethnographic theorizing on this point and phenomena by basing my cultural interpretation on my specific fieldwork experiences in ports, on ships, and at sea.

As such, in addition to being in conversation with interdisciplinary queer studies in the United States (where Global North locations are still largely privileged as sites of study), I aim to dialogue with Philippine Studies, Filipino/a American Studies, and Asian American scholars situated in these fields where heterosexuality (but not necessarily heteronormativity) and conventional biological masculinities and manhoods are often privileged, especially through the figure of the heterosexual Filipino male migrant worker, a key subject in foundational Asian American Studies and Filipino/a American Studies. In addition, I seek to dialogue and debate with Filipina lesbian feminists in the Philippines and diaspora, who regularly advance the idea and narrative that Filipino tomboys are always lesbians, women, and/or female.

For Filipino/a American and Asian American Studies readers, I want to clarify the difference between heterosexuality and heteronormativity here to create improved understanding in our fields. Although Filipino migrant workers in the context of the early twentieth century have been persistently described in heterosexual terms, Filipino migrant men from this period were not necessarily heteronormative or conventional because racism, colonialism, classism, and other forms of social injustices prevented them from living or creating full heteronormative lives (had they desired this kind of existence, which has not been fully substantiated).[20] They were not necessarily heteronormative because many were migratory and highly mobile and, thus, did not or could not live settled lives (settlement can be read as a part of heteronormativity, especially in a U.S. American capitalist context where property or a fixed physical home is valued[21]). They were also majority working-class men of color migrating from a Philippines that was being colonized by the United States, and later they lived and worked in a country that eventually restricted Filipino/a immigration to the United States (as a result of the Tydings-McDuffie Act in 1934). Gendered notions of those who were fit to travel to the United States (e.g., men, not women) and this anti-Filipino and anti-Asian legislation subsequently kept Filipina populations at low levels, which hindered Filipino migrant men's (possible) desires and hopes to marry, build families, and "settle down," all components of heteronormativity in the logics of U.S. capitalism and heterosexual reproduction.[22] As such, my research addresses how Filipino seamen may be heterosexual, but not socially normative.

Because "tomboy" is a term and formation that travels and circulates in and between the Philippines, Southeast Asia, and diasporic locations, I intentionally link queer and transgender with tomboy to indicate my transnationally and diasporically situated subject-position and interpretive framework. My intention here is *not* to transport the terms "queer" or "transgender" to the Philippines in a Western, U.S. American, or Global North colonial or imperialist manner, but rather to emphasize the transnational, transpacific, and transport connections and cultural flows between the Philippines, and regional and diasporic geographies and oceanographies. That is, Filipino/a peoples *and ideas* flow back and forth between the Philippines and diasporic locations. To be sure, I am also trying to point out to readers in the United States or the "West" that a lot can be learned from people situated in the Philippines/Southeast Asia or translocally/transnationally/transPacific-ly when it comes to understanding sex/gender. In other words, it's a multiway flow of Filipino crosscurrents, not simply unidirectional or unidimensional epistemological and bodily traffic.

Keeping this in mind, I connect Philippine and diasporic cultural logics and try to pay close attention to epistemologies in the Philippines as well as in the diaspora (particularly United States) In *Impossible Desires: Queer Diasporas and South Asian Public Cultures,* literary critic and feminist queer studies scholar Gayatri Gopinath forcefully challenges the dominance of Indian nationalist ideologies, which privilege India as a homeland and which marginalize South Asian diasporic communities. Through queer and feminist critical readings of queer South Asian public cultures (music, film, novels, and activism), Gopinath intervenes into the heteronormative and patriarchal logics of Indian nationalist ideologies rooted in India and routed through South Asian diasporas. In doing so, Gopinath significantly and fiercely stresses the queerness of South Asian diasporic public cultures. What is different about my emphasis here (although clearly building on and greatly admiring Gopinath's groundbreaking work), is that my intention in this chapter is *not* to privilege the homeland/nation (Philippines) *or* the diaspora (United States) as sites of sites of cultural authenticity or radical queer possibilities, but rather to keep them in productive tension and dialogue.[23] My analytical and political position is based largely on ethnographic fieldwork and also on personal life experiences, which include regular travel between the United States and Philippines, as well as substantial residency in both locations.[24] As a self-identified Filipino American queer, transgender, tomboy, and immigrant researcher who is situated in translocal, transnational, and transport(ation) contexts in the Philippines and United States, I precisely evoke these multiple identify formations, which have different kinds of currency in the Philippines and diaspora (e.g., United States), to emphasize and highlight the complexities of how tomboy as a term, cultural practice, and embodiment circulates and how tomboy formations are interpreted or read in different Philippine, diasporic, migrant, and immigrant contexts.

The intimate relationalities between Filipino heterosexual (sea)men and Filipino tomboys, as well as the complexities of tomboy formations, became increasingly clearer to me through fieldwork in Manila, in Oakland,

and at sea. As a new ethnographer who lived in the Philippines in the late 1990s, I initially thought that Filipino seamen would speak with me about their lives at sea, the working conditions on ships and in ports, and the politics of Philippine overseas migration policies (since these were my key research areas). Indeed, over the years I have met dozens of Filipino seamen who have shared stories and social commentaries about life at sea and in port(s). However, as the introductory vignette and subsequent examples from fieldwork reveal, I learned that Filipino seamen wanted to converse with me about Filipino masculinities/manhoods/lalaki-ness through the figure of the tomboy. These encounters suggest how my subject position, embodiment, and identification as tomboy enabled, rather than disabled, certain interactions, exchanges, and conversations with Filipino seamen.

During fieldwork, working-class seamen primarily interacted with me as a Filipino male/masculine subject (tomboy), rather than as a Filipina female/feminine subject (woman or lesbian). As I understand these ethnographic encounters, moments, and exchanges they largely occurred because Filipino seamen understood tomboy to be a working-class embodiment of Filipino masculinity/manhood/lalaki-ness that for them was not routed or rooted through or in lesbianism, womanhood, and even femaleness (again because sex/gender is often fluid in Filipino contexts). With this shared understanding, we conavigated conversations by discussing tomboys more generally and more specifically moved toward seamen's stories, memories, thoughts, and feelings about tomboy friends, relatives, and acquaintances. In turn, ethnographic encounters evoked my own memories as a young tomboy in the Philippines.

Filipino Tomboys: Transnational, TransPacific, Transport Meanings

Although I have explained what I mean by tomboy and how I am using or translating the term, embodiment, and identification in this chapter, to more fully understand the significance of the intimate relationalities and proximities among and between Filipino heterosexual masculinities/manhoods/lalaki-ness and Filipino tomboy masculinities/manhoods/lalaki-ness and the queer postcolonial/decolonized reading I aim to develop here, it is useful to situate and discuss the broader cultural politics or landscape of tomboy definitions and interpretations, especially in transnational, transpacific, and transport contexts. In Manila and other locations in the Philippines, "tomboy" is a term deployed to generally describe a range of gender and sexual practices and identities, including the following: (1) female/woman-identified lesbianism often transculturated via white U.S.– or European-based notions of sex, gender, and sexuality; (2) working-class fe/male masculinities and manhoods where tomboys identify and/or live as males/men/lalaki; and/or (3) neither "women," "lesbians," "men," or "males," but an entirely different third or fourth gender formation.[25] Cultural interpretations based on the second and third notions do not frequently circulate in scholarly knowledge production, and self-representations by Filipino tomboys are currently limited due perhaps to a lack of economic and educational access, especially in the Philippines. As a result, the first understanding (tomboys as female lesbian women) has emerged as a dominant academic and political narrative in the Philippines and in some parts of the diaspora. Historically, nontomboy-authored narratives about tomboys have circulated more widely, resulting in more significant cultural capital.

A significant aspect of how many Filipinos understand tomboy practices and identities in the Philippines and some immigrant communities in North America suggests that being poor or working class is central. This understanding is reflected in popular Philippine discourse in which tomboys are often inscribed as poor, working class, unemployed, or working in low-pay service-industry positions such as bus conductors, security guards, factory workers, or overseas migrants. Although not as visible in popular culture as baklas, poor or working-class tomboys can be found in the pages of Manila-based tabloids, as well as in locally made films such as *Tomboy Nora* (1970) and *T-Bird at Ako* (*T-Bird and I*) (1982), both starring popular Philippine actress Nora Aunor. In an activist example, Information Center Womyn for Womyn (ICWFW), a lesbian nongovernmental organization in Manila, conducted a study of what they describe as "working-class lesbians." The organization, which codes tomboys as lesbians, reports that tomboys in their study were employed in positions such as domestic helper, barber, photocopying clerk, street food vendor, train station security guard, tennis court attendant, retail clerk, library assistant, and massage therapist.[26] In a more literary account, Nice Rodriguez (a Filipino tomboy based transnationally in Canada and the Philippines) writes in the short story "Every Full Moon" that the tomboy protagonist "Remy" (a.k.a "Rambo") works as a bus conductor in Metro Manila: "a dangerous job meant for men and butches."[27]

Confirming the precarious economic status of tomboys, the video exposé *Behind the Labels: Garment Workers on U.S. Saipan,* features Filipino tomboy anti–sweatshop activist Chie Abad who worked in a GAP clothing assembly plant for 6 years in Saipan and who later exposed and organized against the GAP's exploitative employment practices.[28] Abad left the Philippines in the early 1990s to find work in an overseas factory in Saipan. In a personal communication Abad stated, "Many [Filipino] tomboys work abroad as overseas contract workers because they can't find jobs in the Philippines. The Philippines is poor and on top of that tomboys do not want to work in some fields because many companies and government agencies require female employees to wear women's clothing like blouses and skirts."[29] While in Saipan, Abad observed that other tomboys also migrated there for economic reasons. Abad's analysis, which emphasizes a more transgender rather than a lesbian as woman framework for tomboy-ness (i.e., Abad is clearly resisting the unity of femaleness with woman-ness) reveals how the Philippine state's, as well as multinational corporations', heteronormative gender essentialism attempts to police and enforce Filipina femininity and womanhood, severely limiting tomboy masculine/manly gender expressions and their/our economic opportunities.

Translating and interpreting tomboy in a U.S. context, Gigi Otálvaro-Hormillosa, a queer performance artist of Colombian and Filipino descent writing from the San Francisco Bay Area asks, "To what extent does the queer Pinay (Filipina) butch enjoy privilege in the U.S. and in the Philippines, since 'butch' or 'tomboy' status deprives her of power in various diasporic settings[?]"[30] Here, Otálvaro-Hormillosa seems to be responding to what she sees as the unequal power relationships between tomboys, who she equates with butch lesbians or dykes, and Filipino gay men in the diaspora. She responds, more specifically, to what she understands as the "infantilisation of the lesbian" through the term "tomboy" as deployed by anthropologist Martin Manalansan. According to Otálvaro-Hormillosa, Manalansan inadequately addresses queer Pinays, tomboys, and butches and she critiques him for his "brief derogatory mentions" of Filipina lesbians.[31] Through her critique, Otálvaro-Hormillosa attempts to underscore the "[power] differences between men and women." That is, she respectively equates baklas and tomboys with manhood and womanhood/lesbianism in an immigrant and diasporic context (the United States.). Unlike the previously mentioned accounts, Otálvaro-Hormillosa does not foreground class as a significant marker of tomboy-ness. Instead, she emphasizes woman-ness and diasporic or immigrant queer positionality as the clear central markers of difference in how she deploys and translates tomboy. Although Otálvaro-Hormillosa cites Michael Tan, cautioning, "It is dangerous to transport Western terms onto sexual practices and identities," she seems to do just that by unequivocally equating tomboy-ness with lesbianism and womanhood in her essay. This indicates how notions of lesbianism may get universally transposed.

An alternative reading of Otálvaro-Hormillosa may also suggest, however, that through transculturation, she seeks to highlight a racialized queer Pinay/Filipina American framework, suggesting that queer Pinays in the diaspora deploy tomboy to refer precisely to *Filipina* butches, lesbians, dykes, and/or queers in a U.S. or North American context. In other words, in a diasporic space Otálvaro-Hormillosa seeks to locally rework, translate, and "Filipina-ize" terms, ideologies, and formations that regularly circulate globally (woman-ness and lesbianism). In this different geopolitical location (in the United States, outside of the Philippines) Otálvaro-Hormillosa clearly underscores a queer lesbian Pinay feminist or "peminist"[32] perspective. This is dissimilar to mainstream Filipina feminist notions in the Philippines, which suggest that tomboys are generally *not* feminist or even antifeminist. While articulating a clear feminist perspective that highlights gender and power differences in the diaspora, Otálvaro-Hormillosa sidelines class as an axis of difference that intersects with race, sex/gender, sexuality, nationality, and location, in a coconstitutive nexus.

What published Filipina feminist analyses situated on both sides of the Pacific have in common is that both often use gender essentialist notions of tomboy. That is, queer Pinay feminists in the United States such as Otálvaro-Hormillosa or Filipina lesbian feminists such as those working for ICWFW in Manila suggest that tomboys are unequivocally women or lesbians. This reading seems to occur because "biological sex" is seen or constructed as a binary (male and female) with fixed or corresponding genders, for example, female = woman = lesbian. This kind of interpretation is reflected, for example, in Amelia M. de Guzman and Irene R. Chia's report on "working-class lesbians in the Philippines" for ICWFW. de Guzman and Chia conducted lengthy interviews with nine tomboys (my term, not the ICWFW researchers') in Manila. Based on the interviews, their oral history project documents topics such as when tomboys "discovered they were lesbians," their employment histories, their recreational habits, their butch-femme relationships, and their religious practices. Throughout their analysis, de Guzman and Chia primarily use the term "lesbian" to describe the research participants, although admitting that, "a unique element that [they] noticed among the participants is their hesitation to say the word lesbian."[33] At another point in their report, de Guzman and Chia write, "All of them said that they like acting like men. They actually want to become men."[34] In my reading of de Guzman and Chia, they seek to advance a Filipina lesbian feminist agenda by applying the term "lesbian" to poor and working-class tomboys who are clearly uncomfortable with lesbian/woman as an identity and in some cases articulate a desire to become men or the reality that they are already living as males/men/lalaki. The tomboys in their study resist a lesbian feminist narrative, subsequently disrupting the correspondence between "biological sex" and gender and notions of fixed and essentialist racialized and classed sex/gender identities.

As a result of how class intersects with Filipino tomboy formations, as well as my own particular embodiment, in Philippine contexts at different moments during fieldwork in ports, on ships, and at sea, the concept of being poor or working class as central to tomboy inspired and produced unstable readings of what my particular embodiment of masculinity meant to others during fieldwork. On any given day in Manila (in different settings), Manileños interpreted my subject-position and embodiment in multifarious ways, for example, as "male," "female," "man," "woman" "bakla," and/or "tomboy." They also identified how these sex, gender, and sexual formations intersect with race, nationality, and/or class background: namely, "Filipino/a" "balikbayan,"[35] "overseas Filipino/a workers (OFWs)," "Japanese," "Chinese," and/or "Korean."[36] But significantly, when I traveled in and through the port area, if I introduced and represented myself as a student researcher (at the time) originally from Malolos, Bulakan, where I was born, my hometown and province in the Philippines, and conversed in Tagalog, Filipino seamen generally interpreted my masculinity and lalaki-ness as tomboy and interacted with me as a masculine/male/lalaki subject. Their reactions to my "local-ness" indicate that the Filipino seamen I encountered also understood tomboy formations in classed ways, namely that tomboys are locally situated, poor, and/or working class. Their reading of me as a transgender tomboy/lalaki and their general understanding of tomboy formations were reinforced if I expressed a working-class sensibility and/or personal genealogy. For example, if I mentioned that I traveled by jeepney (which as I said earlier, I chose to ride regularly during fieldwork to precisely move in working-class spaces of the city) from Quezon City to the port or Ermita (a neighborhood in Manila where lots of seamen congregate) rather than taking a taxi or driving a car, which from some seamen's perspectives is what middle-class, wealthy, or balikbayan Filipinos might use for local transportation, they interacted with me as a transgender tomboy/lalaki. In other cases, if I revealed my family's humble roots in Malolos, or that one of my male cousins was a seaman, or that a female cousin migrated to Kuwait as an OFW, or that an uncle migrated to "Saudi" (Arabia) and lived and worked there for many years, these kinds of personal disclosures marked my genealogy and family, and hence me as being more working class, perhaps middle class, but certainly not elite. This revelation reinforced seamen's understandings of tomboy masculinities, which helped them to "locate" my positionality and interact with me in terms of these logics. In contrast, if I introduced other aspects of identity formation, for example, that I was from the United States, a balikbayan, and an academic, three axes of difference that in the Philippines suggests class privilege, working-class seamen were more apt to interact with me as a "woman." If this occurred, I was moved or pushed to contextualize or situate my tomboy-ness (and lalaki-ness) by deepening conversations that highlighted my family's poor and working-class origins. Once I demonstrated an intelligible and locally informed working-class sensibility, my presence elicited seamen's memories, stories, and thoughts about tomboys. The previous discussion of ethnographic encounters and conversations in port(s) between Filipino seamen and me speak to this point.

In sum, the seamen's stories and memories speak of overlapping and shared social spaces from and through childhood, youth, kinship/family ties, and friendships where different kinds of Filipino masculinities/manhoods/lalaki-ness are cocreated, coproduced, and coexperienced. The seamen's narratives as a whole strongly suggest that Filipino tomboy masculinities/manhoods/lalaki-ness can be, indeed, *are a part of,* Filipino heterosexual male masculinities/manhoods/lalaki-ness and vice versa. That is, some heterosexual Filipino men grow up alongside tomboys, and some tomboys develop meaningful friendships and kinship ties with "bio-boys" and "bio-men" (terms often used in queer and transgender communities in the United States to describe people born as normatively or anatomically "male").

Seamen's commentaries about friendships and family ties with tomboys also collectively reveal an important component of Filipino masculinities/manhoods/lalaki-ness: the ability to emotionally connect and create "one-ness" with each other, understood in Tagalog as "pakikiisa." In a late 1980s Philippines-based ethnographic study, Jane Margold reports that, "masculinity that seeks intimacy and a feeling of trust and oneness with another is a highly desirable state (pakikiisa) (for Ilokanos, a major ethnic group in Northern Luzon in the Philippines)."[37] Critiquing dominant frameworks that define masculinities through processes of "emotional repression and detachment" and that posit the "Filipino man as absolutely macho or patriarchal," Margold emphasizes, instead, *emotional intimacy* between Filipino men and "more fluid [and] contingent gender identities."[38] The Ilokano overseas migrant men in Margold's study created and enhanced pakikiisa through barkadas (friendship groups), which enabled them to endure oppressive social conditions, where employers referred to them as "tools, slaves, and dogs" and where the threat of Arab/employer violence loomed large. Not confined to just males/men/lalaki, pakikiisa as a broader cultural concept stresses the goal of creating "emotional one-ness" through the group, not masculinist individualism, intragroup hierarchies, social competition, and violence, which patriarchal European-based notions of dominant masculinities and "male social bonding" have historically reinforced. Indeed, as sociologist and masculinities studies scholar R. W. Connell writes, "European/American masculinities [are] deeply implicated in the world-wide violence through which European/American culture became dominant."[39]

In contradistinction, situated in Philippine contexts and cultural logics, pakikiisa emphasizes group or collective equality and emotional collaboration, which is directly suggested in pakikiisa's composite parts. Sikolohiyang Pilipino (indigenous Filipino psychology) scholar Virgilio G. Enriquez defines the prefix "paki-pakiki" as "prefix nouns to denote shared humanity/favor/sympathetic sharing/rapport/cooperation."[40] Similarly, Pilipino[41] language studies specialist Teresita V. Ramos writes, "The prefix 'paki' is roughly equivalent to the English word 'please.'. . . The topic or focus of the *paki*-verb may be any semantic element *other than the actor,* such as the object or goal [in this case, "isa-ness" or one-ness is the goal or pakikiisa]. . . . [In other words], the actor of a *paki*-verb. . . is always in a non-focus" [emphasis added].[42] Since paki- and pakiki- refer to a polite request to meet a collective goal, that is, "please collaborate with me to create a sense of emotional one-ness," and *not* a command, pakikiisa suggests that group members value equality and interdependence within the group, which is collectively striving to reach the common goal of isa (emotional one-ness). This collective interdependency continues to suggest the importance of kapwa solidarity (shared identity or unity between self and others discussed in chapter 2) in Filipino/a contexts, as the object or goal, *not individual actors,* is the group's primary focus. That is, pakikiisa suggests that the self or personal ego is subordinate to the group's overall well-being. Although Margold is specifically referring to Ilokanos, her arguments are applicable to other Filipino lowlanders, such as the Tagalogs and Visayans I encountered during fieldwork. This is particularly the case since pakikiisa is defined as a Tagalog word, not Ilokano. In seamen's commentaries, they evoke and remember stories of love, loss, brotherhood, and camaraderie with tomboy cousins, friends, and older relatives, demonstrating how working-class Filipino (sea)men and tomboys cocreate masculinities/manhoods/lalaki-ness through pakikiisa.

Like the working-class Filipino seamen I encountered through traveling fieldwork, I also began to think about moments of pakikiisa with other Filipino males/men/tomboys. Traveling fieldwork encounters with Filipino seamen in Manila, in Oakland, and at sea transported me to memories of earlier balikbayan travel where heterogeneous masculinities (e.g., working-class, straight, tomboy, local, balikbayan, immigrant, Filipino, and Filipino American) coexisted. In the following section, I use a combination of ethnographic description, travelogue, and personal reflection to show another example of how heterogeneous Filipino masculinities/manhoods/lalaki-ness are cocreated through transportation, seafaring, and immigrant, balikbayan, and/or OFW mobilities.

Sunday Cockfights (at Sea and in Malolos, Bulakan, Philippines)

It's early evening on a Sunday on the *Penang Prince,* after a mostly blue sky day at sea. I am on board the *Prince* as a passenger-ethnographer and have been on board for almost two weeks. (See chapter 3 for an introduction to the *Prince*'s Oakland to Hong Kong transpacific voyage.) The sun is beginning its descent into the sea and its always receding horizon. Electric orange light leaks through a few hazy clouds. The five Filipino seamen working on board the *Prince* invited me to join them in the officers' recreation room this early evening to watch cockfights recorded on VCD that one of them purchased in Singapore. When I arrive at the gathering, I notice that the second mate ("Max") has a bottle of Russian vodka and some boxed orange juice, while the chief cook ("Yoyoy") shares small pieces of beef that were marinated in adobo sauce (soy sauce, garlic, vinegar, and bay leaves) and then baked. My contribution to the group is some Carlsberg beer purchased from the captain's store.

Sunday cockfights take me back to my father's mother, lola (Grandmother) Chayong, a small, quiet, and kind woman who in the 1970s ran a food stall at the Malolos Municipal Cockfighting Arena in Bulakan Province. Fortunately for me, my parents'/grandmother's modest home was located directly across from the sabongan (cockfighting arena). As a nine-year-old balikbayan child in 1977, I recall traveling to the Philippines, the cooking frenzy before the cockfights, and then actually watching cockfights with my uncles ("E" and "B") and their tomboy friend ("Jo-Jo"). On Saturday night, my grandmothers, aunts, older female cousins cooked foods such as bibingka (cassava cake) and ube (sweetened purple yam), and on Sunday morning, they prepared the ingredients for Pancit Lug-Lug, a Central Luzon noodle dish that was my lola's specialty.

All of the action occurred in the kitchen in the morning, but once the cockfights were about to begin, the action moved across the street. On this particular balikbayan trip Tito (Uncle) E and B (then in their mid to late twenties), plus Tito B's tomboy friend, Jo-Jo, who lived in my father's barrio (neighborhood) brought me to watch the cockfights in the upper stands. There, I listened to and observed my uncles and Jo-Jo yelling and placing bets across our section of the arena, the absolute quiet of the place just before the gamecocks clashed, and the crowd's eruption into thunderous cheering and more yelling as one of the gamecocks cut into his opponent's body with a knife attached to one of his ankles, drawing first blood. Later, some of the losing cocks were butchered near my lola's eatery.

On the ship, the cockfights are much more subdued compared with my childhood immigrant and balikbayan experiences despite the alcohol we've been drinking; there are only six of us, after all. As the VCD plays on the TV screen, the seamen size up the gamecocks, offering commentary on the cock's overall appearance, noting features like feather color, relative size, personality, and demeanor (e.g., "That one's a beauty; that one's ugly. This cock looks mean; that cock looks cowardly.") On board the *Prince,* no one gambles with real money, only fantasy greenbacks: the third mate bets one million dollars on the large off-white cock, and the electrician prefers the spotted brown one. The second mate bets five million dollars on the indigo ink–colored cock with the orange and white plume feathers; I agree to root for its opponent. We are captivated with each cockfight, which lasts a few minutes or longer. The fights happen in quick succession because we are watching a cockfighting derby in which many elite fighting cocks battled each other at Araneta Coliseum in Metro Manila several months ago. We produce a similar stillness that happens in live cockfights and the eruption of noise as the gamecocks clash! The Filipino seamen and I are yelling and swearing as the fights develop: Ang ganda! (How beautiful!) Sige! (Go on!) Puta! (Whore! When their chosen cocks are slashed or lose.) Naku, patay na ang manok! (Wow, the chicken is dead!) Ang bilis! (How fast [the gamecock lost]!) The third mate excited, yells at me: "Mas maganda ito kay sa World Cup, di ba?!" (This is more beautiful than the World Cup, right?!) (The 2006 World Cup soccer tournament was concluding on the voyage. While the German seamen intensely followed the tournament through satellite reports, Filipino seamen had little interest in this event.)

What these Sunday cockfights show is that there are clearly spaces where different kinds of male/masculine/lalaki subjects (here, working-class Filipino straight men and an immigrant Filipino American tomboy) coexist and cocreate masculinities/manhoods/lalaki-ness in and through seafaring, transportation, and travel, specifically through OFW/immigrant/balikbayan mobilities centered in key masculine social spaces (e.g., seafaring and cockfights). As a result of interacting with one another, heterogeneous Filipino masculinities/manhoods/lalaki-ness participate in and coconstitute different Filipino sex/gender formations. This is *not* to say that heterogeneous (including queer, transgender, and/or tomboy) masculinities/manhood/lalaki-ness are created only through practices of mobility and movement *outside* of the nation-state or "homeland" or primarily in the diaspora. Indeed, my first experiences of masculine/manly/lalaking pakikiisa happened precisely in a "local space" (Malolos). In making this clarification, as stated previously, I aim to dialogue with critiques and concerns raised in Asia where queer studies scholars and activists situated in this region (Asia) suggest that queer (United States) diaspora perspectives have become hegemonic (or even colonial), rendering local/regional queer and Asian sex/gender formations and geographies as "less queer," "more normative," and/or "more traditional."[43] These important knowledge/power critiques situated in Asia are critical to keep in mind as queer studies scholars and activists situated in the United States or Global North dialogue and debate with colleagues, friends, and activists situated in Asia and/or the Global South. Seamen's narratives illustrate that heterogeneous, queer, transgender, and/or tomboy masculinities/manhoods/lalaki-ness are precisely produced in various local, regional, transnational, and global nexuses (e.g., Malolos, Manila, Oakland, and Philippines/United States/Southeast Asia/Pacific Rim), not only in Global North, U.S., or diasporic contexts. As stated previously, although I am invested in understanding queer/transgender/non-normative racialized and classed sexes, genders, and sexualities as they are locally, regionally, transnationally, and globally *rooted in Asia,* I am also committed to showing how heterogeneous masculinities and manhoods (straight, tomboy, queer, transgender) are also coproduced through transit and transport—*via routes in and out of Asia.*

Cross culturally, cockfights have been largely interpreted as purely "men's spaces" where dominant masculinities and manhoods are reproduced. This has been especially true in island Southeast Asian Studies since anthropologist Clifford Geertz's watershed essay "Deep Play: Notes on the Balinese Cockfight" has been required anthropological reading in many anthropology departments (as well as in some gender studies departments or programs). In and through Geertz's widely acclaimed cultural interpretation, the Balinese cockfight has become the signifier par excellence of "(Balinese) men and masculinity." This coupling of maleness at birth with masculinity, however, is linked through essentialist notions that equate biology, anatomy, and sex with gender rather than acknowledging that sex and gender are produced through bodily practices, identifications, and stylized performances. In other words, bodies, sexes/genders are contingent and can be produced through identification, bodily practices, and/or performativity, and thus are not necessarily produced through gendered notions of biology, anatomy, or "sexed" bodies at birth. At the same time (as Judith Butler and others reminds us), we have to remain mindful of various social contexts and institutions that potentially/regularly restrict non-normative gender acts.[44] Although Geertz writes a complex and informative "thick description" of Balinese cockfighting, he narrativizes the cockfights as an absolute male/men's space, missing the ways that women participate on the sidelines of the cockfights through the selling of food, drinks, and admission tickets.[45] It is also quite probable that with this kind of understanding of sex/gender, masculinity/maleness/manhood, he may have entirely missed the Indonesian fe/male men or tombois (as well as children) who may have been watching the cockfights with other males, boys, men, or adult relatives. In December 2008, I went to the cockfights in Malolos with a tomboy second cousin named "V," and I was reminded of this point again as V and I were *not* the only tomboys watching in the stands (we noticed four other tomboys seated in different parts of the cockfighting arena). When I asked V why there weren't more, he said, "Siguro, walang pera." (Probably, they don't have money.) V explained that tomboys (and other men) need money to gamble at the cockfights and since we were at the cockfighting arena during Christmas season, any extra money a tomboy had probably went to gifts for family and friends. (Indeed, V felt a little guilty about gambling away 3,000 pesos [about $60], the Sunday we went to watch the cockfights.) V's explanation also speaks to the way that class and economic access intersect with gender/masculinity/manhood/lalaki-ness, affecting such things as participation at the cockfights, an important site of masculinity/manhood/lalaki-ness production in the Philippines.

In light of the potential gaps in Geertz's interpretation, what at first appears to be a highly normative "heterosexual men's space" (Filipino seamen at sea/watching cockfights) can thus also be read and interpreted through a queer, transgender, transnational/transPacific, and immigrant Filipino American logics if the presence of alternative male/masculinity/lalaki formations—tomboys—are taken into account. In addition, if the intimate relationalities and proximities among and between working-class heterosexual Filipino masculinities/manhoods/lalaki-ness and Filipino transgendered masculinities/manhoods/lalaki-ness and the concept of pakikiisa are treated seriously, an entirely different cultural reading or ethnographic analysis of the scene can be developed.

Instead of seeing a closed, watertight, and dominant Filipino seamen's masculinity and manhood, strongly reinforced by a normative heterosexual reading of cocks (in both senses of this word) and cockfighting (i.e., Geertz's cultural interpretation and the Philippine state's), heterosexual and *transgender* tomboys actually have access to the symbolic meanings and material realities of cockfighting, game/cocks, and/or the phallus. This illustrates the way in which Filipino masculinities/manhoods/lalaki-ness are contingent, fluid, and not naturalized or limited by biology or the body. This dynamic coproduction of and interplay between masculinities/manhoods/lalaki-ness were not only evident through the cockfighting experience, but throughout my fieldwork time on the *Prince*. Filipino seamen during the transpacific voyage engaged a more transgender understanding of Filipino tomboy masculinities and lalaki-ness. As such, the working-class Filipino seamen on board the *Prince* never used the word "lesbian" (the dominant reading in Filipina lesbian/feminist discussions) and like many of the seamen who shared tomboy commentaries at the Ports of Manila and Oakland, they used the term "tomboy" to describe masculine fe/male Filipinos who are guy/male-like (lalaking-lalaki) or those actually living as males/men/lalaki.

An example that further illustrates this point is when Yoyoy (the chief cook on the Prince) told Max in the galley that we (Yoyoy and I) were going to arrange a fake marriage, so that Yoyoy could immigrate to the United States. Yoyoy explained, "Eh, lalaki naman siya (gesturing toward me) kaya o.k. kung mayroon akong girlfriend, o.k. rin kung mayroon siyang ibang girlfriend." (Well, he/Kale is a male/man/boy/guy, so it's OK if I have a girlfriend, it's also OK if he/Kale has [another] girlfriend.) This exchange reveals that although immigration officials would probably read Yoyoy and me as a (married) "man" and "woman" (especially if I was in feminine drag!), Yoyoy understood tomboy-ness not as a form of womanhood or female-ness as some Filipina lesbian/feminists have suggested, but rather as an embodiment of lalaki that is commensurate with his larger, fluid notion of maleness/manhood/masculinity/lalaki-ness. With this inclusive perspective and epistemological understanding, the Filipino seamen on the *Prince* and I shared activities that many Filipino males/men/tomboys/lalaki share in the Philippines, which other seamen substantiated during other conversations in port, on ships, or at sea. We drank liquor and beers, ate pulutan (the food that goes well with alcoholic beverages), talked with each other about sweethearts and lovers (in their case, also wives), discussed relationship and family dramas, sang Tagalog songs available on karaoke

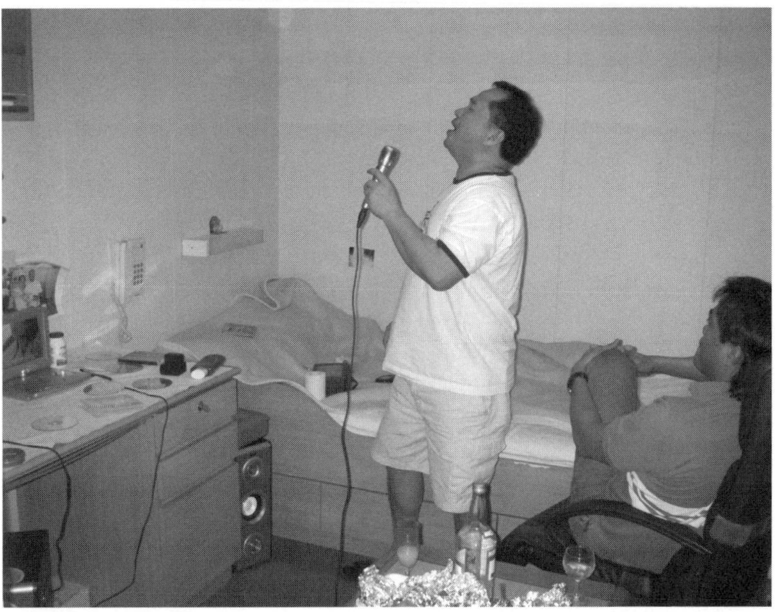

Filipino chief cook singing karaoke in his cabin with Filipino seamen and the author.

VCDs that projected soft pornographic imagery, cheered Filipino boxing champion Manny Pacquiao[46] as we viewed his fights on VCD, and we also watched sabong (cockfighting) on a Sunday.

The ethnographic vignette also reveals how watching cockfights on the ship with the five Filipino seamen clearly transported me to another time/place through memories, evoking past experiences of pakikiisa with other men and relatives in the Philippines (e.g., Uncles E and B and their tomboy friend Jo-Jo). My own immigrant and balikbayan experiences as a young tomboy and later as an adult, participating in Sunday family rituals and watching sabong, reflects many of the seamen's stories from ports and the sea: Filipino fe/males/men/tomboys/lalaki, young and old, spending time together as friends, family, companions, and neighbors cocreating heterogeneous masculinities/manhoods and memorable moments of pakikiisa.

Avast: To Cease Hauling; to Stop (Conclusion)

Filipino seamen's heterogeneous masculinities/manhoods, their memories, and commentaries about tomboy relatives and friends, and the transpacific autoethnographic travelogue and cultural analysis presented in this chapter (and in other chapters of this book) articulate clear counternarratives and alternative "gender realities" (to use Judith Butler's phrase) to U.S. and Japanese colonial, imperialist, capitalist, and misogynistic discourses, which seek to construct the Philippines and Filipino/a peoples as disempowered or feminized victims without agency, discourses, which at the end of the twentieth and beginning of the twenty-first century unfortunately remain persistent. (See the discussion of feminizing discourses of Filipino/as and the Philippines in the introduction and chapter 1 of this book.) Filipino seamen, and now potentially Filipino tomboys/lalaki, provide masculine fe/male alternatives to the figure of the Filipina domestic helper, "prostitute," and/or "mail-order bride," through which to imagine the nation and Filipino (global) migrant labor. However, rather than uncritically naturalizing or celebrating closed and essentialist heteronormative Filipino masculinities/manhoods and understandings of sea-based migration and globalization (the Philippine state's impulse and the state's social/political agenda), in contrast, "Transportation" (this chapter) and *Filipino Crosscurrents* (this book) stress how heterogeneous masculinities/manhoods/lalaki-ness—dominant/state; situated ashore and away; "the heroes" and "the deserters," conventional and tomboy; elite, poor, and working class; migrant, seafarer (OFW), immigrant, balikbayan, and Filipino/Filipino American—are culturally constructed, personally/socially identified or contextualized, performed, and clearly contingent.

Moreover, through transportation and crosscurrents as a theoretical and ethnographic framework that emphasizes the importance of transnational, translocal, transgender cultural logics and cultural memory in anthropological interpretation, as well as transportation, seafaring, and immigrant travel as a key ethnographic practice, this chapter further demonstrates that there are alternative itineraries and trajectories to queer and trans (both as a verb and a noun) in queer studies, masculinity studies, Philippine Studies, Filipino/a American Studies, Asian American Studies, and postcolonial studies. That is, rather than privileging queer sexuality (a common approach in mainstream/European-based lesbian, gay, bisexual, trangender, queer (LGBTQ) studies) or heterosexuality (a foundational approach in Asian American Studies, Philippine Studies, and Filipino/a American Studies), this chapter documents and engages an alternatively queered and "trans-ed" sea-based trajectory, and sex/gender identifications, routed through the nexus of Filipino/a globalization, migration, immigration, and transportation routed in and out of Manila, Oakland, Malolos, Hong Kong, Southeast Asia, and the Northern Pacific Ocean. In doing so, this chapter also shows how projects, which may initially read as "straight" or heteronormative can be queered and trans-ed through closer ethnographic attention to the cultural dynamics of encounter(s); researchers' positionalities, subjectivities, and memories; and by engaging a hybrid interdisciplinary and ethnographic writing style.

In closing, my encounters and conversations with Filipino seamen in ports and on ships, Filipino seamen's memories and commentaries, and my autoethnographic travelogue and analysis clearly illustrate the intimate relationalities and proximities between Filipino seamen and Filipino tomboys. As such, my analysis significantly contradicts and challenges closed and conservative heteronormative notions of Filipino maritime and migrant masculinities and manhoods. Just as importantly, this chapter debates essentialist Filipina/Filipina American lesbian/feminist conceptualizations and narratives of Filipino tomboys as primarily or absolutely female, women, and/or lesbians. In marked difference, I focus and develop a transgender, transnational/transpacific translation of Filipino tomboys, focusing on the connections, fluidities, and sense of oneness (pakikiisa) among and between conventional and alternative Filipino masculinities/manhoods/lalaki-ness. Significantly, this chapter also begins to ethnographically theorize Filipino tomboys as embodiments, identifications, and formations of Filipino masculinities/manhoods/lalaki-ness through an analytical collage that illustrates the importance of addressing the geotemporal place-moments where differently situated Filipino masculinities/manhoods/and lalaki-ness cometogether, contradicting, reinforcing, and/or creating unity among and between each other.

Yes, cockfights at sea are more beautiful than the World Cup.

EPILOGUE

Decolonizing Filipino Masculinities

It is a cold (20°F) and clear early February morning when I begin writing this epilogue. After several days of light snowfall, the South Minneapolis cityscape is covered again by white powder. Is this poetic in/justice that my task is to put closure on this book as I am literally situated in the middle of the North American continent, far removed from the sea? (This is a first reading of place, location, and water; my second reading comes shortly.)

The sea has been speaking to me since childhood (see preface) and still it reaches and finds me across great expanses of terrain, touching me through dreams. One night in Minneapolis, I dream of brown and black island-people living on a seashore. A glassy sea-green sea, probably warm, rolls gently near their beach. This is not a sea of storms or baguios (typhoons), but rather the calm, no whitecaps for miles kind of sea. A lake-like sea. The dream/water scene changes, and the sea now flows like a river, running horizontally across and away from me as I stand on a different shore. The water rushes by quickly, but its force is not scary because although moving rapidly at first, the waters eventually slow down, freezing and finally stopping, frozen in their tracks, resulting in what looks like a frozen Minnehaha Waterfalls turned on its side. (Minnehaha Falls is a famous water feature [fifty-three feet in height] located in South Minneapolis that freezes solid during our cold and usually long winters.)

And so it would seem that a frozen sea suggests a *momentary* stopping point, an apt metaphor for this epilogue. For while the sea freezes in my dreams and while *areas* of Minnesota's great inland sea, Lake Superior (part of the Great Lakes [water-based] border between Canada and the United States), as well as the Mississippi River (which runs through Minneapolis and St. Paul) also freeze in winter, seas generally move freely in non-subarctic or arctic latitudes, flowing, churning, and traveling, creating the various marine currents and weather systems of the world.[1] And although it seems unlikely on a cold February morning in Minnesota that the Superior [inland] Sea and "Big

River" (Mississippi's nickname) will eventually thaw and move again, I know in time, ice will melt. I, therefore, offer this epilogue as a way to update readers on the current status of neoliberal globalization, maritime migration, and masculinities in Philippine, diasporic, and postcolonial contexts. Equally important, this epilogue is not intended as an academic exercise to conclude or foreclose future conversations, scholarly debate, or activist work, but rather my hope is that in this concluding chapter, space is opened up further for other lines of inquiry and dialogue about these intertwined economic and cultural phenomena (seafaring, masculinities, and globalization).

On January 1, 2010, the China-ASEAN (Association of Southeast Asian Nations) (CAFTA) took effect, creating a regional duty-free zone (for 7,000 products) between China and six founding ASEAN countries (Philippines, Indonesia, Singapore, Thailand, Malaysia, and Brunei). By 2015, Vietnam, Laos, Cambodia, and Myanmar are expected to also join CAFTA. With China's "major (economic) engine," importing ASEAN commodities and products, CAFTA's promoters say it will pull ASEAN out of the economic "doldrums" resulting from the global economic recession that started in 2008.[2] In an op-ed, Walden Bello uses a railroad metaphor to describe CAFTA's neoliberal and "free trade" capitalist logics advanced by politicians and economists in Beijing and Manila. He writes, "[Beijing and Malacañang Palace/President Macapagal Arroyo] suggest that it is like "a Chinese locomotive pulling the rest of East [and Southeast] Asia along with it on a fast track to economic nirvana."[3] This trope of transportation resonates with past boating, sailing, and shipping metaphors and imaginaries deployed in Manila a decade earlier, discourses used, for example, to justify the privatization of a maritime port and free trade zone at the Manila Harbour Centre (see chapter 1). However, instead of sailing on a neoliberal yacht in Manila Bay with the hopes that Manila develop into a "global city" in an era of expanding free trade and economic globalization, building on Bello's observation and economic critique, I suggest that CAFTA relies on what I would call China's "tugboat diplomacy" or its economic (as well as military) power and potentials to drag all ASEAN craft (or nations) out of a twenty-first century global capitalist recession and crisis. The Macapagal Arroyo administration's support of CAFTA also illustrates that although presidents and administrations change (or are toppled) through the years at Malacañang Palace, the Philippine state's neoliberal economic and political orientation has not significantly changed. In fact, this orientation is more entrenched than ever.

Not surprisingly, at the same time, the Philippine state also continues to expand and deepen its economic dependency on overseas global migration policies and overseas Fillipino/a workers remittances (including those sent by Filipino seamen). As recent Philippine Overseas Employment Agency (POEA) OFW statistics show, since the early years of my fieldwork, there has been a steady increase in the number people who participate in sea-based migration. In 1998, 193,300 Filipino seafarers worked in maritime industries.[4] Ten years later, 261,614 Filipino/a sea-based migrants (98 percent male and 2 percent female) worked worldwide.[5] Proud of the Philippines's *dependency* on OFW remittances, President Macapagal Arroyo (on her Facebook profile) wrote that the Philippines is doing relatively well (economically) due its "rely[ing] heavily on remittances sent home by overseas Filipino workers, numbering a fourth of the country's workforce."[6] Reporting a more detailed accounting of OFW remittances, 2008 POEA records (the latest data available to me when I wrote this epilogue) show that Filipino/a *sea-based* migrants remitted $3,034,553 of the $16,426,854 "grand total" that all OFWs remitted to the Philippines (the maritime sector's monthly remittance average was $1,368,905 for that year[7]). These employment and remittance figures, as well as Macapagal Arroyo's Facebook boasting suggest that the Philippine state and its private sector partners (e.g., overseas employment manning agencies and multinational shipping companies) have been successful in promoting and advancing the buying and selling of Filipino seamen's labor in the global shipping industry and other maritime transportation industries.[8]

Just as telling, even with the high number of piracy incidents, hijackings, and kidnappings off of the East African coast and the Philippine Foreign Affairs Secretary Alberto Romulo's suggestion to the POEA that Filipino seafarers be *disallowed* on vessels that sail in this specific region (due to the extreme dangers posed to Filipino seamen), the POEA *rejected* Romulo's recommendation.[9] Rather than protect Filipino workers, the state agency created a program that included "double pay" for seamen who travel and work in the piracy- and kidnapping-prone region. John Leonard Monterona, the Saudi Arabia-based Middle East coordinator for *Migrante* (a nongovernmental organization that advocates on behalf of Filipino/a migrants in the region) countered that, "The double hazard pay scheme is simply saying 'Welcome aboard, Filipino seafarers; let all of you be kidnapped but what we need are your precious remittances.'"[10]

And so, while Macapagal Arroyo infamously wined and dined in Manhattan, spending $20,000 at Le Cirque on August 2, 2009, and spending $15,000 at Bobby Van's Steakhouse in Washington, DC on July 30, 2009, OFWs and Filipino/a immigrants around the world worked and labored, subsequently remitting billions of U.S. dollars to the Philippines.

In the end, OFWs and immigrants supported local families and communities, but they also subsidized extravagant presidential trips abroad and foreign debt repayments previously discussed in this book.

Just as it is important to understand how the broader context and politics of Filipino/a global migration has *not* significantly changed in the last decade, it is important to note that the feminization of Filipino/a labor and migration has continued during the early years of the twenty-first century. Journalist Beverly T. Natividad, reporting for *The Inquirer* (based in Manila) writes that recent government reports for 2000 to 2005 indicated that *70 percent* of OFWs deployed overseas were female and female OFWs dominated seven of the top ten country destinations for OFWs.[11] Natividad outlines a few examples from around the world culled from the "State of the Philippine Population Report": 93 percent of OFWs in Hong Kong were [female] domestic workers, while in Kuwait and Japan, they represented 74 percent of all OFWs.[12] These data suggest further that the POEA has continued to promote and advance the buying and selling of women OFW's domestic, reproductive, and sexual labor. As such, it remains important to engage the feminization of labor and migration (discussed in the introduction of this book). Again, because of the racialized and classed feminization of Filipino/as in regional, international, and global scales and relationships, it remains equally important to critically explore and analyze how Filipino migrant masculinities/manhoods are precisely constructed, imagined, and inscribed. In other words, the dialectic between femininities and masculinities remains an important cultural construct or tandem to explore and critique. As *Filipino Crosscurrents* shows, seafaring and shipping are important sites where Filipino masculinization, particularly through the figure of the seaman, is attempted, manipulated, naturalized, and reinforced in the context of feminization. Other Filipino masculinities (migrant and otherwise) need further attention. For example and to give two lines of possible/future inquiry related to maritime transportation industries unaddressed in this book: how are Filipino/a masculinities and femininities constructed through the cruise industry, where Filipino/as work as seafarers, cabin-cleaners, musicians, entertainers, bartenders, photographers, and waiters? How and why does the Philippine state deploy the racialized and classed gender formation of these sea-based workers in particular ways?

In terms of the research analyzed in this book, my participant-observation research and post-fieldwork analyses strongly reveal that Philippine state officials, corporate business leaders, and some Filipino seamen themselves continue to deploy and attempt to naturalize dominant narratives about Filipino seamen, particularly discourses that seek to highlight Filipino seamen's geographic and heterosexual mobility, heroic (bagong bayani) nationalism, heteronormative family values, and macho-ness. Although as I have acknowledged, components of this discourse are applicable to many Filipino seamen, rather than ethnographically consolidating, strengthening, or repeating this hetero-patriarchal understanding, imaginary, and discourse of Filipino seamen's masculinities, my focus in this book has been to develop a cultural critique of dominant narratives and ideologies about Filipino seafaring, maritime/migrant masculinities, and neoliberal globalization through situated traveling fieldwork that is highly attentive to and respectful of marginalized (maritime and migrant) Filipino masculinities.[13]

To do this in *Filipino Crosscurrents,* I articulated a postcolonial, decolonized, queer, and transnational ethnographic cultural critique, which emerged as a result of an ethnographic optic and approach (to fieldwork and writing) that questions, explores, and analyzes the gaps, contradictions, and contingencies in dominant discourses and ideologies of Filipino seafaring, seamen's masculinities, and globalization. Instead of offering a supposedly "neutral," "objective," or positivist analysis (anthropological strategies that have been heavily criticized in postmodern and postcolonial anthropology), I showed in *Filipino Crosscurrents* why it is important to highlight and create ethnographic spaces (in our fieldwork and in our books) for marginalized (i.e., postcolonial/decolonized, feminist, transnational, queer, transgender, and/or immigrant) ethnographic interpretations about Filipino/a migration, racialized and classed sex/genders, and globalized capitalism. As hegemonic discourses are powerful and powerfully supported by their very definition, articulating the aforementioned marginalized perspectives, discourse, and racialized and classed sex/genders remains an important strategy for anthropology, Asian American Studies, Filipino/a Studies, queer studies, and/or American Studies that aim to work *as cultural critique*. Doing so allows us to stress and develop postcolonial/decolonized, feminist, queer, and transgender/transnational optics and analyses that remain necessary in an age of neoliberal and neocolonial globalization.

In addition, my fieldwork observations and cultural close readings of the everyday practices and narratives of working-class Filipino seamen situated in Manila, in Oakland, and at sea; in the national contexts of the Philippines and the United States; in the regional contexts of Southeast Asia and Asia and the Pacific; and in the global economy ethnographically reveal how Philippine state officials and economic elites deploy Filipino maritime histories and figures to promote and advance neoliberal economics, globalized free trade schemes, and dependencies on foreign debts and OFW remittances. My analyses also address the way in which these political and economic processes are deeply implicated in exploitation, social inequalities, and injustice in the Philippines and in diaspora. Whereas these neoliberal and neocolonial nationalist ideological positions are vigorously deployed through hegemonic structures, institutions, and figures in the Philippines and diaspora(s), *Filipino Crosscurrents* emphasizes how Filipino seamen successfully navigate these complex national, regional, and global cultural politics and political economies, subsequently developing their own cultural critiques of capitalist globalization, overseas Filipino/a migration, Philippine neoliberalism and neocolonial nationalism, racism and classism in the global shipping industry, and the intersectionality of race, class, sex/gender, citizenship, and location.

In conavigating these dominant and marginal "currents," Filipino seamen persuasively suggest alternative postcolonial, decolonized, transnational, or diasporic possibilities for understanding, imagining, narrativizing, and embodying Filipino masculinities. Although I agree with sociologist Steven McKay when he cautions that not all Filipino/a diaspora masculinity formations are liberatory, at the same time and from my perspective, it is critical to acknowledge and underscore that there are clearly memorable and identifiable time-spaces when and where Filipino seamen articulate oppositional politics and cultural perspectives, enact oppositional everyday practices, and create oppositional racialized and classed masculinities, especially in relation to the Philippine state, neoliberal and neocolonial nationalism, and the racism and classism many of them experience(d) in the global shipping industry.[14] Because hegemonies are usually forceful and persuasive, I have chosen to precisely focus my "decolonized (ethnographic) eye(s)" (to use Filipino Studies scholar Sarita Echavez See's phrase) on marginalized Filipino maritime/migrant masculinities during fieldwork and in the writing of this book.[15]

I learned through my education with and in the ocean, as well as through fieldwork with Filipino seamen, that where marine currents meet or cross, some of the most abundant and dynamic sea life exists.[16] As a sailor-scholar, I have also learned that although the wind may be coming at you—directly and with great force—it is still possible to sail one's boat "close-hauled" and eventually reach one's desired destination with significant patience and practice. Like waters and winds, many of the Filipino seamen I met in Manila, in Oakland, and at sea teach us many lessons. Although the Philippines and the Filipino/a diaspora have experienced and endured centuries of colonialisms, neocolonialisms, neoimperialisms, and, in the last four decades, neoliberal and neocolonial nationalisms, my fieldwork and life experiences with Filipino/as situated in the Philippines and in diaspora (United States) reveal that working-class migrant and immigrant Filipino/as possess remarkable abilities to endure and thrive under extremely difficult social, economic, political, and cultural conditions. Certainly, as many of the Filipino seamen I had conversations with in Manila, Oakland, and at sea made clear to me over the years, in an era of economic globalization, state-promoted and -advanced overseas migration, and neoliberal and neocolonial Philippine nationalism, critically and creatively understanding and questioning dominant notions and practices of "Filipino/a-ness," especially racialized and classed genders articulated by the neoliberal state, remain vitally important. In doing so, Filipino seamen also creatively and courageously point to and create other time-spaces of solidarity, resistance, critical learning, teaching, and beauty.

Through their understanding and belief in indigenous Filipino/a concepts, practices, and emotional/spiritual states such as kapwa, lakas na loob, pakikiisa, and "the blues," as well as through a more inclusive understanding of lalaki-ness, working-class Filipino seamen stress that despite the extreme force of capitalist globalization, neoliberal and neocolonial nationalism, and the racism and classism many of them experience in the global economy, as well as the very real limitations and difficulties these social, economic, and historical processes pose and create, it is still possible, although not without a struggle, to offer and/or create alternative—decolonized—everyday practices and epistemologies of Filipino-ness and racialized and classed masculinities/manhoods/lalaki-ness. Working-class Filipino seamen and their maritime migrant and traveling work lives in ports and at sea, the practice and work of developing a decolonized ethnographic optic and narrative (through the writing of this book), and the art of sailing teach us that like currents in the sea, it is still possible—indeed, often preferable—to move, sail, live, think, read, relate, and/or write in an opposite, alternative, and/or queer/decolonized direction.[17]

ACKNOWLEDGMENTS

Creating *Filipino Crosscurrents* was a voyage I always wanted to take. Thank you to the many stars who steadfastly guided my way. First and foremost, in Manila, in Oakland, and at sea, maraming salamat po to the many Filipino seamen I was honored to meet. Thank you for your time, stories, and analyses about seafaring, shipping, migration, nationalism, and masculinities.

At the University of California, Santa Cruz, a heartfelt thank you goes to Nancy N. Chen (Anthropology), my advisor, for her important mentoring, for chairing my dissertation committee, and for her friendship over the years. Many thanks also go to Olga Nájera-Ramírez (Anthropology) and Neferti X. Tadiar (History of Consciousness) for their critical feedback and service on my dissertation committee. A special thanks to Neferti, whose scholarship inspired several components of my project. Neferti's important questions and smart critique greatly helped to improve this ethnography. Thank you also to Judy Yung (American Studies) for reading early chapter drafts.

Thanks and appreciation also go to my graduate school friends and colleagues at the University of California, Santa Cruz, especially those with whom I worked closely with through the Research Cluster for the Study of Women of Color in Conflict and Collaboration: Annie Laurie Anderson, Catriona Rueda Esquibel, Charla Ogaz, Darla Thompson, Darshan Campos, Deb Vargas, Isabel E. Velez, Ivelisse Rivera-Bonilla, Joanne Barker, J. Kehaulani Kauanui, Kianga Ford, Keta Miranda, Laura Kuo, Luz Calvo, and Maylei Blackwell. I owe a lot to this fierce crew of women of color who taught me how to organize, intellectually challenge, and dance salsa. A special mahalo nui loha to Kehaulani for giving me practical advice on how to finish the dissertation and, more importantly, for showing us all how it—plus more—can be done. A heartfelt thank you to Teresia Teaiwa, for sharing her love of Oceania and the Pacific Ocean, and her island and sea poetics and politics with me. Teresia taught me that just as there are many islands in Oceania, there are multiple ways to be an intellectual, teacher, artist, and seafarer. In the Anthropology Board, thank you to my friends and colleagues: Ulrika I. Dahl, Lieba Faier, Scott Morgensen, Debbie Klein, Nina Schnall, and Kate Spilde, and professors Lisa Rofel, Carolyn Martin Shaw, Ann Kingsolver, Triloki Pandey, Jacqueline Brown, Anna L. Tsing, and Shelly Errington. A special thank you to Lieba who intellectually engaged my work during key moments of writing, as well as to Lisa, Ann, and Carolyn for pushing my thinking and writing in their graduate seminars. Thank you also to Anna for her innovative scholarship on local/global questions and the politics of fieldwork, which inspired many of us at Santa Cruz. In the History of Consciousness Board, thank you to friends and colleagues Glenn Mimura, Maurice Stevens, and Aureliano De Soto, as well as Professor James Clifford. Professor Clifford's book *Routes* inspired lines of inquiry posed in *Filipino Crosscurrents*. Also in Santa Cruz, thank you to Jane Higashi, Sharon Yamanaka, Martha Duenas Baum, Jean Gier, Afia Walking Tree, and Winona for their friendship and support shared over the years.

In Manila, maraming salamat po to Dr. Alex Calata, Mrs. Gigi Dizon, and other staff and friends at the Philippine American Educational Foundation (PAEF), for supporting my dissertation fieldwork in the Philippines with a Fulbright-Hayes Dissertation Fellowship. Maraming salamat to Ida Mae Fernandez (now at the International Organization for Migration) for sharing important feminist insights and helping me to (re-) fall in love with Manila. Maraming Salamat po to my uncle and aunt, Noli and Sylvia Reyes, for inviting me into their home in Quezon City while I was resettling in Metro Manila. Maraming salamat po to Isabelo A. Samonte, Father Savino Bernardi, Nelson Ramirez, and Rolando Talampas for sharing their vast knowledge of Filipino seafaring.

In the San Francisco Bay Area, thank you to Paul Devine and Barry Binsky for the opportunity to do participant-observation research in Oakland. Thank you also to my friends and colleagues at Global Exchange, especially Executive Director Kirsten Moller, Mariana Bustamante, Michael O'Heaney, and Chie Abad. A special thanks goes to Michael for helping me with my writing. Thank you also to my friends and colleagues at the International Gay and Lesbian Human Rights Commission (IGLHRC), especially Executive Director Surina Khan and Daniel Lee, as well as friends and colleagues at the Asian and

Pacific Islander (A&PI) Wellness Center, especially Executive Director John Manzon-Santos, Javid Syed, Tita Aida, and Tatiana Kaneholani. Working at Global Exchange, IGLHRC, and the A&PI Wellness Center provided me with many opportunities to continue learning about race, class, gender, sexuality, and citizenship in local, regional, and global contexts. Friends in the queer/of color communities in the Bay Area also supported this project through their friendship and inspiration. Thank you to Jane Rabanal, Shaily Matani, Tina D'Elia, Margot Goldstein, Michelle Williams, Neeru Paharia, Alice Hom, Trinity Ordona, Desiree Thompson, Dana Ginn Paredes, Tei Okamoto, Saun-Toy Trotter, Phalla Sar, and Leslie Mah.

A heartfelt thank you also goes to Gayari Gopinath, Jack Halberstam, and ManChui Leung. Thank you to Gayatri and Jack for their friendship and mentoring while I lived in Oakland. Thank you to ManChui for believing in this project and me and for sharing a lot of love, beauty, and joy, which sustained me through crucial years of writing. This book simply would not have been possible without ManChui.

New friends and colleagues in Filipino/a Studies have also helped me to finish this book. Thank you to the many Filipino/a Studies scholars and writers who have inspired me through the years: Martin F. Manalansan IV, Nerissa S. Balce, Linda España-Maram, Allan Isaac, Rick Bonus, Robyn Rodriguez, Sarita See, Theo Gonzalves, Augusto Espiritu, Anna Gonzalez, Jody Blanco, Joe Ponce, Jeffrey Santa Ana, Richard Chu, Kimberly Alidio, Francisco Benitez, Dylan Rodriguez, Victor Roman Mendoza, Vernadette Gonzalez, Arlene De Vera, Victor Bascara, Jean Gier, R. Zamora Linmark, Gina Apostol, Rhacel Salazar Parreñas, Neferti X. Tadiar, Reynaldo Illeto, Vicente Rafael, Catherine Choy, Dorothy Fujita Rony, and Yen Le Espiritu. In the field of Asian American Studies, thank you to David Eng, Kandice Chuh, Gary Okihiro, Jack Tchen, Grace Kyungwon Hong, Lok Siu, and Isabelle Pelaud for their important scholarship.

At the San Diego Maritime Museum, thank you to Mark Allen for his editorial advice and for publishing an early version of chapter 2. At *GLQ: A Journal of Gay and Lesbian Studies*, many thanks go to Eithne Luibhhéid, Special Issues Editor, who patiently worked with me as I wrote and revised an early version of chapter 4. Eithne's editorial feedback significantly pushed my analysis in that essay and subsequent chapter. Thank you to the faculty and students in the Social and Cultural Analysis Department and the Asian/Pacific/American Studies Program at New York University, as well as the Ethnic Studies Department at the University of Hawai'i at Manoa, for inviting me to their campuses and for the opportunity to share drafts of chapter 4. A special thanks to Lisa Duggan for her important questions about (queer) femininities. Thank you also to friends and colleagues in the Ethnic Studies Department at the University of Oregon for inviting me to Eugene to think about globalization and intersectionality just as I was finishing the manuscript. Special thanks go to Lynn Fujiwara, Irmary Reyes-Santos, Michael Hames-Garcia, and Ernesto Martinez.

At the University of Minnesota, Twin Cities (UMNTC), thank you to my colleagues and friends in the Department of American Studies who supported this book project over the last five years: David Noble, Riv-Ellen Prell, Elaine May, Larry May, Brenda Child, Roderick Ferguson, Jennifer Pierce, Trica Keaton, Bianet Castellanos, and David Karjanen. Our department's interest in and support of transnational and intersectional approaches to globalization and migration have been extremely instrumental in shaping this book. A special thanks go to Rod and Elaine, my mentors in American Studies, who provided valuable advice, guidance, and wisdom. In the Asian American Studies Program at UMNTC, thank you to colleagues and friends, Josephine Lee, Jigna Desai, Erika Lee, Karen Ho, Rich Lee, Lisa Park, Teresa Toguchi Swartz, Yuichiro Onishi, and Mai Na M. Lee, all of whom supported this book project. Thank you also to other colleagues and friends working in different departments at Minnesota, especially Kevin Murphy, Dara Strolovitch, Regina Kunzel, David Valentine, Cindy Garcia, David Chang, Tracy Deutsch, Ananya Chatterjea, Maria Damon, Paula Rabinowitz, Jani Scandura, Richa Nagar, Qadri Ismael, and Ann Waltner. Thank you also to Minnesota graduate students who dialogued with me in classes and conferences, especially Elakshi Kumar, Ryan Murphy, Juliana Pegues, Doug Jensen, Tom Sarmiento, Ryan Cartwright, Pamela Butler, Michael David Franklin, Jasmine Tang, Jasmine Mitchell, Marion Traub-Werner, and Jeannie Shinozuka.

At the University of Minnesota Press, a heartfelt thank you to Executive Editor Richard Morrison, for taking this project seriously from the beginning, and for moving the manuscript and book along like an expert boatman. Thank you also to editorial assistants Adam Brunner and Erin Warholm-Wohlenhaus for greatly assisting me during the pre- and postproduction processes, as well as to all of the Press staff and consultants who assisted in copyediting, design, and other facets of the production process. Thank you also to research assistant Emma Nelson, who completed the index. Special thanks also go to the anonymous reviewers of my book manuscript for their constructive criticism, challenging questions, and focused intellectual engagement.

Returning to my earlier years for a moment, many thanks also go to the extraordinary teachers and coaches in Gladstone, Oregon, especially teachers Chris Hedensten, John Dykes, and Dorothy Sawyer; coaches

Joyce Knowlton, Bob Stewart, and Irma Penwell; and Assistant Athletic Director Ann Casey for encouraging me as a student-athlete during high school. Without the lessons I learned from them, this book would not have been completed, nor would I have had access to the educational opportunities at Cornell University where I studied and played as an undergraduate student-athlete. At Cornell, many thanks to professors Kathryn March, Biddy Martin, Joan Brumberg, and Christine White, for teaching me the importance of feminist scholarship, praxis, and research methods.

Maraming salamat to my transnational and translocal family. Thank you to my cousins Erlinda B. Collado, Benjie Gonzales, and Gerry Gonzales for teaching me so much about the Philippines. Maraming salamat po to Tito Dodoy and Tita Dory, as well as to Ninong Nandy and Ninang Mely, for their love, hospitality, and generosity. Muchísimas gracías to my sister, Rosario, in San Juan, Puerto Rico. Rosario invited me into her home when I first began writing the first lines of what would eventually be this book. Writing next to the sea—the Atlantic—for four months was the absolute most perfect way to begin. Many thanks also go to my other sister, Rossiya, for inspiring me with her sharp mind and her joy for living. Thank you also to Rachel, Ella Ruby, Langston Seeger, and Erik for all of their love and encouragement over the years. To my mother, Concepcion: O po, tapos na po ang aking aklat! (Yes, Mom, my book is done!) Please try to relax now! A heartfelt thank you goes to my mother for believing in me and for her many prayers during my life. Maraming salamat po to my father, Leandro, for teaching me how to appreciate, indeed love, the Philippines, and Filipino/a histories. A Pacific-size thank you also goes to Omise'eke Natasha Tinsley, my shipmate in Minneapolis, Minnesota, for voyaging with me in Pacific/Atlantic/Caribbean crosscurrents. Thank you, Omi, for sharing many poetic insights about oceans and seas, salt and sweet waters, and the courageous people who move (or were forced to move) in and through calm and troubled waters. Thank you also to Kidlat, my companion in Minneapolis. And last, but not least, a 7,000+ islands-archipelago of hugs and kisses goes to Baía Amihan for whispering to me before s/he entered the world that it was high time to finish and publish this book already! Thank you, Baía Amihan.

NOTES

Preface

1. This preface is inspired by Pablo Neruda's poem, entitled "First Sea." See Neruda, "First Sea."

2. Filipino language words are not italicized in this book. Following and agreeing with historian Noe Noe Silva's approach, I do not to italicize Filipino language words in this book. Silva states that she does not italicize Hawaiian words in her book *Aloha Betrayed: Native Hawaiian Resistance to American Colonialism* "to resist making the native tongue appear foreign." See Silva, *Aloha Betrayed*, 13.

3. Tricycles are motorcycles with sidecars that are used for short-distance local transportation in the Philippines. One to four people can generally fit on a tricycle (at least the kind found in Malolos; other styles of tricycles are available on other islands, some able to accommodate more passengers).

4. For a compelling analysis of Elvis Presley's *Blue Hawaii*, see Isaac, *American Tropics*.

Introduction

1. Sekula, *Fish Story*.

2. Globalization is defined in Inda and Rosaldo, "Introduction," and world capitalist system is discussed in Wallerstein, "The Rise and Future Demise."

3. Tuan, *Space and Place*.

4. For an insightful ethnography of Wall Street, finance, stockbrokers, and capitalism, see Ho, *Liquidated*.

5. Greenlaw, *The Hungry Ocean*. See also Ghosh, *The Hungry Tide,* and Dyson, *Come Hell or High Water*.

6. Junger, *The Perfect Storm*.

7. Gore, *An Inconvenient Truth.*

8. On choke-points, see Nincic, "Sea Lane Security." On reading Somali piracy as a disruption of economic globalization, see Fajardo, "Piracy in the Gulf of Aden."

9. This figure appears to continue to rise. Despite a recession in several regions of the world, the Philippine Department of Labor and Employment reported that OFW deployment increased by 30 percent in 2008 (compared with 2007). The Philippine Overseas Employment Agency (POEA) reported that 1,376,823 Filipinos left the Philippines in 2008. See Ubalde, "OFW deployment in 2008 up by 30%."

10. Sassen, "Whose City Is It?, 73.

11. Fujita-Rony, "Water and Land."

12. Landingin, "Every Six Hours."

13. "Pinoy Seamen Remit $2 Billion." In 2005 Filipino seamen remitted $1.669 billion to the Philippines; in 2006 $1.949 billion and in 2007 $2.236. For the sake of comparison, in 2008, land-based OFWs (as a whole) contributed $9.879 billion in the first nine months (of 2008), an increase of 12.17 percent.

14. Burgonio, "OFW Remittances up 15.5%."

15. On gender and performativity, see Butler, "Performative Acts and Gender Constitution" and *Gender Trouble.*

16. Halberstam, *Female Masculinity,* 1.

17. On understanding "formation," see Omi and Winant, *Racial Formation in the United States*, 66. Writing against essentialist notions of race, Omi and Winant understand racial formation as historical and political processes. They write, "The racial order is organized and enforced by the continuity and reciprocity between micro-level and macro-level of social relations." Similarly, writing against essentialist notions of gender, Butler theorizes "gender as performance" (via linguistic and bodily repetition, always in social and historical contexts). See Butler, *Gender Trouble.*

18. Halberstam, *Female Masculinity,* 1.

19. On intersectionality, see, for example, Crenshaw, "Mapping the Margins"; Collins, *Black Feminist Thought*; and bell hooks, *Ain't I a Woman?*; among others.

20. Because of space limitations, I am not able to fully explain how and why sex/gender became distinct in European contexts. For a recently published explanation, see Valentine, *Imagining Transgender*, especially chapter 4, "The Making of a Field: Anthropology and Transgender Studies." Drawing significantly from the anthropology of sex/gender in Southeast Asian contexts, Valentine discusses how sex/gender are not usually/rigidly separated in Southeast Asian contexts, and he also discusses the cultural politics of how and why white gay, lesbian, and/or feminist scholars and activists tended to separate sex/gender in the twentieth century.

21. Fajardo, "Transportation."

22. On the possibility of using literature as theory, see Christian, "The Race for Theory" and Tinsley, *Thiefing Sugar*. I thank Omise'eke Natasha Tinsley, who

reminds us of the importance of Christian's scholarship and shows through her own scholarship the theoretical and analytical possibilities of Christian's ideas.

23. For an excellent summary and reader's guide to *Noli Me Tangere*, see Francia, "Introduction to José Rizal's *Noli Me Tangere.*"

24. Rizal, *Noli Me Tangere*, 142.

25. Lorde, "Uses of the Erotic."

26. Ibid., 320.

27. Joaquin, *Manila, My Manila.*

28. Rizal politically supported the women of Malolos who were involved in anti(Spanish)colonial resistance in Malolos, Bulakan. He was, therefore, not entirely masculinist or anti-(proto)feminist. See Rizal, "Letter to the Women of Malolos."

29. Tadiar, *Fantasy-Production* (see especially chapter 4, "Sexual Economies").

30. Ibid. See also Bello, "In the Shadow of Debt."

31. Freedom from Debt Coalition, "Is the Philippine Debt Problem Over?"

32. Ibid.

33. Tadiar, *Fantasy-Production* (see especially chapter 4, "Sexual Economies").

34. Anderson, *Imagined Communities.*

35. San Juan, "Configuring the Filipino Diaspora."

36. España-Maram, *Creating Masculinity in Los Angeles's Little Manila.*

37. Espiritu, *Home Bound*, 29.

38. Ostreng, "Does Togetherness Make Friends?," 7, cited in McKay "Men at Sea," 14.

39. Said, *Orientalism.*

40. Fajardo, "Transportation."

41. Male and female Filipinos work in maritime transportation industries. Indeed, there are growing numbers of Filipinas who work in the restaurant, hospitality, entertainment, and housekeeping sectors of the cruise industry. Although not within the scope of my research, I hope that another researcher or cultural worker can address these important female seafarers in the future. For an overview of the cruise industry, see Klein, *Cruise Ship Blues.*

42. Sekula, *Fish Story,* 12. I first encountered this quote in Bhabha, *The Location of Culture,* 11. Bhabha quotes from Sekula's then unpublished manuscript. In Sekula's manuscript, he writes "Salvadorean" rather than Honduran.

43. Higgott, "Series Preface," 13.

44. Sekula, *Fish Story,* 50.

45. See Goldman, *The Ordinary Seaman,* for a compelling story about a ship registered through a flag of convenience and what happens when Global South seamen (specifically from Guatemala) are abandoned in port (Brooklyn, New York).

46. Chapman, *Trouble on Board.* For a documentary film that reports on some of the dismal working conditions on board ships in the global shipping industry, see also Guy and Smith, *Turbulent Waters.*

47. Talampas, "Struggle of Filipino Seafarers."

48. Gilroy, *The Black Atlantic.*

49. Hau'ofa, "Our Sea of Islands" and "The Ocean in Us."

50. Ghosh, *In an Antique Land.*

51. Glissant, *Caribbean Discourse.*

52. Benítez-Rojo, *The Repeating Island.*

53. Gilroy, *The Black Atlantic,* 4.

54. Foucault, "Of Other Spaces."

55. Tinsley makes a similar observation and assessment in "Black Atlantic, Queer Atlantic."

56. Epeli Hau'ofa passed away on January 11, 2009. I regret I never met him, but I am honored to know several people who knew him and were touched by his life, scholarship, and art. May Epeli Hau'ofa rest or sail in peace.

57. Hau'ofa, "Our Sea of Islands," 31. "Our Sea of Islands" was first published in 1993.

58. Ibid., 31.

59. Ibid., 36.

60. Hau'ofa, *Tales of the Tikongs* and *We Are the Ocean.*

61. Hau'ofa, "The Ocean in Us," in *We Are the Ocean,* 53. (Note that "The Ocean in Us" was first published in Mishra and Guy, *Dreadlocks in Oceania,* 1997.)

62. Chisholm, *The Encyclopædia Britannica,* 651.

63. Because of space limitations and my own areas of specialization, I shall leave Hau'ofa's assertions that Indonesia and Japan are "nonoceanic" for other scholars to comment upon.

64. Linebaugh, and Rediker, *The Many Headed Hydra*; Tchen, *New York before Chinatown*; Brown, *Dropping Anchor, Setting Sail*; Fujita-Rony, *American Workers, Colonial Power*; Brand, *A Map to the Door of No Return*; and Tinsley, "Black Atlantic, Queer Atlantic." See also Tinsley, *Thiefing Sugar.*

65. Abu-Lughod, *Before European Hegemony*, and Shaffer, *Maritime Southeast Asia to 1500.*

66. See Espina, *Filipinos in Louisiana*; Fred Cordova, *Filipinos*; and Bronner, *Lefcadio Hearn's America* (especially chapter 2, "Saint Malo: A Lacustrine Village in Louisiana").

67. See Cortés, *Longitude.*

68. Safina, *Song for the Blue Ocean.*

69. Peletz, *Reason and Passion.*

70. Said, *Orientalism,* and Foucault and Gordon, *Power/Knowledge.*

71. Anzaldúa, *Borderlands/La Frontera.*

72. Rosaldo, *Culture and Truth.*

73. Pratt, *Imperial Eyes.*

74. Ibid.

75. Bhabha, *The Location of Culture.*

76. Fujita-Rony, "Water and Land in Asian Migration," 569. On the "Pacific Question" in Asian American Studies, see Kauanui, "Asian American Studies and the 'Pacific Question'"; Stillman, "Pacific-ing Asian Pacific American History"; and Diaz, "To 'P' or Not to 'P'?"

77. Okihiro, *Common Ground*, 17.

78. Professor Greg Dening, a highly respected scholar in Pacific Studies, died on March 13, 2008. Following writing conventions, I use the past tense when referring to him or his publications.

79. Dening, *Islands and Beaches*, 3.

80. Massey, *for space*, 119.

81. Ibid.

82. See Ong, *Flexible Citizenship*; Manalansan, *Global Divas*; and Alvarez, *Mangos, Chiles, and Truckers*.

83. Clifford, *Routes*.

84. Sassen, *The Global City*.

85. Wallerstein, "The Rise and Future Demise."

86. On time-space compression, see Harvey, *The Condition of Postmodernity*.

87. Sassen, "Global Cities and Survival Circuits."

88. Parreñas, *Servants of Globalization*; Constable, *Maid in Hong Kong* and *Romance on a Global Stage*; and Choy, *Empire of Care*.

89. See, for example, Bulosan, *America Is in the Heart*; Takaki, *Strangers from a Different Shore*; and Cordova, *Filipinos*.

90. On critiques of heteronormative and essentialist analyses in Asian American Studies, see, for example, De Jesús, "Rereading History, Rewriting Desire," and Eng and Hom, "Introduction."

91. See again Butler, "Performative Acts and Gender Constitution" and *Gender Trouble*.

92. Halberstam, *Female Masculinities*, and Fajardo, "Transportation."

93. Clifford, *Routes*, 20–21.

94. Rosaldo, *Culture and Truth*.

95. Narayan, "How Native Is a 'Native' Anthropologist?," 671–72.

96. Clifford and Marcus, *Writing Culture*, and Behar and Gordon, *Women Writing Culture*.

97. Clifford, *Routes*, 12.

98. Tsing, *Friction*, 13.

99. Pratt, "Fieldwork in Common Places."

100. Ibid., 49.

1. The Race of the Century

1. Conversations at the Race of the Century/Manila–Acapulco Commemorative Regatta occurred largely in Filipino, but they are translated here in English.

2. "Rudy" and all names in quotations are pseudonyms. After introducing an "informant" or research participant, I drop the quotations for easier reading.

3. Filipino is in quotes here to indicate that it is a socially and historically constructed term and identity. "Indio" was the term previously used during the Spanish colonial period to describe the indigenous people of the archipelago currently known as the Philippines. Filipino during the Spanish colonial period was usually used to describe Spaniards who were born in Las Filipinas [rather than España] or those who had resided in Las Filipinas for a significant period of time. With the rise of indigenous [Filipino] anticolonial nationalist revolutionary movements in the nineteenth century, the terms "Filipino" or "Filipina" were taken up by "Indios" and "Indias," as well as by [Spanish and Chinese] "mestizos" and "mestizas." For commentary on the terms "Filipino" and "Indio," see Joaquin, *Manila, My Manila*; Rafael, *White Love*; and Tiongson, *The Women of Malolos*.

4. Nelson Ramirez, personal communication, February 10, 1998.

5. Interview with Isabelo A. Samonte, February 17, 1998.

6. Ayala Foundation, *Castles of the Sea*.

7. Thomas Hubbard, personal communication, March 23, 1998.

8. Deocampo, *Memories of Old Manila*.

9. Schurz, *Manila Galleon*.

10. Underwood, "Commerce and Culture of the Manila Galleon."

11. Tchen, *New York before Chinatown* and Ding, *Ancestors in the Americas*.

12. Quirino, "The Mexican Connection."

13. Schurz, *Manila Galleon*.

14. Tiongson, *Women of Malolos*. In full disclosure, I am related to Tecla Chichioco. Tecla's brother, Bonifacio Chichioco, is my (maternal) great grandfather. Tiongson's historical research historicizes the famous women of Malolos, many of whom were Chinese mestizas, who challenged Spanish colonial authorities and demanded education for Filipinas. As a result of their strong intellects and acts of resistance, Dr. Jose Rizal (the Philippines's National Hero) wrote a famous open letter to them.

15. Wilson, *Ambition and Identity*.

16. Tiongson, *Women of Malolos*.

17. Talampas, "Struggle of Filipino Seafarers."

18. Interview with Rolando G. Talampas, March 14, 1998.

19. Phillips, "Spaniards in Hawaii before Cook?"

20. I use the term "corporate globalization" as it is or was often used by communities of often progressive or radical organizers, activists, and scholars in the late 1990s and early 2000s who exposed and creatively resisted the expansion of multinational corporate control worldwide. Activists and community-based social justice organizers during the 1999 World Trade Organization protests in Seattle, Washington (U.S.A.), a mass mobilization that helped put critiques of corporate globalization into the mainstream U.S. media, popularized the term.

21. Martinez and Garcia, "What Is 'Neo-Liberalism?"

22. Maoist International Movement, "New People's Army Fights."

23. Canadian Embassy, *Philippines Investment Brief 2000.*

24. See, for example, Danaher and Burbach, *Globalize This!,* and Black, *Life and Debt.*

25. Brysk, "Globalization."

26. Bello, *Anti-Development State.*

27. Bello, "Fifty Years Is Enough."

28. Bello, "The Change We Need."

29. Maoist International Movement, "New People's Army Fights."

30. Korkalainen, "Illegal Recruitment."

31. Jubilee Australia, "The Philippines' Debt Problem."

32. Dumlao, "23 Million Filipinos." To give a regional perspective: in 2008, the poverty rates in Asia were as follows: India, 65.3 percent; Nepal, 59.2 percent; Bangladesh, 58.2 percent; Laos, 48.8 percent; Mongolia, 40 percent; Indonesia, 39.2 percent; Cambodia, 35.4 percent; and Pakistan, 32 percent. The Philippines's poverty rates are higher than Vietnam's 25.6 percent, Sri Lanka's 18.4 percent, and Thailand's 0.1 percent. Dumlao's journalistic account is based on an Asian Development Bank report.

33. Resurreccion, "Globalization Lends Urgency."

34. Forbes, "Representations of Pacific Asian Metropolis" and "Globalisation, Postcolonialism and New Representations."

35. Ibid., 244.

36. Tyner, "Laboring in the Periphery ," 108.

37. For two examples of scholarship that focuses on professional financial labor in the global economy, see Ong, *Flexible Citizenship*, and Ho, *Liquidated.* On the term "sweatship," see Pabico, "Filipino Seamen Take Their Chance."

38. Ramos, "A Salute to Filipino Seafarers," 26–27.

39. For scholarship on the bagong bayani discourse, see, for example, Rafael, *White Love*; Parreñas, *Servants of Globalization*; and Rodriguez, *Brokering Bodies.*

40. Jaleco, "Manning the Way to Nic-hood," 8.

41. Tadiar, "Sexual Economies," 240.

42. Ileto, "The 'Unfinished Revolution' in Philippine Political Discourse."

43. Omise'eke Natasha Tinsley and Lisa Duggan's critical questions and critiques about state and corporate elite anxieties directed at femininities and feminine subjects were helpful as I thought through this point. Queer femininities and femme subjects are excellent examples of femininities and positionalities that are (potentially) powerfully disruptive, non-(hetero)-normative and nonvictimized. For postcolonial and queer scholarship on same-sex or queer femininities see, for example, Tinsley, *Thiefing Sugar*; Gopinath, *Impossible Desires*; and Wekker, *The Politics of Passion.*

44. Gray, *The Global Assembly Line.*

45. Bello, "The End of the Southeast Asian Miracle?"

46. Ibid.

47. Ibid.

48. Lamorena, 2000.

49. Tadiar, *Fantasy-Production.*

50. For discussions about more sustainable economic development and visions of a more just global society, see, for example, Bello, *Deglobalization*; Tadiar, "Hope"; Hawken, *Blessed Unrest.*

2. Ashore and Away

1. The Philippine Merchant Marine Academy is a well-established educational institution with a long history of promoting (heteronormative) maritime masculinities. Established during Spanish colonial rule, the academy was opened on April 5, 1820, originally as the "Escuela Nautica De Manila." Philippine Merchant Marine Academy, *A Concise History of the Philippine Merchant Marine Academy.*

2. Althusser, "Ideology and Ideological State Apparatuses," 132.

3. Rafael, *White Love and Other Events in Filipino History* (see chapter 8, "Your Grief Is Our Gossip: Overseas Filipinos and Other Spectral Presences"); Parreñas, *Servants of Globalization*; Tadiar, *Fantasy-Production* (see chapter 1, "Sexual Economies," and chapter 3, "Domesticated Bodies"); McKay, "Filipino Sea Men."

4. Connell, "The History of Masculinity." See also Connell, *The Men and the Boys* and *Masculinities.*

5. Almario, *UP Diksiyonaryong Filipino*, 75.

6. Ibid.

7. Center for Southeast Asian Studies Northern Illinois University, "Markers NG and NI/NINA."

8. McKay, "Filipino Sea Men," 72.

9. Butler, *Gender Trouble.*

10. Anderson, *Imagined Communities.*

11. Friedman, *The Horizontal Society,* 82.

12. In an example of a more masculinist translation of the Katipunan, the *Encyclopædia Britannica,* for example, translates the Katipunan as the "Supreme and Venerable Society of the *Sons* of the Nation" (*Encyclopædia Britannica,* "Katipunan").

13. Zarate, "Ang Konsepto ng Bagong Bayani."

14. Rafael, *White Love and Other Events*, 211.

15. Office of the Press Secretary, "Statement of the President."

16. Office of the Press Secretary, "PGMA (President Gloria Macapagal Arroyo)."

17. Ramos, "A Salute to Filipino Seafarers."

18. Enriquez, *From Colonial to Liberation Psychology,* 63, 159.

19. Ibid., 43.

20. This is similar to what historian Noenoe K. Silva documents and analyzes. In the Native Hawaiian/Kanaka Maoli case, one key indigenous spiritual/cultural/political/ecological concept that was abused by U.S. American colonial historians, authorities, and plantation owners is "aloha 'aina." Colonial notions of aloha 'aina

were promoted by these figures in their efforts to overthrow the Hawaiian monarchy and annex their once sovereign nation (Silva, *Aloha Betrayed*).

21. Enriquez, "*Pakikisama o Pakikibaka*." See also Kaut, "*Utang-na-loob*," and Samonte, "*Kabuuan ng mga kahulugan*."

22. Rafael, *Contracting Colonialism*, 128.

23. Ileto, *Pasyon and Revolution*, 12.

24. Ibid., 13.

25. For discussions of the Philippine nation-state as motherland or "ina" (mother), see Ileto, *Pasyon and Revolution*; Rafael, *Contracting Colonialism*; and Tolentino, "*Inangbayan*, The Mother-Nation."

26. Rafael, *Contracting Colonialism*, 128–29.

27. Ibid., 128–29.

28. Ramos, "A Salute to Filipino Seafarers."

29. Bello, *The Anti-Development State*.

30. Another example of Philippine state "gesturing" includes the annual "Bagong Bayani Awards" given by heads of state and other upper level governmental officials to OFWs who have participated in meritorious deeds and acts of courage. For an interesting discussion of President Macapagal Arroyo and the 2005 Bagong Bayani Awards ceremony and Macapagal Arroyo's specific deployment of Bagong Bayani discourse, see Zarate, "Ang Konsepto ng Bagong Bayani," 104.

31. Taussig, *The Magic of the State*.

32. Rodriguez, *Brokering Bodies* and "The Labor Brokerage State."

33. Tiongson, "On Filipinos, Filipino Americans, and U.S. Imperialism" 2006.

34. Several of my primary research subjects in the Visayas requested anonymity. To respect their privacy, I use pseudonyms for them and their hometown(s).

35. As a result of reframing and revising my dissertation into a book, Donding has a less prominent role in this version of *Filipino Crosscurrents*. My dissertation discusses Donding and his Roscan life in greater detail (Fajardo, "Filipino Cross Currents," chapter 3.)

36. McKay, "Men at Sea," 9.

37. Enriquez, *From Colonial to Liberation Psychology*, 1992, 72.

38. Ibid.

39. Ibid., 43.

40. For a fictionalized account of Magellan's attempted circumnavigation, written from the perspective of Enrique de Malaccca, see Cortés, *Longitude*.

41. Joyner, *Magellan*, 48.

42. Pigafetta, *The First Voyage Around the World*. For other interpretations of the Magellan-Elcano circumnavigation, see, for example, Morison, *The European Discovery of America*; Joyner, *Magellan*; Oliveira, *Viagem de Fernão Magalhães*; and Bergreen, *Over the Edge of the World*.

43. Pigafetta, *The First Voyage Around the World*, 63–64.

44. Ibid., 63.

45. Espina, *Filipinos in Louisiana*, 3.

46. Ibid.

47. Ibid., 8.

48. Ibid.

49. Ibid.

50. Ibid.

51. Thomas, *The Slave Trade*, 307. See also Rediker, *The Slave Ship*, 171, 250–51, 270, 321.

52. Richardson, *African American Literacies*, 80.

53. Rediker, *Between the Devil and the Deep Blue Sea*.

54. Ibid., 103.

55. Binghay, "Ensuring Occupational Health and Safety," 149.

56. Pabico, "Filipinos Toil in 'Unworthy' Ships," 5.

57. McKay, "Filipino Sea Men," 76.

58. Jimenez, "Shadowy Trails."

59. Philippine Consulate General in Los Angeles, "Passport Frequently Asked Questions."

60. Ibid.

3. Ethnography in Blue

1. For a discussion of other OFWs who meet in parks, see Constable, *Maid in Hong Kong*, 1. Constable conducted fieldwork with Filipinas working as domestic helpers in Hong Kong who gather at "Sunday Square," a park in Central district. See also Chen, *Breathing Spaces*, and Boellstorff, *A Coincidence of Desires*. Chen conducted fieldwork with qigong practitioners who gathered in Beijing parks; Boellstorff conducted fieldwork with non-normatively gendered Indonesians in various urban parkscapes.

2. Avila, "LapuLapu City Denounces Removal."

3. Avila, "Once More. . . Lapu-Lapu."

4. Harvey, *The Condition of Postmodernity*.

5. Tsing, "Global Situation," 469.

6. Harvey, *The Condition of Postmodernity*, 240.

7. Ibid.

8. Ibid., 145.

9. Ibid.

10. Tsing, "Global Situation," 466.

11. Ibid., 477.

12. Hannerz, "Notes on the Global Ecumene" and *Transnational Connections*; Kearney, "The Local and the Global" and *Reconceptualizing the Peasantry*; and Appadurai, "Introduction" and *Modernity at Large*.

13. Evangelista, "Filipino Seafarers Face Declining Demand."

14. Ibid.

15. United Filipino Seafarers, "Marina Worst STCW Violator."

16. The Philippines did in fact make the "IMO White List" in 2000. See Suarez, "R.P. Included in World Maritime List."

17. The Port of Long Beach (California, United States) is the third largest port in the world behind Hong Kong (China) (number 2) and Singapore (number 1).

18. Port of Oakland, 1998.

19. Ibid.

20. When I asked the *Prince*'s (German) first mate if he or the rest of the crew knew of the contents of the containers, he replied, "We don't get any paperwork for most of the containers. We only know if there is dangerous cargo or if it's a 'reefer cargo' (goods that need to refrigerated and thus transported in special containers)." When I asked if the containers are x-rayed, the first mate chuckled and said, "Most of the containers have not been x-rayed. It would take too long."

21. Sekula, *Fish Story*.

22. Cargo ships are measured by the volume of tonnage each ship carries. The containers that they transport (i.e., steel boxes) were originally built to a standard twenty-foot length, which became known as "twenty-foot equivalent units" or TEUs. Although 20-foot containers are standard, they can be as long or large as fifty feet. The China Ocean Shipping Company (COSCO) (state-owned by the People's Republic of China) has a fleet of five that travels to Oakland weekly. COSCO ships have a capacity of 3,500 TEUs (175 steel containers). Some container ships that have been recently built hold even higher numbers of containers; for example, some have the capacity of 6,000 TEUs. See Port of Long Beach, "Latest Monthly TEUs," 2009.

23. Ramos, *Intermediate Tagalog*, 38.

24. An early article that I published about this transpacific voyage (Fajardo, "Transportation") incorrectly stated that twenty-one seamen worked on the *Prince*. There were actually twenty-two seamen working on the *Prince*.

25. Machinist mates work within the hull of a ship in fire rooms, boiler rooms, engine rooms, or shops. Able-bodied seamen normally have a minimum of one year of service on a vessel. Their duties usually include helm watch, lookout watch, handling lines for tying up and letting go in port, and deck maintenance and they usually work directly with/for the bosun or the mate. Ordinary seamen are entry-level positions that do not require any previous sea time/experience. They are usually responsible for cleaning the ship, deck maintenance, assisting with securing the vessel, and being on lookout.

25a. The Filipino Chief Cook chose the pseudonyms for his Filipino shipmates.

26. A knot is a nautical measure of speed, one knot being equivalent to sailing/traveling at the rate of one nautical mile per hour (6,080 feet/1.51 mph) (Kemp, *The Oxford Companion to Ships*).

27. In addition to seamen's long hours, many duties, and exhaustion, other reasons some seamen do not or cannot go to shore include immigration restrictions post–September 11, 2001, and the high costs of loading or unloading cargo (faster times in ports help to keep costs down and profits up, as shipping

companies do not want their ships in port longer than necessary). See Fajardo, "Filipino Cross Currents" (especially epilogue); Brady, "For Shipbound Sailors"; and Elass, "Angel of the High Seas."

28. Foucault, "Of Other Spaces." Foucault's ideas that heterotopias are sites of "deviance" (in other words, non-normativity), contradiction, and nontraditional time are helpful in thinking through how ships are a part of and create the crosscurrents of masculinities and globalization. Geographer Arun Saldanha has recently exposed and critiqued some of the structuralist "fallacies" with Foucault's framework on heterotopias, which Saldanha writes, "hinders a geography of mobility, unevenness, and differentials of power [e.g., race, class, gender, sexuality, nationality, citizenship status, etc.]." I agree with Saldanha's critique of structuralism, as well as his suggestion that the concept of heterotopia still has productive possibilities, especially when in dialogue with poststructuralist, postcolonial, and feminist critiques (I would also add queer/of color/diaspora studies). See Saldanha, "Heterotopia and Structuralism." For other scholarship that engages Foucault's concept of heterotopias, see Sekula, *Fish Story,* and Casarino, *Modernity at Sea.*

29. For maritime accounts of the slowness (and sometimes melancholia) of sea travel and transportation, see Pigafetta, *The First Voyage Around the World*; Cortés, *Longitude*; and Slocum, *Sailing Alone Around the World*; Heyerdahl, *Kon-Tiki*; and Nicols, *Sea Change.* See also Goldman, *The Ordinary Seaman,* for a fictionalized account of how time-space works differently for ordinary (Guatemalan) seamen who never leave the shore.

30. *Encyclopædia Britannica*, "International Date Line."

31. McKay, "Filipino Sea Men."

32. Sampson, "Transnational Drifters or Hyperspace Dwellers," 256.

33. Ibid.

34. Ibid.

35. Rediker, *Between the Devil and the Deep Blue Sea.*

36. For other accounts of racial discrimination in the contemporary global shipping industry (as well as other human rights violations), see Chapman, *Trouble on Board*; McKay, "Filipino Sea Men"; and Guy and Smith, *Turbulent Waters.*

37. Crouch, "Duke's Blues," 450. For a discussion of eighteenth century European seamen and the blues, see Rediker, *Between the Devil and the Deep Blue Sea*, 160. Rediker writes, "The 'sailor's lament,' an early form of the blues, consisted of wistful songs of separation from wife, children, parents, friends, and home." For a (white, working-class) butch and transgender perspective on the blues, see Feinberg, *Stone Butch Blues.*

38. Rediker, *Between the Devil and the Deep Blue Sea*, 160.

39. Mercado, *Elements of Filipino Philosophy,* 107–18.

40. Dorotheo, *A Bilingual Structural Analysis,* 66–67. See also Mercado, *Elements of Filipino Philosophy,* 107.

41. Mercado, *Elements of Filipino Philosophy.*

42. Espiritu, *Five Faces of Exile*. See especially Espiritu's chapter on Carlos Bulosan (chapter 2). For other accounts of racialized and classed migrant Filipino "suffering" (in early to mid-twentieth century contexts), see Bulosan, *America Is in the Heart* and Scharlin and Villanueva, *Philip Vera Cruz*.

43. Halberstam, *In a Queer Time and Place*, 4–5, 10. For a queer studies critique of Christian heteronormative and reproductive conceptualizations of time, see Boellstorff, *A Coincidence of Desires*, 2007, 28, 32. Engaging Walter Benjamin, Boellstorff writes: "A queer critique could interrupt what Walter Benjamin terms. . . 'messianic' time. . . straight time organized around a climactic end so that 'every second of time was the straight gate through which the Messiah might enter.' See also Benjamin, "Theses on the Philosophy of History," 264.

4. Transportation

1. The first jeepneys were modified army jeeps left by U.S. Americans during World War II. See Tahimik, *Bangungot Mababangong/Perfumed Nightmare*.

2. On the politics of traffic in Metro Manila, see Tadiar, "Manila's New Metropolitan Form." On the importance of interclass contact, see Delaney, *Time Square Red, Time Square Blue*.

3. In the late 1990s, First Lady (at the time) of the Philippines Amelita "Ming" Ramos began the "Piso Para Sa Pasig" (Peso for the Pasig) program in her efforts to mobilize Manileños and businesses to clean up the Pasig River, an important cultural and economic river-based thoroughfare in Metro Manila.

4. As a result of neoliberal and economic globalization policies such as Philippines 2000 (discussed in chapter 1), the Philippines is now *importing rice* from Thailand, rather than exporting it. Historically, the Philippines was a key rice exporting country in Southeast Asia.

5. "Tomboy" (a Tagalog-ized English word with specific Filipino meanings) broadly refers to masculine- or male-identified fe/males or masculine transgendered subjects in the Philippines or diaspora who generally have sexual/emotional relationships with feminine females who identify as "women."

6. In my dissertation, I refer to Percy (and me) using feminine pronouns and identities. After returning to Manila in 1997 (and experiencing my racialized and classed gender in different ways when compared with contexts in the United States) and later, after moving to and living in a city where a dynamic queer and transgender community exists (e.g., Oakland / San Francisco Bay Area) in 1998, as well as learning more about gender and queer theory and different kinds of embodiment, over the last ten years, I have been seriously rethinking tomboy masculinities. That is, I have been *returning to the notion* that they/us are masculine-identified fe/males or transgendered men/guys/boys, an idea I had as a child (a three-year-old to be exact) in the Philippines and as a young immigrant in the United States. This particular transgender "gender

reality," however (to use Judith Butler's term), has not always been supported by or understood by straight communities or by lesbian feminist communities in the United States and the Philippines (including parts of Asian/Asian American lesbian feminist communities in the San Francisco Bay Area). My rethinking and returning is reflected in my ethnographic writing, gender expression, and identity and in cultural/political shifts that have taken place in different queer/transgender subcultures (as collective rethinking and returning occurs). These related phenomena demonstrate the fluidities of time, racialized and classed gender performances, personal and collective identities; the phenomena of everyday (racialized and classed) gender practices changing; and the force of oppositional knowledge-production.

7. Marcus and Fischer, *Anthropology as Cultural Critique*.

8. Anthropologist Scott Morgensen uses the phrase "intimate relationalities" to describe the historically close political and cultural relationships between U.S. sexual minority formations and two-spirit (American Indian) formations. See Morgensen's *Settler Sexualities*. On racial/sexual intimacies, see Faier, *Intimate Encounters,* and Stoler, *Carnal Knowledge and Imperial Power*.

9. For an ethnography of transgender as a category, see Valentine, *Imagining Transgender*.

10. See Boellstorff, *A Coincidence of Desires*, xiii. See also Fajardo, "Boellstorff, Tom" (a book review of Boellstorff's ethnography). Boellstorff italicizes "gay" and "lesbi" (in *A Coincidence of Desires*) to "indicate that [these terms] are Indonesian language terms that are not reducible to the English terms 'gay' and 'lesbian,' despite clear links to them." I discuss in the body of this chapter why I choose *not* to italicize "tomboy" (and other Filipino terms). Despite this difference in approach, my understanding of "tomboy" as a Filipino language term resonates with Boellstorff's understanding of "gay" and "lesbi" as having specific local/Southeast Asian meanings.

11. Silva, *Aloha Betrayed*, 13.

12. Anak is a gender-neutral Tagalog word for child/offspring, and there are no equivalent Tagalog words for "son" or "daughter." A speaker may say, however, "anak na lalaki" (child that is a male/boy) or "anak na babae" (child that is female/girl) to indicate gender. Jonas used the word anak and did not include "na babae" (that is, female). So as to not infantilize the tomboy Jonas was referring to, I do not translate anak here as "child." Anak can also refer to adult children.

13. On the importance of "abiding" in postcolonial studies/praxis, see Ismail, *Abiding Sri Lanka*.

14. Clifford, *Routes*, 11.

15. Foucault, *Discipline and Punish*.

16. See Bhaba, *Location of Culture*, for an influential theory of cultural hybridity.

17. Many examples from diverse literary traditions can substantiate this point. Selected examples that articulate or imagine the interconnections between different kinds of masculinities and journeying, remembering, and meditating include: Bashō, "Narrow Road to the Interior" and "Travelogue of Weather-Beaten Bones" in *The*

Essential Bashō, 1–36 and 37–52 (see also Shirane, *Traces of Dreams*); Ghosh, *In an Antique Land*; Bulosan, *America Is in the Heart*; Pham, *Catfish and Mandala*; Pigafetta, *The First Voyage Around the World*; Nichols, *Sea Change*; and Kerouac, *On the Road*. Selected examples of ethnographies that engage different modes of transportation or movement for the purposes of cultural interpretation include Tsing, *In the Realm of the Diamond Queen* (walking/hiking); Valentine, *Imagining Transgender* (biking); and Alvarez, *Mangoes, Chiles, and Truckers* (trucking).

18. Sinnott. *Toms and Dees*.

19. Blackwood. "*Tombois* in West Sumatra."

20. De Jesús, "Rereading History, Rewriting Desire."

21. On the importance of property and settlement in colonial America, see O'Brien, *Dispossession by Degrees*.

22. Halberstam, *In a Queer Time and Place*.

23. Gopinath. *Impossible Desires*.

24. I immigrated to the United States in 1973 and have been traveling regularly to the Philippines since the 1980s. Trips have lasted from ten days to ten months. The years when trips occurred are 1977, 1978, 1987, 1988–1989, 1992, 1994, 1996, 1997–1998, 2000, 2005, 2006, 2008, 2009, 2010, and 2011.

25. The other gender formation often discussed in Filipino/a contexts is bakla (a Filipino/a fe/male femininity / gay men's / transgender / transsexual formation). See Manalansan, *Global Divas* and Benedicto, "The Haunting of Gay Manila."

26. de Guzman and Chia, "Working Class Lesbians in the Philippines."

27. Rodriguez, *Throw It To The River*, 26.

28. *Behind the Labels*.

29. Chie Abad, personal communication, February 15, 2002.

30. Otálvaro-Hormillosa, "Performing Citizenship."

31. My position is that in *Global Divas* Manalansan does not significantly focus on Filipina tomboys, lesbians, and dykes primarily because it was not within the scope of his study to address these racialized gender/sexuality formations.

32. De Jesus, *Pinay Power*.

33. de Guzman and Chia, "Working Class Lesbians in the Philippines," 14.

34. Ibid., 18.

35. Balikbayan historically refers to Filipino/as from North America who return to the Philippines. The (Ferdinand) Marcos Dictatorship coined this term and promoted tourism with Filipino/a immigrants in Canada and the United States in the 1970s. See Rafael, "Your Grief is Our Gossip."

36. As previously discussed in chapter 3, various readings emerged quickly upon first meetings with Filipino/as during fieldwork. Filipino language specialist and scholar Teresita V. Ramos writes, "Filipinos are usually not inhibited about initiating conversations because talking to a stranger is generally not considered intrusive. If thrown together for almost any reason, someone will break the ice. A common conversation opener is *Tagasaan ka?* 'Where are you from?'" (Ramos, *Intermediate Tagalog*, 38).

37. Margold, "Narratives of Masculinity and Transnational Migration," 279.

38. Ibid., 18.

39. Connell, "The History of Masculinity," 185. See also Kimmel, *Manhood in America.*

40. Enriquez, *From Colonial to Liberation Psychology*, 160.

41. Filipino—largely based on Tagalog—is the Philippines's national language.

42. Ramos, *Conversational Tagalog*, 134.

43. I anecdotally heard about these critiques from U.S.-based queer studies scholars who attended the "Sexualities, Genders, and Rights in Asia—1st International Conference of Asia Queer Studies," in Bangkok, Thailand (July 7–9, 2005).

44. Butler, *Gender Trouble*. See also Davis, "Situating Fluidity."

45. Guggenheim, "Cock or Bull," 149.

46. As I revise this chapter in August 2009, Manny Pacquiao's record is forty-nine wins (thirty-seven by knockout), three losses, and two draws. Pacquiao has held titles as World Boxing Council (WBC) Lightweight world champion, WBC Super Featherweight world champion, International Boxing Federation Super Bantamweight world champion, and WBC Flyweight world champion.

Epilogue

1. In addition to Lake Superior, the Mississippi River is also on my mind because it is a river that I cross regularly in my everyday life. The University of Minnesota, Twin Cities campus (where I teach) is situated on both east and west banks of the river in Minneapolis. For information on marine currents, see Neumman, *Ocean Currents,* and Hidy, *The Waves: The Nature of Sea Motion.*

2. Bello, "The China-Asean Free Trade Area."

3. Ibid.

4. Philippine Overseas Employment Agency, "Deployed Landbased." 1.

5. Philippine Overseas Employment Agency, "Compendium of OFW Statistics (2008)," 21.

6. Arroyo, "PGMA's Legacy."

7. Philippine Overseas Employment Agency, "Compendium of OFW Statistics (2008)," 21.

8. See Rodriguez, *Migrants for Export.*

9. Landingin, "Every 6 Hours."

10. Ibid.

11. Natividad, "Female OFWs Overtaking Males."

12. Ibid.

13. Marcus and Fischer, *Anthropology as Cultural Critique.*

14. See McKay's caution in McKay, "Filipino Sea Men," 80.

15. See, *The Decolonized Eye.*

16. When I write "in the ocean," I mean to say that in addition to the fieldwork conducted at sea, since I began this project I have also been learning the art of

sailing, first, in the San Francisco Bay, later at Lake Harriet (Minneapolis) and Lake Superior (in Northern Minnesota).

17. In sailing, two maneuvers that allow a sailor to change a boat's direction include the tack and the jibe. When tacking (or "coming about"), the bow of the boat first crosses or turns into the wind (during the turn). By taking this maneuver, the direction from which the wind blows changes from one side to the other. During a jibe, as the boat is running before the wind (in other words, sailing in front of the wind), the sailor steers the boat's stern into the wind. As a result, the wind direction changes from one side of the boat to the other (the sails are also moved to the opposite side). I thank my sailing teacher and friend Professor Peter Lock (Emeritus, French Department, University of Minnesota, Twin Cities) for helping me to improve my maritime skills and for our thought-provoking discussions about theory, gender, sexuality, and race while sailing during our fine summer days in Minneapolis.

BIBLIOGRAPHY

Abu-Lughod, Janet L. *Before European Hegemony: The World System A.D. 1250–1350*. New York: Oxford University Press, 1989.

Almario, Virgilio S., ed. *UP Diksiyonaryong Filipino*. Pasig City, Philippines: Anvil Publishing Inc., 2001.

Althusser, Louis. "Ideology and Ideological State Apparatuses (Notes Towards an Investigation)." In *Lenin and Philosophy and Other Essays*, translated by Ben Brewster. New York: Monthly Review Press, 1971.

Alvarez, Robert, Jr. *Mangoes, Chiles, and Truckers: The Business of Transnationalism*. Minneapolis: University of Minnesota Press, 2005.

Anderson, Benedict. *Imagined Communities: Reflections on the Origins and Spread of Nationalism*. London: Verso, 1987.

Anderson, Sarah. *Views from the South: The Effects of Globalization and the WTO on Third World Countries*. San Francisco: International Forum on Globalization, 1999.

Anzaldúa, Gloria. *Making Face, Making Soul, Hacienda Caras, Critical and Creative Perspectives by Women of Color*. San Francisco: Aunt Lute Foundation, 1975.

———. *Borderlands/La Frontera: The New Mestiza*. San Francisco: Aunt Lute, 1987.

Anzaldúa, Gloria, and Cherrie Morraga, eds. *This Bridge Called My Back: Writings by Radical Women of Color*. New York: Kitchen Table Women of Color Press, 1983.

Appadurai, Arjun. "Introduction: Commodities and the Politics of Value." In *The Social Life of Things*, edited by Arjun Appadurai. Cambridge, UK: Cambridge University Press, 1986.

———. "Sovereignty without Territoriality." In *Geographies of Identity*, edited by Patricia Yaeger. Ann Arbor: University of Michigan Press, 1996.

———. *Modernity at Large: Cultural Dimensions of Globalization*. Minneapolis: University of Minnesota Press, 1996.

Aranas, Simeon. *Kaligaligayang Bundok ng Banahaw* (awit). 2 vols. Manila: P. Sayo, 1927.

Arroyo, Gloria Macapagal. "PGMA's Legacy: A Stable Economy, Free Elections." December 23, 2009, http://www.facebook.com/pages/President-Gloria-Macapagal-Arroyo/106858983263#!/notes/president-gloria-macapagal-arroyo/pgmas-legacy-a-stable-economy-free-elections/214546724500.

Ashley, Ray. "Anson's Arrival in the Pacific." *Mains'l Haul: A Journal of Pacific Maritime History* 38, nos. 1 and 2 (2002): 36–39.

Asian Art Museum of San Francisco. *At Home and Abroad: 20 Contemporary Filipino Artists*. San Francisco: Asian Art Museum, 1998.

Atkinson, Jane Monnig, and Shelly Errington, eds. *Power and Difference in Island Southeast Asia*. Stanford, Calif.: Stanford University Press, 1990.

Avila, Bobit S. "LapuLapu City Denounces Removal of Statue from Rizal Park." *Cebu Star*, June 21, 2004.

———. "Once More. . . Lapu-Lapu Stands at the Luneta!" *Cebu Star*, 2005.

Ayala Foundation. *Castles of the Sea: A History of the Manila Galleon*. Makati City, Philippines: Ayala Foundation, 1997. CD-ROM.

Bagwell, Beth. *Oakland: The Story of a City*. Oakland, Calif.: Oakland Heritage Alliance, 1982.

Barthes, Roland. *Mythologies*. New York: Hill and Wang, 1957.

Bascara, Victor. "Hitting Critical Mass, (Or, Do Your Parents Still Say 'Oriental' Too?)" *Critical Mass: A Journal of Asian American Cultural Criticism*, 1.1 (1993): 3–38.

———. *Model-Minority Imperialism*. Minneapolis: University of Minnesota Press, 2006.

Bashō, Matsuo. *The Essential Bashō*. Translated by Sam Hamill. Boston: Shambhala, 1999.

Behar, Ruth. *Translated Woman: Crossing the Border with Esperanza's Story*. Boston: Beacon Press, 1993.

Behar, Ruth, and Deborah Gordon, eds. *Women Writing Culture*. Berkeley: University of California Press, 1996.

Behind the Labels: Garment Workers on U.S. Saipan. Video. Produced/directed by Tia Lessin. Brooklyn, N.Y.: WITNESS, 2001.

Bello, Walden. "The End of the Southeast Asian Miracle?" *Focus Bulletin*, no. 17, August 1997, http://www.focus.org (accessed June 15, 1998).

———. "Back to the Third World? The Asian Financial Crisis Enters Its Second Year." *Focus on Trade*, no. 27, July 1998, http://www.focus.org (accessed August 15, 1998).

———. "Fifty Years Is Enough." September 6, 2000, http://www.50years.org (accessed November 1, 2000).

———. "In the Shadow of Debt." *Business Mirror*, April 22, 2008, http://www.businessmirror.com.ph/04222008 (accessed May 1, 2008).

———. "The Change We Need." January 22, 2009, http://www.fdc.ph/index.php?option=com_content&view=article&id=401:the-change-we-need&catid=88:by-walden-bello (accessed February 20, 2009).

———. "The China-Asean Free Trade Area: Propaganda and Reality." January 14, 2010, http://opinion.inquirer.net/viewpoints/columns/view/20100114-247344/The-China-Asean-Free-Trade-Area-Propaganda-and-Reality.

———. *Deglobalization: Ideas for a New World Economy*. New York: Zed Books, 2002.

———. *The Anti-Development State: The Political Economy of Permanent Crisis in the Philippines*. Diliman: Department of Sociology, College of Social Sciences and Philosophy, University of the Philippines, Diliman and Focus on the Global South, A Program of Development Policy Research, Analysis and Action, 2004.

Benedicto, Bobby. "The Haunting of Gay Manila: Global Space-Time and the Specter of *Kabaklaan*." *GLQ* 14, no. 2/3 (2008): 317–39.

Benítez-Rojo, Antonio. *The Repeating Island: The Caribbean and the Postmodern Perspective*. Durham, N.C.: Duke University Press, 1992.

Benjamin, Walter. "Theses on the Philosophy of History." In *Illuminations: Essays and Reflections*, edited and with an introduction by Hannah Arendt. New York: Schocken Books, 1955.

Bergreen, Laurence. *Over the Edge of the World*. New York: HarperCollins, 2003.

Bernad, Miguel. "A Booming Inter-Island Trade." In *Filipino Heritage, the Making of a Nation*. Edited by Alfredo Roces. Vol. 3, *The Age of Trade and Contacts, Visitors from Across the Seas*, 645–50. Manila: Lahing Pilipino Publishing Foundation, 1977–78.

Bhabha, Homi K. *The Location of Culture*. New York: Routledge, 1994.

Binghay, Virgel C. "Ensuring Occupational Health and Safety for Overseas Filipino Seafarers," Paper presented at 8th International Society for Labor and Social Security Law Regional Congress, Taipei, Taiwan, 2005.

Black, Stephanie, producer/director. *Life and Debt*. Film. New York, NY: New Yorker Video, 2003.

Blackwood, Evelyn. "*Tombois* in West Sumatra: Constructing Masculinity and Erotic Desire." *Cultural Anthropology* 13, no. 4 (1998): 491–521.

Blanc-Szanton, Cristina. "Collision of Cultures: Historical Reformulations of Gender in the Lowland Visayas, Philippines." In *Power and Difference in Island Southeast Asia*, edited by Jane Monnig Atkinson and Shelly Errington, 345–84. Stanford, Calif.: Stanford University Press, 1990.

Boellstorff, Tom. *A Coincidence of Desires: Anthropology, Queer Studies, Indonesia*. Durham, NC: Duke University Press, 2007.

Bonus, Rick. *Locating Filipino Americans: Ethnicity and the Cultural Politics of Space*. Philadelphia: Temple University Press, 2000.

Brady, Emily. "For Shipbound Sailors, a Smiling Personal Shopper." *New York Times*, May 25, 2008, 7.

Brand, Dionne. *A Map to the Door of No Return*. Vintage Canada, 2002.

Breitwieser, Sabrine, ed. *Allan Sekula: Performance Under Working Conditions*. Vienna: Generali Foundation, 2003.

Brettell, Caroline. *Anthropology and Migration: Essays on Transnationalism, Ethnicity, and Identity*. Walnut Creek, Calif.: AltaMira Press, 2003.

Broad, Robin. *Plundering Paradise: The Struggle for the Environment in the Philippines.* Berkeley: University of California Press, 1998.

Bronner, Simon J., ed. *Lefcadio Hearn's America: Ethnographic Sketches and Editorials.* Lexington: University of Kentucky Press, 2002.

Brown, Jacqueline Nassy. *Dropping Anchor, Setting Sail: Geographies of Race in Black Liverpool.* Princeton, N.J.: Princeton University Press, 2005.

Brysk, Alison. "Globalization, the Double-Edged Sword," *NACLA Report on the Americas* XXXIV, no. 1 (July 2001), 29–33.

———. "Transnational Threats and Opportunities." In *Globalization and Human Rights.* Berkeley: University of California Press, 2002.

———. *Globalization and Human Rights.* Berkeley: University of California Press, 2002.

Bulosan, Carlos. *America Is in the Heart.* Seattle: University of Washington Press, 1973.

Burgonio, Maricel E. "OFW Remittances up 15.5%." *The Manila Times,* December 16, 2008, http://www.manilatimes.net/national/2008/dec/16/yehey/top_stories/20081216top1.html (accessed January 17, 2009).

Butler, Judith. "Performative Acts and Gender Constitution: An Essay in Phenomenology and Feminist Theory," *Theatre Journal* 40, no. 4 (1988): 519–31.

———. *Gender Trouble: Feminism and the Subversion of Identity.* New York: Routledge, 1990.

Campomanes, Oscar V. "Filipinos in the United States and Their Literature of Exile." In *Discrepant Histories, Translocal Essays on Filipino Cultures,* edited by Vicente Rafael. Manila and Philadelphia: Anvil Press and Temple University Press, 1995.

Canadian Embassy. *Philippines Investment Brief 2000.* February 15, 2000.

Cannell, Fenella. *Power and Intimacy in the Christine Philippines.* Cambridge, UK: Cambridge University Press, 1999.

Carlisle, Rodney. *Sovereignty for Sale: The Origins and Evolution of the Panamanian and Liberian Flags of Convenience.* Annapolis, Md.: Naval Institute Press, 1981.

Casarino, Cesare. *Modernity at Sea: Melville, Marx, Conrad in Crisis.* Minneapolis: University of Minnesota Press, 2002.

Casiño, Eric S. "A Family of Boats." In *Filipino Heritage, the Making of a Nation.* Edited by Alfredo Roces. Vol. 3, *The Age of Trade and Contacts, Visitors from Across the Seas,* 711–13. Manila: Lahing Pilipino Publishing Foundation, 1977–78.

Center for Southeast Asian Studies Northern Illinois University, "The Markers NG and NI/NINA," http://www.seasite.niu.edu/Tagalog/Grammar%20Activities/Grammar%201/Markers/Ng&Ni.htm (accessed August 7, 2009).

Chapman, Paul. *Trouble on Board: The Plight of International Seafarers.* Ithaca, NY: Cornell University, School of Industrial and Labor Relations Press, 1992.

Chen, Nancy N. *Breathing Spaces: Qigong, Psychiatry, and Healing in China.* New York: Columbia University Press, 2003.

Chisholm, Hugh. *The Encyclopædia Britannica: A Dictionary of Arts, Sciences, Literature and General Information.* Charlottesville, University of Virginia Press, 1910.

Choy, Catherine Ceniza. *Empire of Care: Nursing and Migration in Filipino American History.* Durham, N.C.: Duke University Press, 2008.

Choy, Curtis, director. *Fall of the I-Hotel.* Film/VHS. Produced and distributed by National Asian American Telecommunications Association, 1983.

Christian, Barbara. "The Race for Theory." *Making Face, Making Soul/ Hacienda Caras: Creative and Critical Perspectives By Women of Color,* ed. Gloria Anzaldúa, 335–45. San Francisco: Aunt Lute, 1990.

Chuh, Kandice. *Imagine Otherwise: An Asian Americanist Critique.* Durham, N.C.: Duke University Press, 2003.

Clifford, James. *The Predicament of Culture: Twentieth Century Ethnography, Literature, and Art.* Cambridge, Mass.: Harvard University Press, 1988.

———. *Routes: Travel and Translation in the Late Twentieth Century.* Cambridge, Mass.: Harvard University Press, 1997.

Clifford, James, and George Marcus, eds. *Writing Culture: The Poetics and Politics of Ethnography.* Berkeley: University of California Press, 1986.

Coates, Austin. *Rizal: Philippine Nationalist and Martyr.* London: Oxford University Press, 1968.

Collins, Patricia Hill. *Black Feminist Thought: Knowledge, Consciousness and the Politics of Empowerment.* Boston: Unwin Hyman, 1990.

Connell, R. W. *The Men and the Boys.* Berkeley: University of California Press, 2000.

———. "The History of Masculinity." In *Masculinities Reader,* edited by Rachel Adams and David Savran. Oxford: Blackwell Publishing, 2002.

———. *Masculinities.* Berkeley: University of California Press, 2005.

Constable. Nicole, *Maid to Order in Hong Kong: An Ethnography of Filipina Workers.* Ithaca, N.Y.: Cornell University Press, 1997.

———. *Romance on a Global Stage: Pen Pals, Virtual Ethnography and "Mail Order Marriages."* Berkeley, University of California Press, 2003.

Constantino, Renato. *The Philippines: A Past Revisited.* Quezon City, Philippines: Tala Publishing Services, 1975.

———. *Neo-Colonial Identity and Counter Consciousness: Essays on Decolonization.* London: Merlin Press, 1993.

Cordova, Fred. *Filipinos: Forgotten Asian Americans.* Dubuque, Iowa: Kendall/ Hunt Publishing Company, 1983.

Correy, Stan. "Background Briefing: The Bad Shipping News: Ports, Freight and Security." By Australian Broadcasting Corporation Radio National, Radio Program, August 31, 2003.

Cortés, Cárlos. *Longitude.* Quezon City: University of the Philippines Press, 1998.

Crenshaw, Kimberlé. "Mapping the Margins: Intersectionality, Identity Politics, and Violence Against Women of Color." *Stanford Law Review* 43, no. 6 (1991): 1241–99.

Crouch, Stanley. "The Duke's Blues." In *African Philosophy: An Anthology,* edited by Emmanuel Chukwudi Ezep, 447–54. Hoboken, NJ: Wiley-Blackwell, 1998.

Danaher, Kevin, and Roger Burbach, eds. *Globalize This!* Monroe, Maine: Common Courage Press, 2000.

Davis, Erin Calhoun. "Situating Fluidity: (Trans) Gender Identification and Regulation of Gender Diversity." *GLQ: A Journal of Gay and Lesbian Studies* 15, no. 1 (2008): 97–130.

de Guzman, Amelia M., and Irene R. Chia. "Working Class Lesbians in the Philippines," 2005, www.icwow.org/WCL/WCLenglish.pdf.

De Jesús, Melinda L., ed. "Rereading History, Rewriting Desire: Reclaiming Queerness in Carlos Bulosan's America Is in the Heart and Bienvenido Santos' Scent of Apples." *Journal of Asian American Studies* 5, no. 2 (2002): 91–111.

———. *Pinay Power: Peminist Critical Theory: Theorizing the Filipina/American Experience.* New York: Routledge, 2005.

De La Cruz, Khavn. *Nang Gabing Umiyak Ang Dagat.* Directed by Ruelo Lozendo, http://www.youtube.com/watch?v=2FCFYpqtCfM&feature=related (accessed July 25, 2008).

Delaney, Samuel. *Time Square Red, Time Square Blue.* New York: New York University Press, 2001.

Delgado, James P. *To California by Sea: A Maritime History of the California Gold Rush.* Columbia: University of South Carolina Press, 1990.

Delgado, James, and Foster, Kevin. "Scow Schooner *Alma* National Historic Landmark Study," n.d., http://www.nps.gov/history/maritime/nhl/alma.htm (accessed March 3, 2008).

Deocampo, Nick, director. *Memories of Old Manila,* Film/VHS. 1993. Manila: Nick Deocampo.

Dening, Greg. *Islands and Beaches: Discourse on a Silent Land, Marquesas, 1774–1880.* Honolulu: University of Hawai'i Press, 1980.

Desai, Jigna. *Beyond Bollywood: The Cultural Politics of South Asian Diasporic Film.* New York: Routledge, 2003.

Diaz, Vicente M. "To 'P' or Not to 'P'?": Marking the Territory Between Pacific Islander and Asian American Studies." *Journal of Asian American Studies* 7, no. 3 (2004): 183–208.

Ding, Loni. *Ancestors in the Americas: Coolies, Sailors, Settlers: Voyage to the New World.* VHS. 1995. San Francisco: Center for Educational Telecommunications,

Dirlik, Arif. "Globalism and the Politics of Place." In *Globalisation and the Asia-Pacific: Contested Territories,* edited by Kris Olds, Peter Dicken, Philip F. Kelly, Lily Kong, and Henry Wai-chung. London: Routledge Press, 1999.

Dirlik, Arif, ed. *What Is in a Rim? Critical Perspectives on the Pacific Region Idea.* Oxford: Rowman Littlefield Publishers, Inc., 1988.

Dorotheo, Paz Ruiz. *A Bilingual Structural Analysis to Justify Theoretically the Cebuano Induced Verb Errors in English.* Cebu City, Philippines: San Carlos Publications, 1966.

Dumlao, Doris. "23 Million Filipinos Living Below Asia-Pacific Poverty Line." *The Inquirer,* August 27, 2008, http://globalnation.inquirer.net/news/breakingnews/view/20080827-157167/23-million-Filipinos-living-below-Asia-Pacific-poverty-line (accessed July 1, 2009).

Dunn, Geoffrey, and Mark Schwartz, producers/directors. *Dollar a Day, Ten Cents a Dance: A Historic Portrait of Filipino Farmworkers in America.* VHS/DVD. New York, N.Y.: The Cinema Guild, Inc., 2007.

Dyson, Michael Eric. *Come Hell or High Water: Hurricane Katrina and the Color of Disaster.* New York: Basic Civitas Books, 2007.

Elass, Rasha. "The Angel of the High Seas." *The National,* July 9, 2008, http://www.thenational.ae/article/20080708/PAGETHREE/901516436/1119/NEWS&profile=1119 (accessed August 10, 2009).

Encyclopædia Britannica. "International Date Line." *Encyclopædia Britannica Online,* http://www.search.eb.com/eb/article-9042582 (accessed July 1, 2009).

———. "Katipunan." *Encyclopædia Britannica Online,* http://www.britannica.com/EBchecked/topic/313286/Katipunan (accessed July 15, 2009).

Eng, David L. *Racial Castration: Managing Masculinity in Asian America.* Durham, N.C.: Duke University Press, 2001.

Eng, David L., Judith Halberstam, and José Esteban Muñoz. "What's Queer About Queer Studies Now?" *Social Text* 23, no. 3–4, 84–85 (Fall–Winter 2005): 1–18.

Eng, David, and Alice Hom. "Introduction. Q&A: Notes on a Queer Asian America." In *Q & A: Queer in Asian America,* edited by David Eng and Alice Hom, 2–21. Philadelphia: Temple University Press, 1998.

Enloe, Cynthia. *Bananas, Beaches, and Bases: Making Feminist Sense of International Politics.* Berkeley: University of California Press, 1990.

Enriquez, Virgilio G. "*Pakikisama o Pakikibaka:* Understanding the Psychology of the Filipino." Paper presented at the Conference on Philippine Culture, Bay Area Bilingual Education League, Berkeley, California, April 29–30, 1977.

———. *From Colonial to Liberation Psychology: The Philippine Experience.* Diliman, Quezon City: University of the Philippines Press, 1992.

Errington, Shelly. "Recasting Sex, Gender, and Power: A Theoretical and Regional Overview." In *Power and Difference in Island Southeast Asia,* edited by Jane Monnig Atkinson and Shelly Errington, 1–58, Stanford, Calif.: Stanford University Press, 1990.

España-Maram, Linda. *Creating Masculinity in Los Angeles's Little Manila: Working Class Filipinos and Popular Culture in the United States.* New York: Columbia University Press, 2006.

Espina, Marina. *Filipinos in Louisiana.* New Orleans, La.: A. F. Laborde & Sons, 1988.

Espiritu, August Fauni. *Five Faces of Exile: The Nation and Filipino American Intellectuals.* Stanford, CA: Stanford University Press, 2005.

Espiritu, Yen Le. *Filipino American Lives.* Philadelphia: Temple University Press, 1995.

———. *Home Bound: Filipino American Lives Across Cultures, Communities and Countries.* Berkeley: University of California Press, 2003.

Evangelista, Sonny. "Filipino Seafarers Face Declining Demand." *Philippines Today,* November 15–December 14, 2002.

Faier, Lieba. *Intimate Encounters: Filipina Women and the Remaking of Rural Japan.* Berkeley: University of California Press, 2009.

Fajardo, Kale Bantigue. "Of Galleons and Globalization." *Mains'l Haul: A Journal of Pacific Maritime History* 38, nos. 1 and 2 (2002): 61–66.

———. "Filipino Cross Currents: Seafaring, Masculinities, and Globalization," 2004. Ph.D. Dissertation. University of California, Santa Cruz.

———. "Transportation: Translating Filipino/Filipino American Tomboy Masculinities through Global Migration and Shipping." *GLQ* 14, no. 2/3 (2008): 403–424.

———. "Piracy in the Gulf of Aden," December 9, 2008, http://www.youtube.com/watch?v=sA30hwJpivM (accessed July 28, 2009).

———. Boellstorff, Tom. "A Coincidence of Desires: Anthropology, Queer Studies, Indonesia." *Journal of the Royal Anthropological Institute,* 16, no. 2 (2010): 421–22.

Feinberg, Leslie. *Stone Butch Blues.* Ithaca, N.Y.: Firebrand, 1993.

Ferguson, Roderick. *Abberrations in Black: Toward a Queer of Color Critique.* Minneapolis: University of Minnesota Press, 2004.

———. "Sissies at the Picnic." In *Feminist Waves, Feminist Generations: Life Stories from the Academy,* edited by Hokulani K. Aikau, Karla A. Erickson, and Jennifer Pierce. Minneapolis: University of Minnesota Press, 2007.

Forbes, Dean. "Globalisation, Postcolonialism and New Representations of the Pacific Asian Metropolis." In *Globalisation and the Asia-Pacific: Contested Territories,* edited by Kris Olds, Peter Dicken, Philip F. Kelly, Lily Kong, and Henry Wai-chung. London: Routledge Press, 1999.

Foucault, Michel. *Discipline and Punish.* New York, Pantheon Books, 1978.

———. "Of Other Spaces." *Diacritics* 16, no. 1 (1986): 22–27.

Foucault, Michel, and Colin Gordon. *Power/Knowledge: Selected Interviews and Other Writings, 1972–1977.* New York: Pantheon Books, 1980.

Francia, Luis H., ed. *Brown River, White Ocean: An Anthology of Twentieth Century Philippine Literature in English.* New Brunswick, N.J.: Rutgers University Press, 1993.

———. *Eye of the Fish: A Personal Archipelago.* New York: Kaya Press, 2001.

———. "Introduction to José Rizal's *Noli Me Tangere.*" n.d. http://us.penguingroup.com/static/rguides/us/noli_me_tangere.html.

Freedom from Debt Coalition. "Is the Philippine Debt Problem Over?" *Manila Times,* January 20, 2008, http://www.manilatimes.net/national/2008/jan/20/yehey/top_stories/20080120top2.html (accessed June 18, 2009).

Friedman, Lawrence Meir. *The Horizontal Society.* New Haven, Conn.: Yale University Press, 1999.

Fujita-Rony, Dorothy. *American Workers, Colonial Power: Philippine Seattle and the Transpacific West, 1919–1941.* Berkeley: University of California Press, 2002.

———. "Water and Land: Asian Americans and the U.S. West." *Pacific Historical Review* 76, no. 4 (2007): 563–74.

Gardner, Jinky. "Snapshots of a Treasure Trade." In *Mains'l Haul: A Journal of Pacific Maritime History* 38, no. 1 and 2 (2002): 50–56.

Geertz, Clifford. *The Interpretation of Cultures.* New York: Basic Books, 1973.

Ghosh, Amitav. *In an Antique Land; History in the Guise of a Traveler's Tale.* New York: Random House, 1992.

———. *The Hungry Tide.* New York: Mariner Books, 2006.

———. *Sea of Poppies.* New York: Picador, 2009.

Giddens, Anthony. *The Consequences of Modernity.* Stanford, Calif.: Stanford University Press, 1990.

Gier, Jean Vengua. ". . . 'to Have Come from Someplace': October Light, America Is in the Heart, and 'Flip' Writing After the Third World Strikes." *Critical Mass: A Journal of Asian American Cultural Criticism* 2, no. 2 (1995): 1–33.

Gilroy, Paul. *The Black Atlantic; Modernity and Double Consciousness.* Cambridge, Mass.: Harvard University Press, 1993.

Glavin, Terry. *The Last Great Sea; a Voyage Through the Human and Natural History of the Northern Pacific Ocean.* Vancouver, BC: David Suzuki Foundation, 2000.

Glissant, Edouard. *Caribbean Discourse: Selected Essays.* Charlottesville: University of Virgina Press, 1999.

Goldman, Francisco. *The Ordinary Seaman.* New York: Grove Press, 1997.

Gopinath, Gayatri. *Impossible Desires: Queer Diasporas and South Asian Public Cultures.* Durham, N.C.: Duke University Press, 2005.

Gore, Al. *An Inconvenient Truth: The Planetary Emergency of Global Warming and What We Can Do About It.* DVD. Directed by Davis Guggenheim. Hollywood, CA: Paramount Classics, 2006.

Gray, Lorraine, producer/director. *The Global Assembly Line.* VHS. Harriman, N.Y.: New Day Films, 1986.

Greenlaw, Linda. *The Hungry Ocean: A Swordboat Captain's Journey.* Washington, D.C.: Compass Press, 2000.

Guggenheim, Scott. "Cock or Bull: Cockfighting, Social Structure, and Political Commentary in the Philippines," in *The Cockfight: A Casebook,* ed. Alan Dundes. Madison: University of Wisconsin Press, 1994.

Guy, Malcolm and Smith, Michelle, directors. *Turbulent Waters.* DVD. 2004, Oley, Pa.: Bullfrog Films.

Hagedorn, Jessica. *Dogeaters.* New York: Penguin, 1990.

———. *Jungle Dream.* New York: Viking Press, 2003.

Hall, Stuart. "Cultural Identity and Diaspora." In *Identity: Community, Culture, Difference,* edited by J. Rutherford, 222–37. London: Lawrence and Wishart, 1990.

Halberstam, Judith/Jack. *Female Masculinities.* Durham, N.C.: Duke University Press, 1998.

———. "Female Masculinities." In *The Masculinity Studies Reader,* edited by Rachel Adams and David Savran. Malden, MA/Oxford, UK: Blackwell Publishing, 2002.

———. *In a Queer Time and Place: Transgender Bodies, Subcultural Lives.* New York: New York University Press, 2005.

Hannerz, Ulf. "Notes on the Global Ecumene." *Public Culture* 1, no. 2 (1989): 66–75.

———. *Transnational Connections.* New York: Routledge, 1996.

Harris, Edward. "Pact Gives U.S. Search Rights Over Ships." *Associated Press,* February 13, 2004.

Harvey, David. *The Condition of Postmodernity.* Cambridge, Mass.: Blackwell Publishers, 1989.

Hau'Ofa, Epeli. "Our Sea of Islands." In *A New Oceania: Rediscovering Our Sea of Islands,* edited by E. Waddel, V. Naidu and E. Hau'ofa. Suva, Fiji: School of Economic Development, University of the South Pacific in Association with Beake House, 1993.

———. *Tales of the Tikongs.* Honolulu: University of Hawai'i Press, 1994.

———. "The Ocean is in Us." *Dreadlocks in Oceania* 1 (1997): 124–48.

———. *We Are the Ocean: Selected Works.* Honolulu: University of Hawai'i Press, 2008.

Hawken, Paul. *Blessed Unrest: How the Largest Largest Movement in the World Came into Being and Why No One Saw It Coming.* New York: Penguin, 2007.

Hearn, Lafcadio. "Saint Malo: A Lacustrine Village in Louisiana." In *Lefcadio Hearn's America: Ethnographic Sketches and Editorials,* edited by Simon J. Bronner, 54–62. Lexington: University of Kentucky Press, 2002.

Heng, Geraldine, and Janadas Devan. "State Fatherhood: The Politics of Nationalism, Sexuality, and Race in Singapore." In *Bewitching Women, Pious Men; Gender and Body Politics in South East Asia,* edited by Aiwa Ong and Michael G. Peletz, 195–215. Berkeley: University of California Press, 1995.

Henry, Pat. *By the Grace of the Sea: A Woman's Solo Odyssey Around the World.* New York: International Marine/McGraw-Hill, 2003.

Herod, Andrew. "Labor as an Agent of Globaization and as a Global Agent." In *Spaces of Globalization: Reasserting the Power of the Local,* edited by Kevin R. Cox, 167–200. New York: Guilford Press, 1997.

Heyerdahl, Thor. *Kon-Tiki: Across the Pacific by Raft.* Chicago: Rand McNally, 1950.

Hidy, George M. *The Waves: The Nature of Sea Motion.* New York: Van Nostrand Reinhold Company, 1971.

Higgott, Richard. "Routledge/Warwick Studies in Globalisation, Series Preface." In *Globalisation and the Asia-Pacific; Contested Territories,* edited by Kris Olds, Peter Dicken, Philip F. Kelly, Lily Kong, and Henry Wai-chung. New York: Routledge, 1999.

Ho, Karen Z. *Liquidated: An Ethnography of Wall Street.* Durham, N.C.: Duke University Press, 2009.

Holstege, Sean. "The Scourge of Modern Piracy." *Oakland Tribune*, March 14, 2004.

Hong, Grace Kyungwon. *The Ruptures of American Capital: Women of Color Feminism and the Culture of Immigrant Labor.* Minneapolis: University of Minnesota Press, 2006.

hooks, bell. *Ain't I a Woman? Black Women and Feminism*. Boston: South End Press, 1981.

———. *Yearning: Race, Gender, and Cultural Politics*. Boston: South End Press, 1990.

Hu-DeHart, Evelyn. "Latin America in Asia-Pacific Perspective." In Arif Dirlik, *What Is in a Rim? Critical Perspectives on the Pacific Region Idea,* 2nd revised edition. Lanham, Md.: Roman and Littlefield, 1997.

Hu-DeHart, Evelyn, ed. *Across the Pacific; Asian Americans and Globalization.* Philadelphia: Temple University: 1999.

Ileto, Reynaldo Clemeña. *Pasyon and Revolution.* Metro Manila: Ateneo de Manila University Press, 1979.

———. "The Past in the Present Crisis." In *The Philippines After Marcos*. Sydney, Australia: Croom Helm Limited, 1985.

———. "The 'Unfinished Revolution' in Philippine Political Discourse." *Southeast Asian Studies* 31, no. 1 (1993): 62–82.

Imao, Abdulmari. "Boatbuilding Beehive in Sibuti." In *Filipino Heritage, the Making of a Nation.* Edited by Alfredo Roces, Vol. 3, *The Age of Trade and Contacts, Visitors from Across the Seas,* 625–29. Manila: Lahing Pilipino Publishing Foundation, 1977–78).

Inda, Jonathan Xavier, and Renato Rosaldo, eds. *The Anthropology of Globalization: A Reader.* Malden, Mass.: Blackwell Publishing, 2002.

———. "Introduction: A World in Motion." In *The Anthropology of Globalization: A Reader,* edited by Jonathan Xavier Inda and Renato Rosaldo, 1–34. Malden, Mass.: Blackwell Publishing, 2002.

Isaac, Allan Punzalan. *American Tropics: Articulating Filipino America.* Minneapolis: University of Minnesota Press, 2006.

Ismail, Qadri. *Abiding Sri Lanka: On Peace, Place, and Postcoloniality.* Minneapolis: University of Minnesota Press, 2005.

Iyer, Pico. *Video Nights in Kathmandu.* New York: Vintage, 1989.

———. *The Global Soul: Jet Lag, Shopping Malls, and the Search for Home.* New York: Vintage Departures, 2000.

Jaleco, Rodney. "Manning the Way to NIC-hood." *Philippine Magazine,* September 1997, 8–9.

Jimenez, Cher S. "Shadowy Trails: Stories of the Undocumented" ABS-CBN News Online, http://www.abs-cbnnews.com/pinoy-migration/07/01/08/shadowy-trails-stories-undocumented (accessed July 5, 2008).

Joaquin, Nick. *Manila, My Manila.* Makati, Philippines: Bookmark, 1999.

John, Mary. *Discrepant Dislocations: Feminism, Theory, and Postcolonial Histories.* Berkeley: University of California Press, 1975.

Johnson, Mark. *Beauty and Power; Transgendering and Cultural Transformation in the Southern Philippines*. New York: Oxford University Press, 1997.

Jose, F. Sionil. "We Who Stayed Behind," August 18–25, 2003, http://www.time.com/time/asia/2003/journey/letters-jose.html (accessed March 16, 2004).

Joyner, Tim. *Magellan*. Camden, Maine: International Marine, 1992.

Jubilee Australia. "The Philippines' Debt Problem and the Continued Accumulation of Illegitimate Debt Has Once Again Been Put in the Spotlight," March 26, 2008, http://www.jubileeaustralia.org/_bpost_795/The_Philippines%E2%80%99_debt_problem_and_the_continued_accumulation_of_illegitmate_debt_has_once_again_been_put_in_the_spotlight (accessed July 27, 2009).

Junger, Sebastian. *The Perfect Storm: A True Story of Men Against the Sea*. New York: W.W. Norton and Company, 1997.

Katigbak, Maria Kalaw. "The Tagalogs." In *Filipino Heritage, the Making of a Nation*. Edited by Alfredo Roces, Vol. 4, *The Spanish Colonial Period (16th Century): The Day of the Conquistador*, 1025–33. Manila: Lahing Pilipino Publishing Foundation, 1977–78.

Kauanui, J. Kehaulani. "Asian American Studies and the 'Pacific Question.'" In *Asian American Studies after Critical Mass*, edited by Kent A. Odo, 123–43. Malden, Mass.: Blackwell Publishing, 2005.

Kaut, Charles R. "*Utang-na-loob:* A System of Contractual Obligation among Tagalogs." *Southwestern Journal of Anthropology* 17 (1961): 256–72.

Kearney, Michael. "The Local and the Global; the Anthropology of Globalization and Transnationalism." *Annual Review of Anthropology* 24 (1995): 547–65.

———. *Reconceptualizing the Peasantry: Anthropology in Global Perspective*. Boulder, Colo.: Westview Press, 1996.

Kemp, Peter, Ed. *The Oxford Companion to Ships and the Sea*. London: Oxford University Press, 1976.

Kerouac, Jack. *On the Road*. New York: Viking Press, 1957.

Kimmel, Michael. *Manhood in America*. New York: The Free Press, 1996.

Kincaid, Jamaica. *A Small Place*. New York: Penguin Books, 1919.

Klein, Ross A. *Cruise Ship Blues: The Underside of the Cruise Ship Industry*. Gabriola Island, BC: New Society Publishers, 2002.

Korkalainen, Sari. "Illegal Recruitment of Overseas Filipino Workers." *Kakampi Report* (Newsletter), no. 4 (April 2000).

Kumar, Amitava. *Passport Photos*. Berkeley: University of California Press, 2000.

Landingin, Roel R. "Every Six Hours, Pirates Seize a Filipino Seaman." Philippine Center for Investigative Journalism, November 26, 2008, http://www.pcij.org/i-report/2008/seafarers.html (accessed February 20, 2009).

Laus, Emiliano. "A Question of Seasoning." In *Filipino Heritage, the Making of a Nation*. Edited by Alfredo Roces. Vol. 3, *The Age of Trade and Contacts, Visitors from Across the Seas*, 813–18. Manila: Lahing Pilipino Publishing Foundation, 1977–78.

Linebaugh, Peter, and Rediker Marcus. *The Many Headed Hydra: The Hidden History of the Revolutionary Atlantic*. Boston: Beacon Press, 2000.

Lorde, Audre. "Uses of the Erotic: The Erotic as Power." In *Sister Outsider: Essays and Speeches*. Trumansburg, N.Y.: Crossing Press, 1984.

Lowe, Lisa. *Immigrant Acts*. Durham, N.C.: Duke University Press, 1996.

Maglipon, Jo-Ann. "DH in HK." In *Primed: Selected Stories, 1972–1992,* 45–53. Pasig City, Philippines: Anvil Publishing, Inc. 1993.

Malinowski, Bronislaw. *Argonauts of the Western Pacific*. New York: E. P. Dutton, 1961.

Manalansan, Martin F. *Global Divas; Filipino Gay Men in the Diaspora*. Durham, N.C.: Duke University Press, 2003.

Mandap, Daisy C.L. "Hong Kong: The Call of the Sea (and Its Men)." *Inter Press Service*, n.d.

Maoist International Movement. "New People's Army Fights U.S. Imperialism." in Maoist International Movement Notes, 2000.

Marcus, George E., and Michael M.J. Fischer. *Anthropology as Cultural Critique: An Experimental Moment in the Human Sciences*. Chicago: University of Chicago Press, 1986.

Margold, Jane. "Narratives of Masculinity and Transnational Migration: Filipino Workers in the Middle East." In *Bewitching Women, Pious Men: Gender and Body Politics in South East Asia,* edited by Aiwa Ong and Michael G. Peletz, 274–98. Berkeley: University of California Press, 1995.

Martinez, Elizabeth and Garcia, Arnoldo. "What Is 'Neo-Liberalism," http://www.globalexchange.org/economy (accessed March 1, 2000).

Massey, Doreen. *for space*. Thousand Oaks, Calif.: Sage Publications, 2005.

Mathes, W. Michael. "The Unfulfilled Contract of an Unlucky Galleon Pilot." *Mains'l Haul: A Journal of Pacific Maritime History,* 38, nos.1 and 2 (2002): 30–35.

McCarthy, William. J. "The Fiesta de las Señas." *Mains'l Haul: A Journal of Pacific Maritime History* 38, nos. 1 and 2 (2002): 20–29.

McKay, Steven C. "Men at Sea: Migration and the Performance of Masculinity." Paper presented at the American Sociology Association, Montreal, Canada, August 2006.

———. "Filipino Sea Men: Identity and Masculinity." In *Asian Diasporas: New Formations, New Conceptions*, edited by Rhacel S. Parreñas and Lok C. D. Siu, 63–84. Stanford, Calif.: Stanford University Press, 2007.

Mercado, Leonardo N. *Elements of Filipino Philosophy.* Tacloban City, Philippines: Divine World Publications, 1974.

Mishra, Pankaj. "Border Crossing." *Travel and Leisure* (August 2003): 128–32.

Mishra, Sudesh, and Elizabeth Guy. *Dreadlocks in Oceania*. Suva, Fiji: University of the South Pacific Press, 1997.

Mohanty, Chandra Talpade. "Under Western Eyes: Feminist Scholarship and Colonial Discourses." In *Third World Women and the Politics of Feminism,* edited by Chandra Talpade Mohanty, Ann Russo, and Lourdes Torres, 1–80. Bloomington: Indiana University Press, 1991.

Morgensen, Scott. *Settler Sexualities and the Politics of Indigeneity.* Minneapolis: University of Minnesota Press, forthcoming.

Morison, Samuel Eliot. *The European Discovery of America: The Southern Voyages.* New York: Oxford University Press U.S.A, 1974.

Muroga, Nobuo. "So There We Are." In *Filipino Heritage, the Making of a Nation.* Edited by Alfredo Roces, Vol. 3, *The Age of Trade and Contacts, Visitors from Across the Seas,* 873–74. Manila: Lahing Pilipino Publishing Foundation, 1977–78.

Myrick, Conrad. "Pulse of the Walled City." In *Filipino Heritage, the Making of a Nation.* Edited by Alfredo Roces, Vol. 3, *The Age of Trade and Contacts, Visitors from Across the Seas,* 875–81. Manila: Lahing Pilipino Publishing Foundation, 1977–78.

Nair, J. K. M. "Steering Success." *Times Shipping Journal,* November 2003.

Natividad, Beverly T. "Female OFWs Overtaking Males, Gov't Report Says," *The Inquirer,* November 21, 2007, http://globalnation.inquirer.net/news/breakingnews/view/20071121-102338/Female_OFWs_overtaking_males%2C_gov%92t_report_says.

Narayan, Kirin. "How Native Is a "Native" Anthropologist?" *American Anthropologist* 95, no. 3 (1993): 671–83.

Neruda, Pablo. "First Sea," in *Neruda: On the Blue Shore of Silence; Poems of the Sea.* New York: HarperCollins, 2003.

Neumman, Gerhard. *Ocean Currents.* New York: Elsevier Publishing Company, 1968.

Nichols, Peter. *Sea Change: Alone Across the Atlantic in a Wooden Boat.* New York: Penguin Books, 1997.

Nimmo, Arlo. *The Songs of Salanda and Other Stories of Sulu.* Seattle: University of Washington Press, 1993.

Nincic, Donna J. "Sea Lane Security and U.S. Maritime Trade: Chokepoints as Scarce Resources." In *Globalization and Maritime Power,* edited by Sam J. Tangredi. Washington D.C.: National Defense University, 2002.

Nurthen, William A. "Homeland Security: How Are We Protecting Our Ports." Speech delivered at Economic Development Association of New Jersey, October 3, 2003.

O'Brien, Jean M. *Dispossession by Degrees: Indian Land and Identity in Natick, Massachusetts, 1650–1790.* Lincoln: University of Nebraska Press, 2003.

Office of the Press Secretary. "Statement of the President on the Release of Angelo dela Cruz," July 20, 2004, http://www.ops.gov.ph/speeches2004/speech-2004july20.htm (accessed July 17, 2009).

———. "PGMA (President Gloria Macapagal Arroyo) Says OFWs 2005 Remittances Could Hit $12B," December 12, 2005, http://www.news.ops.gov.ph/archives2005/dec12.htm (accessed August 19, 2009).

Okihiro, Gary Y. *Common Ground: Reimagining U.S. History.* Princeton, N.J.: Princeton University Press, 2001.

Old, Kris. "Questions in a Crisis: The Contested Meanings of Globalisation in the Asia-Pacific." In *Globalisation and the Asia-Pacific: Contested Territories,* edited by Kris Old, Peter Dicken, Philip F. Kelly, Lily Kong, and Henry Wai-chung. London: Routledge Press, 1999.

Old, Kris, Peter Dicken, Philip F. Kelly, Lily Kong, and Henry Wai-chung, eds. *Globalisation and the Asia-Pacific: Contested Territories.* London: Routledge Press, 1999.

Oliveira, Fernando. *Viagem de Fernão Magalhães / The Voyage of Ferdinand Magellan.* Manila: National Historical Institute, 2002.

Omi, Michael, and Howard Winant. *Racial Formation in the United States: From the 1960s to the 1990s.* New York: Routledge, 1986.

Ong, Aihwa. *Spirits of Resistance and Capitalist Discipline.* Albany: State University of New York Press, 1985.

———. *Flexible Citizenship: The Cultural Logics of Transnationality.* Durham, N.C.: Duke University Press. 1999.

Ong, Aihwa, and Michael Peletz, eds. *Bewitching Women, Pious Men: Gender and Body Politics in Southeast Asia.* Berkeley: University of California Press, 1995.

Opiniano, Jeremiah. "Convention Drafts Magna Carta for Seafarers Amid Doubt, Concern Over Feasibility." *Philippines Today,* November 15–December 14, 2002.

Ortner, Sherry. "Theory in Anthropology Since the Sixties." In *Culture Power/History,* edited by Nicholas B Dirks, Geoff Eley and Sherry Ortner, 372–411. Princeton, N.J.: Princeton University Press, 1994.

Ostreng, Dorte. "Does Togetherness Make Friends? Stereotyping and Intergroup Contact on Multiethnic-Crewed Ship." Unpublished paper, 2000. Cited in Steven McKay, "Men at Sea: Migration and the Performance of Masculinity." Paper presented at the American Sociology Association, Montreal, Canada, August 2006.

Otálvaro-Hormillosa, Gigi. "Performing Citizenship and 'Temporal Hybridity' in a Queer Diaspora," http://www.devilbunny.org/temporal_hybridity.htm (accessed February 16, 2007).

Pabico, Alecks P. "Filipino Seamen Take Their Chance in the World's 'Sweatships.'" *Philippine Center for Investigative Journalism* July 14–15, 2003.

———. "Filipinos Toil in 'Unworthy' Ships." *Philippines Today*, July 2003, http://www.philippinestoday.net/ofwcorners/July03/ofw703_2.htm (accessed January 28, 2009).

Parker, Andrew, Mary Russo, Doris Sommer, and Patricia Yaeger, eds. *Nationalisms and Sexualities.* New York: Routledge, 1992.

Parreñas, Rhacel Salazar. *Servants of Globalization: Women, Migration, and Domestic Work.* Stanford: Stanford University Press, 2001.

Parreñas, Rhacel, and Lok Siu, eds. *Asian Diasporas: New Formations, New Conceptions.* Stanford: Stanford University Press, 2007.

Patanñe, E. P. "Overseas Trade Before Magellan." In *Filipino Heritage, the Making of a Nation.* Edited by Alfredo Roces, Vol. 3, *The Age of Trade and*

Contacts, Visitors from Across the Seas, 767–69. Manila: Lahing Pilipino Publishing Foundation, 1977–78.

———. "The Outrigger in the Maritime Scene; Balancing on Philippine Seas." In *Filipino Heritage, the Making of a Nation.* Edited by Alfredo Roces, Vol. 3, *The Age of Trade and Contacts, Visitors from Across the Seas,* 716–18. Manila: Lahing Pilipino Publishing Foundation, 1977–78).

Peletz, Michael G. *Reason and Passion: Representations of Gender in Malay Society.* Berkeley: University of California Press, 1996.

Peters, Jens. *Philippines: A Travel Survival Kit.* Singapore: Singapore National Printers Ltd., 1994.

Pham, Andrew X. *Catfish and Mandala: A Two-Wheeled Voyage Through the Landscape and Memory of Vietnam.* New York: Farrar, Straus and Giroux, 1999.

Phelan, John Leddy. *The Hispanization of the Philippines: Spanish Aims and Filipino Responses.* Madison: University of Wisconsin Press, 1959.

Philippine Consulate General in Los Angeles. "Passport Frequently Asked Questions," n.d., http://www.philippineconsulatela.org/FAQs/FAQS-passport.htm (accessed August 4, 2008).

Philippine Merchant Marine Academy. "A Concise History of the Philippine Merchant Marine Academy," http://www.accessmaritime.com/pmma/history.php (accessed October 22, 2008).

Philippine Overseas Employment Agency, "Deployed Landbased and Seabased Workers (1984–2002)," http://www.poea.gov.ph/html/statistics.html.

———. "Compendium of OFW Statistics (2008)," http://www.poea.gov.ph/html/statistics.html.

Phillips, Carla Rahn. "Spaniards in Hawaii before Cook?" *Mains'l Haul: A Journal of Pacific Maritime History* 38, nos. 1 and 2 (2002): 10–18.

Pigafetta, Antonio. *The First Voyage Around the World: An Account of Magellan's Expedition,* introduction and translation by T. J. Cachey, Jr., New York: Marsilio Publishers, 1995.

"Pinoy Seamen Remit $2 Billion," *Sun-Star Manila,* November 22, 2008, http://www.sunstar.com.ph/static/man/2008/11/22/bus/pinoy.seamen.remit.$2.billion.html (accessed January 7, 2009).

Pratt, Mary Louise. "Fieldwork in Common Places." In *Writing Culture.* Berkeley: University of California Press, 1986.

———. "Arts of the Contact Zone." *Profession* 91 (1991): 33–40.

———. *Imperial Eyes: Travel Writing and Transculturation.* New York: Routledge, 1992.

Quirino, Carlos. "The Chronicles of Piggafetta." In *Filipino Heritage, the Making of a Nation.* Edited by Alfredo Roces, Vol. 3, *The Age of Trade and Contacts, Visitors from Across the Seas,* 828–32. Manila: Lahing Pilipino Publishing Foundation, 1977–78.

———. "Limahong." In *Filipino Heritage, the Making of a Nation.* Edited by Alfredo Roces, Vol. 3, *The Age of Trade and Contacts, Visitors from*

Across the Seas, 906. Manila: Lahing Pilipino Publishing Foundation, 1977–78.

———. "The Mexican Connection; the Cultural Cargo of the Manila-Acapulco Galleons." In *Filipino Heritage, the Making of a Nation: The Age of Trade and Contact; Visitors From Across Many Seas.* Edited by Alfredo Roces, Vol. 3, *The Age of Trade and Contacts, Visitors from Across the Seas,* 933–37. Manila: Lahing Pilipino Publishing Foundation, 1977–78.

———. "Old River Kingdom: The Oldest Settlement on the Pasig Was Namayan." In *Filipino Heritage, the Making of a Nation.* Edited by Alfredo Roces, Vol. 3, *The Age of Trade and Contacts, Visitors from Across the Seas,* 625–29. Manila: Lahing Pilipino Publishing Foundation, 1977–78.

———. "The Philippines in Old Geography." In *Filipino Heritage, the Making of a Nation.* Edited by Alfredo Roces, Vol. 3, *The Age of Trade and Contacts, Visitors from Across the Seas,* 889–92. Manila: Lahing Pilipino Publishing Foundation, 1977–78.

Raes, Peter. "Background Briefing: The Bad Shipping News: Ports, Freight and Security." By Australian Broadcasting Corporation Radio National, Radio Program, August 31, 2003.

Rafael, Vicente. *Contracting Colonialism: Translation and Christian Conversion in Tagalog Society Under Early Spanish Rule.* Durham, N.C.: Duke University Press, 1988.

———. "The Cultures of Area Studies in the United States." *Social Text,* no. 41 (1995): 91–111.

———. "Your Grief Is Our Gossip; Overseas Filipinos and Other Spectral Presences." In *White Love and Other Events in Filipino History,* 204–26. Durham, N.C.: Duke University Press, 2000.

———. *White Love and Other Events in Filipino History.* Durham, N.C.: Duke University Press, 2000.

Rafael, Vicente, ed. *Discrepant Histories: Translocal Essays on Filipino Cultures.* Philadelphia: Temple University Press, 1995.

Rafael, Vince. "A Short History of the Mega-Mall." In *The Flip Reader: Being a Greatest Hits Anthology from Flip: The Official Guide to World Domination,* edited by Jessica Zafra. Pasig City, Philippines: Anvil, 2008.

Ramirez, Nelson. "The President, the Seafarers and China." *Tinig ng Marino,* November–December 2001.

Ramos, Fidel V. "A Salute to Filipino Seafarers." *Ahoy Magazine,* September–November 1997, 26–27.

Ramos, Teresita V. *Conversational Tagalog, A Functional-Situational Approach.* Honolulu, University of Hawai'i Press, 1985.

———. *Intermediate Tagalog, Developing Cultural Awareness through Language.* Honolulu, University of Hawai'i Press, 1981.

Rediker, Marcus. *Between the Devil and the Deep Blue Sea: Merchant Seamen, Pirates, and the Anglo-American Maritime World, 1700–1750.* Cambridge, UK: Cambridge University Press, 1987.

———. *The Slave Ship: A Human History.* New York: Penguin, 2008.

Reid, Anthony. *Southeast Asia in the Age of Commerce, 1450–1680.* New Haven, Conn.: Yale University Press, 1985.

Resurreccion, Lyn. "Globalization Lends Urgency to Call to Raise R&D Budgets," January 10, 2004, http://www.bic.searca.org/feature/resurreccion-globalization.html (accessed May 17, 2009).

Richardson, Elaine B. *African American Literacies,* New York, Routledge, 2002.

Rizal, José. *A Letter to the Women of Malolos,* Manila, Philippines: Bureau of Printing, 1932.

———. *Noli Me Tangere.* New York: Penguin Classics, 2006.

———. *El Filibusterismo.* Honolulu: University of Hawai'i Press, 2007.

Rodriguez, Nice. *Throw It To The River.* Toronto, ON: Women's Press, 1993.

Rodriguez, Robyn Magalit. "The Labor Brokerage State and the Globalization of Filipina Care Workers." In *Signs: Journal of Women in Culture and Society* 33, no. 4 (2008): 794–800.

———. *Brokering Bodies: The Philippine State and the Globalization of Migrant Labor.* Minneapolis: University of Minnesota Press, 2010.

Rogers, Richard W. "European Influences in Ancient Hawaii." *Mains'l Haul: A Journal of Pacific Maritime History* 38, nos. 1 and 2 (2002): 19.

Rosaldo, Renato. *Ilongot Headhunting, 1883–1974, a Study in Society and History.* Stanford: Stanford University Press, 1980.

———. *Culture and Truth: The Remaking of Social Analysis.* Boston: Beacon Press, 1993.

Rosca, Ninotchka. *Endgame: The Fall of Marcos.* New York: Franklin Watts, 1987.

Safina, Carl. *Song for the Blue Ocean; Encounters Along the World's Coasts and Beneath the Seas.* New York: Henry Holt and Company, 1997.

Said, Edward W. *Orientalism.* New York: Vintage Books, 1978.

Saldanha, Arun. "Heterotopia and Structuralism." *Environment and Planning A* 40, no. 9 (2008): 2080–96.

Samonte, Elena. *"Kabuuan ng mga kahulugan ng mga salita sa larangang leksikal ng 'loob'"* ("The meaning of the words in the lexical domain of 'loob'"). Unpublished manuscript. Diliman, Quezon City: University of the Philippines, 1973.

Samonte, Isobelo A. Interview with Kale Bantigue Fajardo, February 6, 1997.

Sampson, Helen. "Transnational Drifters or Hyperspace Dwellers: An Exploration of the Lives of Filipino Seafarers Aboard and Ashore." *Ethnic and Racial Studies* 26, no. 2 (2003): 253–77.

San Juan, Epifanio. *Crisis in the Philippines, the Making of a Revolution.* South Hadley, Mass.: Bergin and Garvey Publishers, 1986.

———. *Racial Formations/Critical Transformation, Articulations of Power in Ethnic and Racial Studies in the United States.* Atlantic Highlands, N.J.: Humanities Press, 1992.

———. "Configuring the Filipino Diaspora in the United States." *Diaspora,* no. 3. (1994): 117–32.

Sassen, Saskia. "Identity in the Global City: Economic and Cultural Encasements." In *Geographies of Identity,* edited by Patricia Yaeger. Ann Arbor: University of Michigan Press, 1996.

———. "Whose City Is It? Globalization and the Formation of New Claims." In *The Globalization Reader,* edited by Frank J. Lechner and John Boli. Maden, Mass.: Blackwell, 2000.

———. "Global Cities and Survival Circuits." In *Global Woman: Nannies, Maids, and Sex Workers in the New Economy,* edited by Barbara Ehrenreich and Arlie Russell Hochschild. New York: Metropolitan Books, 2002.

Scharlin, Craig, and Villanueva, Lilia V. *Philip Vera Cruz: A Personal History of Filipino Immigrants and the Farmworkers Movement.* Seattle: University of Washington Press, 2000.

Schirmer, Daniel and Stephen Rosskamm Shalom, eds. *The Philippines Reader: A History of Colonialism, Neocolonialism, Dictatorship and Resistance.* Boston: Southend Press, 1987.

Schurz, William Lytle. *Manila Galleon.* Quezon City, Philippines: RP Garcia Publishing, 1939.

See, Sarita Echavez. *The Decolonized Eye: Filipino American Art and Performance.* Minneapolis: University of Minnesota Press, 2009.

Sekula, Allan. *Photography Against the Grain: Essays and Photoworks 1973–1983.* Halifax: Press of the Nova Scotia College of Art and Design, 1984.

———. *Fish Story.* Dusseldorf: Richter Verlag, 1995.

———. *Geography Lesson: Canadian Notes.* Vancouver, BC: Vancouver Art Gallery, 1997.

———. *Dismal Science; Photoworks 1972–1996.* Normal: University Galleries Illinois State University, 1999.

Shaffer, Lynda Norene. *Maritime Southeast Asia to 1500.* Armonk, N.Y.: M. E. Sharpe, 1996.

Shirane, Haruo. *Traces of Dreams: Landscape, Cultural Memory, and the Poetry of Bashō.* Stanford: Stanford University Press, 1998.

Silva, Noenoe K. *Aloha Betrayed: Native Hawaiian Resistance to American Colonialism.* Durham, N.C.: Duke University Press, 2004.

Singapore Ministry of Information and the Arts. *Mission Statement,* 1997, http://app.mica.gov.sg/Default.aspx?tabid=61.

Sinnott, Megan J. *Toms and Dees: Transgender Identity and Female Same-Sex Relationships in Thailand.* Honolulu: University of Hawai'i Press, 2004.

Sison, Marites. "Wives Close Eyes to Seafarers' Casual Sex." *Inter Press Service,* May 17, 2001.

———. "A Girl in Every Port." *Inter Press Service,* February 20, 2004.

Slocum, Joshua. *Sailing Alone around the World: The First Solo Voyage around the World.* 1900. Reprint, Dobbs Ferry, N.Y.: Sheridan House, 1999.

Small, Cathy A. *Voyages: From Tongan Villages to American Suburbs.* Ithaca, N.Y.: Cornell University Press, 1997.

Springer, Haskell, ed. *America and the Sea.* Athens: University of Georgia Press, 1995.

Steinberg, David Joel, ed. *In Search of Southeast Asia: A Modern History.* Honolulu: University of Hawai'i Press, 1985.

Stewart, Kathleen. *A Space on the Side of the Road: Cultural Poetics in an "Other" America.* Princeton, N.J.: Princeton University Press, 1993.

Stillman, Amy Ku'leialoha. "Pacific-ing Asian Pacific American History." *Journal of Asian American Studies* 7, no. 3 (2004): 241–70.

Stoler, Ann Laura. *Carnal Knowledge and Imperial Power: Race and the Intimate in Colonial Rule.* Berkeley: University of California Press, 2010.

Suarez, E.T. "R. P. Included in World Maritime List." *Manila Bulletin,* December 7, 2000, http://www.articlearchives.com/trends-events/talks-meetings/275651-1.html (accessed April 4, 2004).

Suñas, Lorela. "The Vulnerabilities of Filipino Seafarers to HIV/STIs." Remedios AIDS Foundation, Inc., August 8, 2003.

Tadiar, Neferti X. "Manila's New Metropolitan Form." In *Discrepant Histories: Translocal Essays on Filipino Cultures,* edited by Vicente L. Rafael. Manila: Anvil Publishing, 1995.

———. *Fantasy-Production: Sexual Economies and Other Philippine Consequences for the New World Order.* Hong Kong: Hong Kong University Press, 2004.

———. "Hope" in *Fantasy-Production: Sexual Economies and Other Philippine Consequences for the New World Order.* Hong Kong: Hong Kong University Press, 2004.

———. "Sexual Economies in the Asia/Pacific Community." In *What Is in a Rim? Critical Perspectives on the Pacific Region Idea,* edited by Arif Dirlik. Oxford, UK: Rowman and Littlefield Publishers, Inc., 1998.

———. *Things Fall Away: Philippine Historical Experience and the Makings of Globalization.* Durham, N.C.: Duke University, 2009.

Tahimik, Kidlat. *Perfumed Nightmare (Bangungot Mababangong).* Film. Produced by Kidlat Tahimik (Eric de Guia). Manila: Tahimik Productions, 1977.

Takaki, Ronald. *Strangers from a Different Shore.* New York: Penguin, 1985.

Talampas, G. Rolando. "Struggle of Filipino Seafarers: An Historical Overview." Unpublished manuscript, 1998.

———. Interview with Kale Bantigue Fajardo, Quezon City, Philippines, March 14, 1998.

———. "Anti-Colonial Seafarer's Movement in the Early 1900s." Paper presented at 9th Annual Manila Studies Association, June 26, 1997.

———. *Marino: An Introduction to the History of Filipino Seamen.* Manila: Maritime Education and Research Center, 1991.

Tangredi, Sam J., ed. *Globalization and Maritime Power.* Washington, D.C.: National Defense University, 2002.

Taussig, Michael. *The Magic of the State.* New York: Routledge, 1997.

Tchen, John Kuo Wei. *New York before Chinatown: Orientalism and the Shaping of American Culture, 1776–1882.* Baltimore: Johns Hopkins University Press, 1999.

Teaiwa, Teresia K. "Displaced and Traveling: The Native in a Militourist Pacific." Qualifying Exam, University of California, Santa Cruz, 1994.

———. "Militarism, Tourism, and the Native: Articulations in Oceania." Ph.D. diss., University of California, Santa Cruz, 2001.

Teaiwa, Teresia K., and Vilsoni Hereniko. *Last Virgin in Paradise.* Suva, Fiji: Mana Publications, 1993.

Thomas, Hugh. *The Slave Trade.* New York: Simon and Schuster, 1999.

Tinsley, Omise'eke Natasha. "Black Atlantic, Queer Atlantic: Queer Imaginings of the Middle Passage." *GLQ: A Journal of Gay and Lesbian Studies* 14, no. 2/3 (2008): 191–216.

———. *Thiefing Sugar: Eroticism between Women in Caribbean Literature.* Durham, N.C.: Duke University Press, 2010.

———. *Desiring the Blue Lagoon: Sea Crossings and Fluid Identities in Caribbean Literature.* (Forthcoming).

Tiongson, Antonio T. "On Filipinos, Filipino Americans, and U.S. Imperialism: Interview with Oscar V. Campomanes." In *Positively No Filipinos Allowed: Building Communities and Discourse,* edited by Antonio Tiongson, Ricardo Gutierrez, and Edgardo Gutierrez, 26–42. Philadelphia: Temple University Press, 2006.

Tiongson, Nicanor G. *Women of Malolos.* Quezon City: Ateneo de Manila University Press, 2004.

Toer, Pramoedya Ananta. *Child of All Nations.* New York: Penguin Books, 1974.

Tolentino, Rolando. "*Inangbayan*, the Mother-Nation, in Lino Brocka's *Bayan Ko: Kapit Sa Patalim* and *Orapronobis.*" *Screen* 37, no. 4 (1996): 368–88.

Trajano, Christian. "Four Centuries of Filipinos in California." *Mains'l Haul: A Journal of Pacific Maritime History* 38, no. 1 and 2 (2002): 67.

Trask, Haunani-Kay. *From a Native Daughter, Colonialism and Sovereignty in Hawaii.* Monroe, Maine: Common Courage Press, 1996.

Trinh, T. Minh-Ha. *Surname Viet, Given Name Nam.* Film/VHS. New York: Women Make Movies, 1989.

———. *Woman, Native, Other: Writing Postcoloniality and Feminism.* Bloomington: Indiana University Press, 1989.

———. *Framer Framed.* New York: Routledge, 1990.

———. *When the Moon Waxes Red: Representation, Gender, and Cultural Politics.* New York: Routledge, 1990.

Troung, Monique. *The Book of Salt.* New York: Houghton Mifflin Company, 2003.

Tsing, Anna Lowenhaupt. *In the Realm of the Diamond Queen: Marginality in an out-of-the Way Place.* Princeton, N.J.: Princeton University Press, 1993.

———. *Friction: An Ethnography of Global Connection.* Princeton, N.J.: Princeton University Press, 2005.

———. "The Global Situation," in *The Anthropology of Globalization: A Reader*, edited by Jonathan Xavier Inda and Renato Rosaldo. Malden, Mass.: Blackwell Publishing, 2002

Tuan, Yi-Fu. *Space and Place: The Perspective of Experience.* Minneapolis: University of Minnesota Press, 1977.

Tyner, James A. "Laboring in the Periphery: The Place of Manila in the Global Economy." In *Relocating Global Cities: From the Center to the Margins,* edited by M. Mark Amen, Kevin Archer, and M. Martin Bosman. Oxford, UK: Rowman & Littlefield Publishers, 2006.

Ubalde, Mark Joseph. "OFW Deployment in 2008 up by 30%," http://www.gmanews.tv/story/146465/OFW-deployment-in-2008-up-by-30 (accessed June 6, 2009).

Ulin, David L. "The Lost Art of Reading." *Los Angeles Times*, August 9, 2009, http://www.latimes.com/entertainment/news/arts/la-ca-reading9-2009aug09,0,4905017.story (accessed August 9, 2009).

Underwood, Robert A. "Commerce and Culture of the Manila Galleon: Linking the Philippines, Guam, The Americas, and Spain." Paper delivered at Smithsonian Institution, May 14, 1998.

United Filipino Seafarers. "Marina Worst STCW Violator." In *Tinig ng Marino,* January–February 1997.

Valentine, David. *Imagining Transgender: An Ethnography of a Category.* Durham, NC: Duke University Press, 2007.

Vanzi, Jose. "LapuLapu City Denounces Removal of Statue from Rizal Park." In *Cebu Star*, June 21, 2004, http://www.newsflash.org/2004/02/ht/ht004464.htm (accessed July 3, 2004).

Velasco Shaw, Angel. *Nailed.* VHS. New York: Mabuhay Productions, 1990.

Vergara, Benito M. *Displaying Filipinos: Photography and Colonialism in Early 20th Century Philippines.* Manila: University of the Philippines Press, 1995.

———. *Pinoy Capital: The Filipino Nation in Daly City.* Philadelphia: Temple University Press, 2008.

Villaviray, Johnna R. "4 Filipino Sailors Killed in Ship Fire." *The Manila Standard,* July 22, 1997, 2.

Visweswaran, Kamala. *Fictions of Feminist Ethnography.* Minneapolis: University of Minnesota Press, 1994.

Von der Porten, Edward. "Uncovering a Lost Galleon." *Mains'l Haul: A Journal of Pacific Maritime History* 38, nos. 1 and 2 (2002): 10–18.

Wallerstein, Immanuel. "The Rise and Future Demise of the World Capitalist System." In *The Globalization Reader,* edited by Frank J. Lechner and John Boli, 63–69. Malden, Mass.: Blackwell, 2000.

Wilson, Andrew R. *Ambition and Identity: Chinese Merchant Elites in Colonial Manila 1880–1916.* Honolulu: University of Hawai'i Press, 2004.

Wolf, Eric. *Europe and People Without History.* Berkeley: University of California Press, 1982.

Wolf, Margery. *A Thrice Told Tale: Feminism, Postmodernism, and Ethnographic Responsibility.* Stanford: Stanford University Press, 1992.

Yaeger, Patricia, Ed. *The Geography of Identity*. Ann Arbor: University of Michigan Press, 1998.

Zafra, Jessica. "An Alternate History of the World." In *The Flip Reader: Being a Greatest Hits Anthology from Flip: The Official Guide to World Domination.* Jessica Zafra, 16–19. Pasig City, Philippines: Anvil, 2008.

Zafra, Jessica, ed. *The Flip Reader: Being a Greatest Hits Anthology from Flip: The Official Guide to World Domination*. Pasig City, Philippines: Anvil, 2008.

Zaragoza, Ramón. *Old Manila.* Oxford, UK: Oxford University Press, 1990.

Zarate, Ma. Jovita. "Ang Konsepto ng Bagong Bayani sa mga Naratibo ng *Overseas Filipino Workers.*" *Malay* 20, no. 1 (2007): 103–9.

INDEX

Kale Bantigue Fajardo is an assistant professor in the Department of American Studies and the Asian American Studies Program at the University of Minnesota, Twin Cities.